Chicana/Latina Testimonios as Pedagogical, Methodological, and Activist Approaches to Social Justice

While the genre of *testimonio* has deep roots in oral cultures and in Latin American human rights struggles, the publication and subsequent adoption of *This Bridge Called My Back* (Moraga & Anzaldúa, 1983) and, more recently, *Telling to Live: Latina Feminist Testimonios* (Latina Feminist Group, 2001), have demonstrated the power of *testimonio* as a genre that exposes brutality, disrupts silencing, and builds solidarity among women of color. Within the field of education, scholars are increasingly taking up *testimonio* as a pedagogical, methodological, and activist approach to social justice, which transgresses traditional paradigms in academia. Unlike the more usual approach of researchers producing unbiased knowledge, the *testimonio* challenges objectivity by situating the individual in communion with a collective experience marked by marginalization, oppression, or resistance. This approach has resulted in new understandings about how marginalized communities build solidarity, and respond to and resist dominant culture, laws, and policies that perpetuate inequity.

This book contributes to our understanding of *testimonio* as it relates to methodology, pedagogy, research, and reflection in pursuit of social justice. A common thread among the chapters is a sense of political urgency to address inequities within Chicana/o and Latina/o communities.

This book was originally published as a special issue of *Equity & Excellence in Education.*

Dolores Delgado Bernal is Professor of Education and Ethnic Studies at the University of Utah, Salt Lake City, Utah, USA. Her community-engaged research focuses on the educational (in)equity of students of color, Latina/o educational pathways, and Chicana feminist methodologies and pedagogies.

Rebeca Burciaga is an Assistant Professor of Educational Leadership at San José State University, California, USA. Her work focuses on understanding and challenging educational practices and structures that (re)produce racial, ethnic, gender, and class inequalities. She uses Chicana feminist methodologies and pedagogies to study *educación* (informal learning/socialization) as epistemological and ontological knowledge production.

Judith Flores Carmona is Assistant Professor in the Department of Curriculum and Instruction and in the Honors College at New Mexico State University, Las Cruces, New Mexico, USA. Her work focuses on critical multicultural education, borderlands theory in education, critical race theory, and *testimonio* methodology and pedagogy.

Chicana/Latina Testimonios as Pedagogical, Methodological, and Activist Approaches to Social Justice

Edited by
**Dolores Delgado Bernal, Rebeca Burciaga
and Judith Flores Carmona**

LONDON AND NEW YORK

First published 2016 by Routledge

2 Park Square, Milton Park, Abingdon, Oxfordshire OX14 4RN
711 Third Avenue, New York, NY 10017

Routledge is an imprint of the Taylor & Francis Group, an informa business

First issued in paperback 2017

British Library Cataloguing in Publication Data
A catalogue record for this book is available from the British Library

ISBN 13: 978-1-138-96297-2 (hbk)
ISBN 13: 978-1-138-30238-9 (hbk)

Typeset in Times New Roman
by RefineCatch Limited, Bungay, Suffolk

Publisher's Note
The publisher accepts responsibility for any inconsistencies that may have
arisen during the conversion of this book from journal articles to book chapters,
namely the possible inclusion of journal terminology.

Disclaimer
Every effort has been made to contact copyright holders for their permission to
reprint material in this book. The publishers would be grateful to hear from any
copyright holder who is not here acknowledged and will undertake to rectify
any errors or omissions in future editions of this book.

Contents

CONTENTS

Citation Information

The chapters in this book were originally published in *Equity & Excellence in Education*, volume 45, issue 3 (July–September 2012). When citing this material, please use the original page numbering for each article, as follows:

Introduction
Chicana/Latina Testimonios*: Mapping the Methodological, Pedagogical, and Political*
Dolores Delgado Bernal, Rebeca Burciaga, and Judith Flores Carmona
Equity & Excellence in Education, volume 45, issue 3 (July–September 2012) pp. 363–372

Chapter 1
Testimonios *of Life and Learning in the Borderlands: Subaltern Juárez Girls Speak*
Claudia G. Cervantes-Soon
Equity & Excellence in Education, volume 45, issue 3 (July–September 2012) pp. 373–391

Chapter 2
Chicana/Latina Testimonios *on Effects and Responses to Microaggressions*
Lindsay Pérez Huber and Bert María Cueva
Equity & Excellence in Education, volume 45, issue 3 (July–September 2012) pp. 392–410

Chapter 3
Pedagogies from Nepantla: Testimonio*, Chicana/Latina Feminisms and Teacher Education Classrooms*
Linda Prieto and Sofia A. Villenas
Equity & Excellence in Education, volume 45, issue 3 (July–September 2012) pp. 411–429

Chapter 4
Chicana and Black Feminisms: Testimonios *of Theory, Identity, and Multiculturalism*
Cinthya M. Saavedra and Michelle Salazar Pérez
Equity & Excellence in Education, volume 45, issue 3 (July–September 2012) pp. 430–443

Chapter 5

The Process of Reflexión *in Bridging* Testimonios *Across Lived Experience*
Michelle M. Espino, Irene I. Vega, Laura I. Rendón, Jessica J. Ranero, and
Marcela M. Muñiz
Equity & Excellence in Education, volume 45, issue 3 (July–September 2012) pp. 444–459

Chapter 6

Making Curriculum from Scratch: Testimonio *in an Urban Classroom*
Cindy Cruz
Equity & Excellence in Education, volume 45, issue 3 (July–September 2012) pp. 460–471

Chapter 7

Getting There Cuando No Hay Camino *(When There Is No Path): Paths to Discovery*
Testimonios *by Chicanas in STEM*
Norma E. Cantú
Equity & Excellence in Education, volume 45, issue 3 (July–September 2012) pp. 472–487

Chapter 8

Testimonio *as Praxis for a Reimagined Journalism Model and Pedagogy*
Sonya M. Alemán
Equity & Excellence in Education, volume 45, issue 3 (July–September 2012) pp. 488–506

Chapter 9

Digital Testimonio *as a Signature Pedagogy for Latin@ Studies*
Rina Benmayor
Equity & Excellence in Education, volume 45, issue 3 (July–September 2012) pp. 507–524

Chapter 10

Testimonio*: Origins, Terms, and Resources*
Kathryn Blackmer Reyes and Julia E. Curry Rodríguez
Equity & Excellence in Education, volume 45, issue 3 (July–September 2012) pp. 525–538

For any permission-related enquiries please visit:
http://www.tandfonline.com/page/help/permissions

Notes on Contributors

Sonya M. Alemán is an Associate Professor in the Mexican Studies program at the University of Texas at San Antonio, TX, USA. Both her research and teaching explore issues of race, racism, representation, and access for communities of color – particularly Latina/o and Chicana/o communities – in media and in educational systems. She draws on critical race theory and Chicana Feminism to inform both her scholarship and pedagogy. Dr. Alemán previously taught at the University of Utah, where she served as Advisor to the campus' only bilingual Chicana/o student newspaper and as Faculty Coordinator for a first year retention program for students of color.

Rina Benmayor is Professor Emerita in the Division of Humanities and Communication at California State University Monterey Bay, CA, USA. She has taught and published widely on community oral history, testimonio, Latina literature, and digital storytelling. She is co-editor of *Memory, Subjectivities, and Representation: Approaches to Oral History in Latin America, Portugal, and Spain* (Palgrave, forthcoming, 2016).

Kathryn Blackmer Reyes is a Librarian and Director of the Cultural Heritage Center which houses the US Race/Ethnic Studies Collections at the Dr. Martin Luther King, Jr. Library of San Jose State University, CA, USA. Her research areas include: Latino Digital Library Resources, Latino Comics, Elizabeth 'Betita' Martinez's works, and Chicano popular culture. She is the founder of the Kaya Sugiyama Endowment at the CHC which supports Asian American and Chicano Studies collections. Most recently she curated the Luis Valdez and El Teatro Campesino 50th Anniversary exhibit.

Rebeca Burciaga is an Assistant Professor of Educational Leadership at San José State University, California, USA. Her work focuses on understanding and challenging educational practices and structures that (re)produce racial, ethnic, gender, and class inequalities. She uses Chicana feminist methodologies and pedagogies to study *educación* (informal learning/ socialization) as epistemological and ontological knowledge production.

Norma E. Cantú is Professor of Latino/Latino Studies and English at the University of Missouri, Kansas City, and Professor Emerita at the University of Texas at San Antonio, TX, USA. She is the founder and director of the Society for the Study of Gloria Anzaldúa and co-founder of CantoMundo, an organization of US Latin@ poets.

Claudia G. Cervantes-Soon is an Assistant Professor of Bilingual/Bicultural Education at the University of Texas at Austin, TX, USA. Her research interests include critical perspectives on bilingual and dual language education, critical pedagogy, cultural studies, and Chicana feminist theories in education with a special emphasis on subaltern women in the US–Mexico borderlands.

Cindy Cruz is an Assistant Professor at the University of California, Santa Cruz, CA, USA. Her research interests are with queer street youth, resistance, youth and violence, and decolonizing pedagogies. In particular, she is pursuing research that centers the thinking of feminists of color.

Julia E. Curry Rodríguez teaches in Chicana and Chicano Studies at San José State University, CA, USA. Her research and advocacy focuses on undocumented student advocacy, pioneer women's oral histories, immigrant women and children, and feminist immigration policy. See her chapter, "Mothers on the Move" in Andrea O'Reilly, editor., *Mothers, Mothering and Motherhood Across Cultural Differences* (2014). Dr. Curry is the SJSU Distinguished Service Professor (2013–2014).

Dolores Delgado Bernal is Professor of Education and Ethnic Studies at the University of Utah, Salt Lake City, Utah, USA. Her community-engaged research focuses on the educational (in)equity of students of color, Latina/o educational pathways, and Chicana feminist methodologies and pedagogies.

Michelle M. Espino is an Assistant Professor in Higher Education, Student Affairs, and International Education Policy at the University of Maryland, College Park, MD, USA. Her research interests centre on Latina/o educational pathways, particularly graduate education, as well as on employing critical methodologies in higher education research.

Judith Flores Carmona is Assistant Professor in the Department of Curriculum and Instruction and in the Honors College at New Mexico State University, Las Cruces, New Mexico, USA. Her works focuses on critical multicultural education, borderlands theory in education, critical race theory, and *testimonio* methodology and pedagogy.

Marcela M. Muñiz is a scholar specializing in higher education policy and diversity, and a regional director of alumni affairs and development for the Faculty of Arts and Sciences at Harvard University.

Lindsay Pérez Huber is an Assistant Professor in the Social and Cultural Analysis program in the College of Education at California State University, Long Beach, CA, USA. She is also visiting researcher in the Chicano Studies Research Center at UCLA, Los Angeles, CA, USA. Her research areas include race and immigration in education, critical race theory and critical race methodologies, microaggressions, and Latina/o education pipeline analysis.

Linda Prieto earned her doctorate in Curriculum and Instruction with an emphasis in Cultural Studies in Education and a Graduate Portfolio in Mexican American Studies at the University of Texas at Austin, TX, USA. She is currently an Independent Scholar working in various areas, such as bilingual education, teacher formation, culturally efficaciousness, social justice issues, biliteracy development, and teaching the Nahua mathematical figurative model–Nepohualtzitzin.

Jessica J. Ranero is a scholar-practitioner who has devoted her career to the field of higher education.

Laura I. Rendón is a Professor of Higher Education, and Co-Director of the Center for Research and Policy in Education, in the College University of Texas-San Antonio, TX, USA.

Cinthya M. Saavedra is an Associate Professor of Diversity and ESL Education at Utah State University, Logan, UT, USA. Her research interests include Chicana/Latina feminist(s), investigations of childhood studies, teacher education, and immigrant educational experiences.

Michelle Salazar Pérez is an Assistant Professor of Early Childhood Education at New Mexico State University, Las Cruces, USA. Her research interests include using critical qualitative methodologies and Black feminist thought to examine dominant constructions of childhood/s, particularly how they influence public policy and subjugate the lived experiences of marginalized people/s and communities.

Irene I. Vega is a doctoral student in Sociology at the University of California, Los Angeles, CA, USA. Her research interests are in international migration, racial and political group formation, and educational inequality. Her work has appeared in the *American Behavioral Scientist*, *Equity and Excellence in Education*, and the *Journal of Hispanic Higher Education*.

Sofia A. Villenas is an Associate Professor in the Department of Anthropology, and the director of the Latina/o Studies Program, at Cornell University, Ithaca, NY, USA. Her scholarship draws from Latina/Chicana and women of color feminisms and critical race studies to explore pedagogy and everyday social movement, and Latina/o education and civic life.

Chicana/Latina *Testimonios*: Mapping the Methodological, Pedagogical, and Political

Dolores Delgado Bernal
University of Utah

Rebeca Burciaga
San Jose State University

Judith Flores Carmona
New Mexico State University

While the genre of *testimonio* has deep roots in oral cultures and in Latin American human rights struggles, the publication and subsequent adoption of *This Bridge Called My Back* (Moraga & Anzaldúa, 1983) and, more recently, *Telling to Live: Latina Feminist Testimonios* (Latina Feminist Group, 2001) by Chicanas and Latinas, have demonstrated the power of *testimonio* as a genre that exposes brutality, disrupts silencing, and builds solidarity among women of color (Anzaldúa, 1990). Within the field of education, scholars are increasingly taking up *testimonio* as a pedagogical, methodological, and activist approach to social justice that transgresses traditional paradigms in academia. Unlike the more common training of researchers to produce unbiased knowledge, *testimonio* challenges objectivity by situating the individual in communion with a collective experience marked by marginalization, oppression, or resistance. These approaches have resulted in new understandings about how marginalized communities build solidarity and respond to and resist dominant culture, laws, and policies that perpetuate inequity. This special issue contributes to our understanding of *testimonio* as it relates to methodology, pedagogy, research, and reflection within a social justice education framework. A common thread among these articles is a sense of political urgency to address educational inequities within Chicana/o and Latina/o communities.

In what follows, we map the *testimonio* genre with a focus on the ways in which Chicana/Latina scholars have contributed to and reshaped it. We begin with a discussion of the contours of the genre including its political purpose. We then take up both the methodology and pedagogy of *testimonio*. Throughout, we discuss how scholars using *testimonio* in this issue have unveiled new approaches to understanding and addressing issues of inequity in the field of education.

MAPPING THE *TESTIMONIO* GENRE

Testimonio writing has a long and varied history; it is most often seen as a voice from the margins or from the subaltern—a political approach that elicits solidarity from the reader. *Testimonios* were first used to convey the experiences and enduring struggles of people who have experienced persecution by governments and other socio-political forces in Latin American countries (Behar, 1993; Burgos-Debray, 1984; Lomas & Joysmith, 2005). *Testimonio* is and continues to be an approach that incorporates political, social, historical, and cultural histories that accompany one's life experiences as a means to bring about change through consciousness-raising. In bridging individuals with collective histories of oppression, a story of marginalization is re-centered to elicit social change.

Testimonio differs from oral history or autobiography in that it involves the participant in a critical reflection of their personal experience within particular sociopolitical realities. That is, it links "the spoken word to social action and privileges the oral narrative of personal experience as a source of knowledge, empowerment, and political strategy for claiming rights and bringing about social change" (Benmayor, Torruellas, & Juarbe, 1997, p. 153). *Testimonio* transcends descriptive discourse to one that is more performative in that the narrative simultaneously engages the personal and collective aspects of identity formation while translating choices, silences, and ultimately identities (Beverley, 2005; Latina Feminist Group, 2001; Lopez & Davalos, 2009). As such, *testimonio* is pragmatic in that it engages the reader to understand and establish a sense of solidarity as a first step toward social change.

There has been an explosion of *testimonio* scholarship in academia, with "*testimonios*" appearing in 36 dissertations and theses from 1990–1999 and soaring to 835 during the 2000–2009 period (Blackmer Reyes & Curry Rodriguez, this issue). Much of the growth in *testimonio* scholarship has been within the field of education, focuses on the experiences of Chicana/o and Latina/o communities in the United States, and is largely being produced by Chicanas and Latinas. This may be due to the fact that *testimonio* as a methodology provides modes of analysis that are collaborative and attentive to myriad ways of knowing and learning in our communities. It might also be attributed to the ways in which *testimonios* align with a strong *feminista* tradition of theorizing from the brown female body, breaking silences, and bearing witness to both injustice and social change (Anzaldúa, 1990; Cruz, 2006; Moraga & Anzaldúa, 1983). *Testimonio*, then, can be understood as a bridge that merges the brown bodies in our communities with academia as we employ *testimonio* methodology and pedagogy in educational practices.

Telling to Live: Latina Feminist Testimonios (2001) is part of this *feminista* tradition and the book opens by the authors reflecting upon their *papelitos guardados*—the protected papers written and roles filled in times of transition. *Papelitos guardados* are both concrete and abstract notions of self during various points in one's life. Some are shared openly with others, yet other *papelitos* are written in journals or filed in one's mind. In *Telling to Live, papelitos guardados* are explored through the method of *testimonio*. To this end, *testimonio* is process (methodology), product (inclusive of text, video, performance, or audio), and a way of teaching and learning (pedagogy). As a process, *testimoniar* (to give testimony) is the act of recovering *papelitos guardados*—previous experiences otherwise silenced or untold—and unfolding them into a narrative that conveys personal, political, and social realities. One's *testimonio* reveals an epistemology of truths and how one has come to understand them. *Testimonio* bridges or serves to connect generations of displaced and disenfranchised communities across time. In the next section, we look at how the methodology of *testimonio* also serves as a bridge to connect the lived experience as a "data" collecting tool and as the analytical process.

TESTIMONIO AS A METHODOLOGICAL TOOL

Testimonio is both a product and a process. While the methodological strategy of *testimonio* is by no means limited to the research conducted by or with Chicanas/Latinas, the ways in which it has been articulated and enacted by these scholars mirror a sensibility that allows the mind, body, and spirit to be equally valuable sources of knowledge and embrace the engagement of social transformation. The methodological concerns of *testimonio* are often around giving voice to silences, representing the other, reclaiming authority to narrate, and disentangling questions surrounding legitimate truth. Most of the methodological and epistemological discussions regarding *testimonios* focus on an approach in which an interlocutor, who is an outside activist and/or ally, records, transcribes, edits, and prepares a manuscript for publication. Within this approach, a *testimonialista*[1] works closely with the recorder/researcher/journalist to bring attention to her community's experiences. When translating, for example, terms of endearment, underlying meaning can get lost in translation. One must be cautious to translate conceptually rather than literally because in translating particular terms, nuances get lost, and we run the risk of reproducing language marginalization. Translating *testimonios* from Spanish into English includes translating culturally-specific knowledge that can shift meaning and reproduce negative connotations associated with gendered or racialized terms of endearment[2]. When translating we become a sort of interlocutor, a translator whose knowledge of English and Spanish becomes a filter to move from one language to another and the knowledge of the languages might affect the *testimonios* (Flores Carmona, 2010). In this act, the *testimonialista* is the holder of knowledge thereby disrupting traditional academic ideals of who might be considered a producer of knowledge (Delgado Bernal, 2009).

This type of *testimonio* scholarship places the Chicana/Latina scholar as the "outside" ally and activist who brings attention to the conditions of a particular group of Latinas/os. For example, in this issue, Claudia G. Cervantes-Soon ("*Testimonios* of Life and Learning in the Borderlands: Subaltern Juárez Girls Speak") presents the *testimonios* of two high-school girls who attend a school with a critical pedagogy orientation and are coming of age in one of the most marginalized areas of Ciudad Juárez, Mexico. These *testimonios* shed light on their experiences and identity formation, attesting to their struggle for freedom, dignity, and life on the South side of the border. In order to understand the effects of microaggressions as embodied systemic oppression, Lindsay Pérez Huber and Bert María Cueva also serve as "outside" allies and activists in "Chicana/Latina *Testimonios* on Effects and Responses to Microaggressions" as they present the *testimonios* of undocumented and U.S.-born Chicana/Latina students. The students' *testimonios* are analyzed from a Latina/o critical race and Chicana feminist theoretical lens that allows us to name some of the oppressions encountered in schools and to better understand how Chicana/Latina students respond to and heal from oppressive experiences. In both of these articles, the authors, who hold multiple insider and outsider positionalities, take care in addressing their methodology and some of the concerns surrounding issues of voice, representation, truth, and their role as researchers.

Their work also exemplifies and displays a Chicana/Latina *feminista* sensibility and attempts to situate the researcher-participant in a reciprocal relationship where genuine connections are made between the researcher and community members.

Another type of *testimonio* scholarship that can raise different methodological concerns is that in which the *testimonialista* is both researcher and participant where, for example, a formally educated Chicana/Latina documents her own collective story in or out of academia (see Burciaga & Tavares, 2006; Delgado Bernal, 2008; Flores Carmona, 2010; Hurtado, Hurtado, & Hurtado, 2008; Latina Feminist Group, 2001; Russel y Rodríguez, 2007; Turner, 2008). Bypassing the role of an interlocutor, these *testimonialistas* narrate their own stories and also challenge dominant notions of who can construct knowledge. They (re)claim *testimonio* as a text written by and for Latinas (or other marginalized groups) to theorize oppression, resistance, and subjectivity (Latina Feminist Group, 2001).

There have been important discussions around the idea that attaining a privileged status might remove one from the possibility of writing one's subaltern or marginalized life. We align with Delgado Bernal and Elenes (2011) and quote them at length to contend that for most Chicana/Latina scholars and other scholars of color, group marginalization continues to exist in academia even when one holds a relatively privileged status.

> Some scholars point to the idea that the very possibility of "writing one's life" (Beverley, 2005, p. 548) implies that the narrator is no longer in the situation of marginality and subalternity that her narrative describes. Part of Gayatri Spivak's (1988) argument is that "being subaltern means . . . not mattering, not being worth listening to, or not being understood when one is 'heard'" (Beverley, 2005, p. 551). Stated another way, if the narrator has attained the cultural status of an author (and generally speaking middle or upper class status), she has transitioned from the subaltern group identity to an individualized identity. We argue that for most Chicana/Latina scholars this is not the case: A group identity and group marginalization continues to exist in academia even when we have attained a relatively privileged status. (p. 111)

Indeed, the *testimonios* of Latinas in academia such as those in Telling To Live: Latina Feminist *Testimonios* (Latina Feminist Group, 2001) or *Speaking from the Body: Latinas on Health and Culture* (Chabram-Dernersesian & de la Torre, 2008) expose experiences of rape, attempted suicide, migrations, chronic health problems, struggles within educational institutions, health care access, and the labor of academia. In doing so, their stories "tell how our bodies are maps of oppression, of institutional violence and stress, of exclusion, objectification, and abuse" (Latina Feminist Group, 2001, p. 12). Our bodies also tell stories of transformational resistance (Solorzano & Delgado Bernal, 2001) talking back, and surviving in academia.

In this special issue, a number of scholars present their own *testimonios* as educators, re-searchers, and/or scholars. For example, in "Pedagogies from *Nepantla*: *Testimonio*, Chicana/Latina Feminisms, and Teacher Education Classrooms," Linda Prieto and Sofia A. Villenas provide us with their *testimonios* as two teacher educators committed to compassionate pedagogy and transformative teaching. They share how their experiences as child translators, young activists, children of caring immigrant parents, college students in predominately white universities, and racialized, gendered, and classed Chicanas inform their pedagogy of *nepantla* in teacher education classrooms. They conceptualize a pedagogy of *nepantla* that exposes tensions, contradictions, and possibilities for exploring how we might engage in transformative teaching. Cinthya M. Saavedra and Michelle Salazar Pérez are teacher and early childhood educators who also by-pass the interlocutor to narrate their own *testimonios*. They draw from their theoretical homes,

Chicana feminism and Black feminism, respectively, in their article, "Chicana and Black Feminisms: *Testimonios* of Theory, Identity, and Multiculturalism" to theorize their shifting identities and privileges in and out of educational institutions, the healing of their mind, body, and spirit, and the us/them binary often found in multicultural education. They translate their theorizations into pedagogical lessons for collective social justice work in classrooms and local and global communities. Another example of scholars narrating their own *testimonios,* is the collaborative work of Michelle M. Espino, Irene I. Vega, Laura I. Rendón, Jessica J. Ranero, and Marcela M. Muñiz. These scholars provide an intergenerational perspective ("The Process of *Reflexión* in Bridging *Testimonios* Across Lived Experience") that bears witness to the critical challenges, consequences, and benefits of academic life for both emerging and *veterana* scholars. They suggest the process of *reflexión* as a way to theorize the status of Latinas in academia through the eyes of two different generations. The process of *reflexión* allows us to learn and listen to our elders' wisdom to preserve knowledge(s) that will not be learned in schools. Their article not only names and critiques oppressive educational structures, but the authors affirm healing pathways for our fractured minds, bodies, and spirits.

Whether as an ally or a *testimonialista*, Chicanas/Latinas in this issue have used *testimonio* as a methodology to transgress and as a venue to speak about educational inequities and systemic oppressions. Simultaneously, these *testimonios* demonstrate the possibility of social change and transformation of self and society. They seek what "Anzaldúa calls a healing image, one that transforms consciousness, bridges our mind, body, and spirit, and reconnects us with others" (Delgado Bernal, 2009, p. 4). Using *testimonio* as a methodological tool, these articles have highlighted the political urgency needed to address educational inequities, and they have unveiled new approaches to understanding the individual in connection with a collective experience marked by marginalization, oppression, or resistance.

TESTIMONIO AS A PEDAGOGICAL TOOL

Trained in the philosophical context of Western metaphysical dualism, many of us have accepted the notion that there is a split between the body and the mind. Believing this, individuals enter the classroom to teach as though only the mind is present, and not the body. (hooks, 1994, p. 191)

Testimonios focus on collective experiences of conditions that have contributed to oppression, as well as the agency of those who suffer under these conditions. As such, *testimonio* is a pedagogical tool that lends itself to a form of teaching and learning that brings the mind, body, spirit, and political urgency to the fore. Whether in a formal classroom or in myriad informal learning environments, such as the home, *testimonio* has the potential to provide a way to theorize and learn from bodily experiences of oppression and resistance. *Testimonios* represent what Moraga (2002) calls theory in the flesh. That is, *testimonio* is a tool for inscribing struggles and understandings, creating new knowledge, and affirming our epistemologies—*testimonio* is about writing what we know best, "*familia, barrio,* life experiences" (Rendón, 2009, p. 3). Through *testimonio* pedagogy we are able to hear and read each other's stories through voices, silences, bodies, and emotions and with the goal of achieving new *conocimientos*, or understandings. The pedagogical practice and process is far from perfect, but when approached with reverence for the process, it is one that can be creative, innovative, and nurturing of various ways of knowing. *Testimonio* pedagogy is based on "wholeness and inclusiveness" (Rendón, 2009, p. 14)—a pedagogy that pieces together our mind, body, and spirit as well as our head, heart, and hands, and where teaching and learning are not disconnected and theory and praxis are intrinsically dependent on each other. It is a process that brings together critical consciousness and the will to take action to connect with others with love and compassion to bring collective healing (Rendón, 2009). Because *testimonios* can take various forms, including written, oral, and digital, they have the potential to reach many audiences.

No matter what form a *testimonio* takes, listening is central to the pedagogical practice of *testimonio*. Hearing a *testimonio* is not the same as listening to a *testimonio* (Lenkersdorf, 2008). In this genre, listening is the precursor to telling. As a listener, another's *testimonio* is much like a gift—the listener unwraps the *testimonio* to reveal the heart of the matter. In doing so, the listener's responsibility is to engage the *testimonialista* in an effort to understand. *"Si no se habla no escuchamos nada. Y si, en cambio, se habla y no escuchamos, las palabras se dirigen al aire . . . el hablar y el escuchar, ambas se complementan y se requieren mutuamente"* (Lenkersdorf, 2008, p. 12).[3] In this space of exchange between listener and *testimonialista*, we are able to open doors into another's world, open hearts and minds and at times, become invited participants—we become *emparejados*—aligned, next to each other, in solidarity (Lenkersdorf, 2008).

If speakers and listeners are open to hearing perspectives that may be different from ones they have lived, *testimonio* pedagogy can incite personal growth through a reciprocal process of exchange. Through *testimonios* we are invited to be participants, and it is not uncommon to encounter experiences that are difficult to hear, including those that are violent, frightening, and tragic. A goal of intervention is central to a pedagogy of *testimonio*. However, one must first listen to the *testimonio* in an effort to understand before one can be moved to action. Through this process, a pedagogy of *testimonio* can help transcend pain toward a space for healing and societal transformation. Listening to, sharing, and transcending struggles, pain, hopes, and dreams yields a type of interdependent solidarity, or *in lak'ech*—a Mayan philosophy that can be translated as, *"Tu eres mi otro yo"* or "You are my other me." This type of interdependent solidarity allows people to connect across social positions, across differences, across language, across space, and across time (Flores Carmona & Delgado Bernal, 2012).

In listening to the story of one, we learn about the conditions of many. When we pay close attention, we learn that all stories are collective accounts of how various forces including culture, history, and society at large, have shaped our understandings of life. Cindy Cruz ("Making Curriculum from Scratch: *Testimonio* in an Urban Classroom") provides a rich example of this in her excerpt from a queer street youth whose *testimonio* about homelessness is both an individual and collective story. Within this young person's *testimonio* is an analysis and critique of the national crises our country continues to face with realities that include homelessness, poverty, and the marginalization of queer youth. When others read the *testimonio*, it becomes a teaching tool that has the potential to connect people across social positions and build solidarity among both those who are familiar and unfamiliar with the experiences of the *testimonio*.

In this issue, Norma Cantú ("Getting There *Cuando No Hay Camino* [When There is No Path]: Paths to Discovery *Testimonios* by Chicanas in STEM") also employs solidarity praxis as she uses *testimonio* theory to analyze the published *testimonios* of Chicanas in science, technology, engineering, and math (STEM) fields. She acknowledges how their *testimonios* of challenge and triumph have the potential to motivate and inspire students who are struggling to continue their studies in STEM. However, her analysis does not stop there. She delves deeper into the systemic and structural elements that need to be in place so that all Chicanas/Latinas

6

can successfully navigate the educational system in STEM areas, and translates these into policy recommendations. Her work demonstrates the pedagogical potential of *testimonios* at both an individual and systemic level.

Testimonio is deeply rooted in raising critical consciousness or what Brazilian pedagogue Freire (1973) refers to as *conscientização*. This concept focuses on achieving an in-depth understanding of the world—allowing for the perception and exposure of perceived social and political contradictions—to become concretized in our classrooms. Critical consciousness also includes taking action against the oppressive elements that are illuminated by that understanding. For example, in "*Testimonio* as Praxis for a Reimagined Journalism Model and Pedagogy," Sonya M. Alemán presents us with the pedagogical possibilities when Chicana/o journalism students enact a raced-and-gendered conscious journalism practice. The students in her university classroom employ a *testimonio* pedagogy that allows them to reflect on their academic privilege in representing "others" and to simultaneously collaborate with their sources to write and edit stories for an alternative bilingual campus newspaper. Their pedagogy allows them to "pursue traditionally neglected stories, incorporate reciprocity as an element of newsgathering, and position student journalists as agents in the representation and transformation of their communities." She demonstrates how by shifting power relations of news consumers and news producers, the students co-produce stories of political urgency that foster social change.

Rina Benmayor ("Digital *Testimonio* as a Signature Pedagogy for Latin@ Studies") also provides us with pedagogical insights from her university classroom that contribute to the *conscientização* of her students. Her critical "signature pedagogy" is about providing students with texts and teaching that help them name their realities. That is by "taking inspiration from Latina writings, students write, record, produce, publish, and theorize their own *testimonios*, building new knowledge from personal and collective experience." In this process, Benmayor guides students to construct a "historical and theoretical understanding" of who they are as holders and producers of knowledge, in the twenty-first century. Her article and the work of her students demonstrate that *testimonio* is a tool for inscribing our own struggles and understandings, by which we control the authorial process and in which we become subject and object of inquiry, create new knowledge, and affirm our epistemology.

Alemán, Cruz, and Benmayor utilize *testimonio* pedagogies that require building trust (by employing various activities, such as writing exercises, sharing/producing in duos, quick writes, and movement activities) to generate *convivencia* (being with each other) and to develop a genuine interest in listening to each other. When people share intimate or vulnerable parts of themselves, *testimonio* pedagogy asks the listeners for openness, respect, and self-reflexivity to forge connections between people who otherwise might never coalesce or build solidarity. All parts of people enter the pedagogical space as sharing and memory often prompt all our senses when reliving or listening to the stories. Feelings, emotions, knowledges, silences, and identities are integral to learning and connecting with *testimonios*—to enter a new site of knowledge—a space of reclamation.

To enter a new site of knowledge, Kathryn Blackmer Reyes and Julia E. Curry Rodríguez present us with another type of integral tool to learn and connect with *testimonios*. Their article, "*Testimonio*: Origins, Terms, and Resources," offers guidance for the educator or scholar interested in conducting bibliographic research on *testimonio* scholarship and provides a short bibliography divided into three parts: Latin American *Testimonios* Roots/Origins; Chicana/o and Latina/o Narrative/*Testimonios* in Education; and *Testimonios* and Dissertations. They begin by outlining the difficulty in searching for "*testimonio*" and give an exploration of terms used for bibliographic searches, as well as suggestions on how to navigate the Library of Congress key words. They point out, "As researchers we are constrained in research and scholarly production by mainstream terms as defined by librarians who may or may not understand the nuanced bilingual and bicultural use of a term such as *testimonios*." They make clear that there is a rich history of *testimonio* scholarship and that the educational teacher or scholar (with some effort) can unearth and draw upon this scholarship to employ *testimonio* as a methodological or pedagogical tool.

FINAL REFLECTIONS

We took on the editing of this special issue as an academic, political, and personal endeavor. We come to *testimonio* work with different backgrounds and different types of expertise, but we have each taught courses on *testimonio*, have used *testimonio* as a research methodology, have written about *testimonios* within the field of education, and have produced *testimonios* of our own. The editing of this special issue has allowed us to nurture and expand our own ideas and understandings of *testimonio* scholarship, but perhaps most importantly we know that as a collection of scholarship, the contribution of these articles to the field of education is monumental. The authors help us understand the possibilities of engaging *testimonios* in education, and they contribute to how we all understand and address the educational inequities within communities of color, and specifically Chicana/o and Latina/o communities.

Of the 45 original submissions, we were able to include 10 of them between the covers of this issue. We would like to be clear that even though we were unable to accept all of the submissions, the personal, political, and intellectual lessons from the authors whose work we were unable to accept in this issue are groundbreaking. For those submissions that we were not able to accept, we invested time in providing the authors with substantial feedback and often, suggestions for different publication outlets. We know that their work has or will soon contribute to the literature on *testimonio* methodology, pedagogy, research, and reflection within a social justice education framework. As co-editors we made sure that we constantly called and responded to each other on employing a *feminista* editorial process. This process definitely reaffirmed the importance of listening to each other and of growing from mentoring that took place throughout the reading and editing process.

Testimonios are a critical tool for understanding the educational experiences of communities of color in general and Chicana/o and Latina/o communities in particular. It is striking that *testimonio* is becoming more popular in the field of education just when institutions of learning are banning Ethnic Studies and Mexican American Studies programs, specifically, in secondary schools and threatening institutions of higher education with similar cuts (e.g., Arizona). As such, we believe the growth of *testimonio* into the field of education is a challenge to the status quo—a reclamation of intellect that would have otherwise been dismissed by power structures in academia. The growth of *testimonio* in academia is the result of the political urgency to pursue social justice education for communities of color, generally, and Chicana/o and Latina/o communities, in particular. *Testimonio* in academia disrupts silence, invites connection, and entices collectivity—it is social justice scholarship in education.

Putting this special issue together has been a labor of love grounded in political urgency. Our academic training insists that we work in solitude, yet the work of *testimonio* calls us back to reclaim solidarity with one another. The educational opportunities not provided to communities of color in general and Chicana/o and Latina/o communities in particular demand this of us as educators. We offer this special issue to building bridges between us and among us—as a call for political solidarity as *testimonialistas*.

NOTES

1. There are many terms used to describe someone who is giving *testimonio*. In this introduction, we use *testimonialista*. (translanguaging?)
2. Spanish is used throughout this Special Issue. At times it is translated and at other times it is not translated into English for these various reasons. (translanguaging)
3. "If we don't talk, we don't hear anything. And if, in turn, we talk and don't hear, the words dissolve into the air . . . to talk and listen, the two are complimentary and require mutualism."

REFERENCES

Anzaldúa, G. E. (1990). *Making face, making soul/haciendo caras: Creative and critical perspectives of feminists of color*. San Francisco, CA: Aunt Lute Books.

Behar, R. (1993). *Translated woman: Crossing the border with Esperanza's story*. Boston: Beacon.

Benmayor, R., Torruellas, R. M., & Juarbe, A. L. (1997). Claiming cultural citizenship in East Harlem: "Si esto puede ayudar a la comunidad mia. . ." In W. V. Flores & R. Benmayor (Eds.), *Latino cultural citizenship: Claiming identity, space, and rights* (pp. 152–209). Boston, MA: Beacon.

Beverley, J. (2005). Testimonio, subalternity, and narrative authority. In N. K. Denzin & Y. S. Lincoln (Eds.), *Handbook of qualitative research* (pp. 555–565). Thousand Oaks, CA: Sage.

Burciaga, R., & Tavares, A. (2006). Our pedagogy of sisterhood: A testimonio. In D. Delgado Bernal, C. A. Elenes, F. E. Godinez, & S. Villenas (Eds.), *Chicana/Latina feminist pedagogies and epistemologies of everyday life: Educación en la familia, comunidad y escuela* (pp. 133–142). New York, NY: State University of New York Press.

Burgos-Debray, E. (1984). *I, Rigoberta Menchú, an Indian woman in Guatemala. (A. Wright, Trans.)* New York, NY: Verso.

Chabram-Dernersesian, A., & de la Torre, A. (Eds.). (2008). *Speaking from the body: Latinas on health and culture*. Tucson, AZ: The University of Arizona Press.

Cruz, C. (2006). Toward an epistemology of a brown body. In D. Delgado Bernal, C. A. Elenes, F. E. Godinez, & S. Villenas (Eds.), *Chicana/Latina education in everyday life: Feminista perspectives on pedagogy and epistemology* (pp. 59–75). New York, NY: SUNY Press.

Delgado Bernal, D. (2008). La trenza de identidades: Weaving together my personal, professional, and communal identities. In K. P. Gonzalez & R. V. Padilla (Eds.), *Doing the public good: Latina/o scholars engage civic participation* (pp. 134–148). Sterling, VA: Stylus.

Delgado Bernal, D. (2009) Introduction: Our testimonios as methodology, pedagogy, and a messy work in progress. In S. Alemán, D. Delgado Bernal, J. Flores Carmona, L. Galas, & M. Garza (Eds.), *Unidas we heal: Testimonios of mind/body/soul. Latinas telling testimonios* (pp. 4–6). Salt Lake City, UT: University of Utah. [Edited in-house book.]

Delgado Bernal, D., & Elenes, C. A. (2011). Chicana feminist theorizing: Methodologies, pedagogies, and practices. In R. R. Valencia (Ed.), *Chicano school failure and success: Present, past, and future* (3rd ed., pp. 99–140). New York, NY: Routledge.

Flores Carmona, J. (2010). Transgenerational Educación: Latina mothers' everyday pedagogies of cultural citizenship in Salt Lake City, Utah. Unpublished dissertation, University of Utah.

Flores Carmona, J., & Delgado Bernal, D. (2012). Oral histories in the classroom: Home and community pedagogies. In C. E. Sleeter & E. Soriano Ayala (Eds.), *Building solidarity between schools and marginalized communities: International perspectives*. New York, NY: Teachers College Press.

Freire, P. (1973). *Pedagogy of the oppressed*. New York, NY: Seabury.

hooks, b. (1994). *Teaching to transgress: Education as the practice of freedom*. New York, NY: Routledge.

Hurtado, A., Hurtado, M. A., & Hurtado, A. L. (2008). Tres hermanas (Three sisters): A model of relational achievement. In K. González & R. Padilla (Eds.), *Doing the public good: Latina/o scholars engage civic participation* (pp. 39–81). Sterling, VA: Stylus.

Latina Feminist Group. (2001). *Telling to live: Latina feminist testimonios*. Durham, NC: Duke University Press.

Lenkersdorf, C. (2008). *Aprender a escuchar: Enseñanzas maya-tojolabales*. Mexico, DF: Editora Plaza y Valdés. S.A de C.V..

Lomas, C., & Joysmith, C. (Eds.). (2005). *One wound for another/Una herida por otra: Testimonios de Latin@s in the U.S. through cyberspace (11 de septiembre de 2001–11 de marzo de 2002)*. Mexico, MX: Universidad Nacional Autonoma de Mexico.

López, T. A., & Davalos, K. M. (2009). Knowing, feeling, doing: The epistemology of Chicana/Latina studies. *Chicana/Latina Studies: The Journal of Mujeres Activas en Letras y Cambio Social, 8*, 10–22.

Moraga, C. (2002). Theory in the flesh. In C.Moraga & G. E.Anzaldúa (Eds.), *This bridge called my back: Writings by radical women of color* (3rd ed., p. 21). San Francisco, CA: Aunt Lute Press.

Moraga, C., & Anzaldúa, G. (1983). *This bridge called my back: Writings by radical women of color*. Brooklyn, NY: Kitchen Table: Women of Color Press.

Rendón, L. I. (2009). *Sentipensante (Sensing/thinking) pedagogy: Educating for wholeness, social justice and liberation*. Sterling, VA: Stylus.

Russel y Rodriguez, M. (2007). Messy spaces: Chicana testimonio and the undisciplining of ethnography. *Chicana/Latina Studies: A Journal of Mujeres Activas en Letras y Cambio Social, 7*(1), 86–121.

Solorzano, D. G., & Delgado Bernal, D. (2001). Examining transformal resistance through a critical race and latcrit theory framework: Chicana and Chicana students in Urban context. *Urban Education, 36*(3), 308–342.

Turner, C. S. (2008). Toward public education as a public good: Reflections from the field. In K. González & R. Padilla (Eds.), *Doing the public good: Latina/o scholars engage civic participation* (pp. 97–111). Sterling, VA: Stylus.

Testimonios of Life and Learning in the Borderlands: Subaltern Juárez Girls Speak

Claudia G. Cervantes-Soon

University of North Carolina at Chapel Hill

This article presents the *testimonios* of two high school girls coming of age in one of the most marginalized areas of Ciudad Juárez, México who attend a school with a critical pedagogy orientation (Freire, 1970). Ciudad Juárez is a city on the U.S-México border and considered one of the most violent in the world today. These *testimonios* shed light on the life experiences and identity formation of young women coming of age in the south side of the border and reveal the knowledge and wisdom they have gained in their struggle for freedom, dignity, and life. They also expose the epistemological and pedagogical nature of young women's discourse and wisdom characterized by *testimonios* as counter-narratives, confessions, and *consejos*; and the role of a critical school in promoting such discourse. This article offers insight into the potential of schools to become sites of organic healing, critical consciousness, and agency in dystopic times by cultivating the use of *testimonios* as a way to center and legitimize subaltern knowledge.

The eyes of the world have been on Ciudad Juárez, México for the last few decades. Images and stories of crime, feminicides[1], violence, impunity, gendered cheap labor, drug trafficking, industrialization, and social inequalities abound in the literature and popular culture depicting this city along the U.S.-México border. Despite the numerous analyses that exist about Juárez, the voices of youth are typically absent. This article presents the *testimonios* of two high school girls coming of age in one of the most marginalized areas of Juárez. These *testimonios* offer salient depictions of experiences, identity formation, and epistemologies on the south side of the border where women's freedom is constantly contested and poor youth are continuously criminalized. Yet, their *testimonios* offer a language of hope and insight into the potential of schools to promote healing, critical consciousness, and agency in dystopic times. Through their *testimonios*, these young Juárez women use counter-narratives to interrupt the media-driven discourse, raise consciousness, and reclaim their humanity. Moreover, their *testimonios* have become part of a habitual discourse of confessions and *consejos*[2], which they use as a pedagogical instrument for survival, healing, and collective learning.

TESTIMONIOS AS THEORY AND METHOD

This article utilizes *testimonio* as a way to bring to the surface a narrative of urgency in the dystopic condition of Juárez and a potential tool to decolonize pedagogical and research practices. These ideas are grounded on Moraga and Anzaldúa's (1981) notion of "theory in the flesh" (p. 23), an organic theory that emerges in urgency and that privileges the real experiences, voices, and knowledge of subaltern women of color demanding attention and action. This is a "struggle of the flesh, and struggle of borders, an inner war" (Anzaldúa, 1987, p. 100) in which women's brown bodies are the mediums, witnesses, and agents (Cruz, 2001). Brown bodies thus constitute the very sites of collision between the First and Third Worlds and of identity negotiation, where the personal becomes political, and knowledge and theory are generated and materialized through experience. If theory in the flesh is the unification of the mind and body (Cruz, 2001), then the personal narrative becomes a means for agency. As the narrator tells her story, she breaks the silence, negotiates contradictions, and recreates new identities beyond the fragmentation, shame, and betrayal brought about by oppression, colonization, and patriarchy (Moraga, 1993). *Testimonios* allow us to put the scattered pieces together of a painful experience in a new way that generates wisdom and consciousness:

> You've chosen to compose a new history and self—to rewrite your *autohistoria* [self-story]. You want to be transformed again; you want a keener mind, a stronger spirit, a wiser soul. Your ailing body is no longer a hindrance but an asset, witnessing pain, speaking to you, demanding touch. *Es tu cuerpo que busca conocimiento* [It's your body that seeks knowledge]; along with dreams your body's the royal road to consciousness. (Anzaldúa, 2002, pp. 558–559)

Testimonios thus offer the opportunity to develop and expose theory in the flesh and urge the audience to action as "the voice that speaks to the reader through the text in the form of an 'I' . . . that demands to be recognized" (Beverley, 2000, p. 548). *Testimonios* originated in Latin American, indigenous, emancipatory struggles, calling attention to painful events or series of oppressions and recognition of indigenous peoples' knowledge (Menchú, 1984; Smith, 2005). Other subaltern women of color have also used *testimonios* to advance their emancipatory goals. The Latina Feminist Group (2001) used *testimonios* to reveal both painful and enriching experiences that have given way to their complex identities while collectively interrupting the silence and isolation that served to perpetuate their oppression both in their communities and in the academy. N. González (2006) presented the *testimonios* of immigrant mothers' struggles and excruciating experiences to reveal their epistemologies and forms of agency, as well as their redefinitions of motherhood and pedagogy, and Elenes (2000) discussed the role of Chicana testimonial texts in destabilizing the hegemony of Western academic knowledge and notions of truth.

The *testimonios* I present here exemplify the possibilities of *mujerista* pedagogical and epistemological theory—that which centers *mujeres'* "articulations of teaching and learning, along with ways of knowing—rooted in the diverse and everyday living of Chicanas/Latinas as members of families, communities, and a global society" (Villenas, Godinez, Delgado Bernal, & Elenes, 2006, p. 3). These *testimonios* reflect some of the ways in which the young women in this study develop and share knowledge and agency in their daily lives despite the dystopic living conditions afforded to them.

The *testimonios* emerged from a year-long ethnography that I conducted at Preparatoria Esperanza (pseudonym) in Ciudad Juárez. My goal was to learn from Mexican border girls who were born into a city, infamous for its feminicides and considered one of the most violent in the world. Furthermore, I was interested in learning about the possibilities of agency within a school context characterized by a strong critical pedagogy orientation.

I began my fieldwork in August 2010, more than a year into the vicious drug war and four months after the most massive militarization in the city's history. I interviewed eight working-class girls from Preparatoria Esperanza and had numerous ethnographic conversations and informal interviews with teachers and several other students in the school. I also spent significant time conducting observations in the classrooms, as well as in other school settings, including the hallways, the courtyards, the library, and locations where students had extracurricular activities. During my year-long stay in the community, I collected multiple *testimonios* from all the girls I interviewed and from others with whom I had an opportunity to converse and observe. The *testimonios* that I chose to share here, while very different, are representative of the multiple strategies and approaches to different ways of knowing utilized by many of the girls whom I met. I selected the *testimonios* of young women that demonstrate some of the ways in which their brown bodies experience the material realities of their context and whose experiences and narratives of survival, healing, and transformation embody consciousness, agency, and theory (Cruz, 2001).

As a critical ethnographer (Foley, 2002) and as their interlocutor, I abandoned assumptions of positivist, detached objectivism, and instead sought to speak from "a very particular race, class, gender, and sexual identity location" (Foley & Valenzuela, 2000, p. 218). Thus, I conducted this research from a Chicana feminist standpoint; I was a native of Juárez who became a border crosser from an early age and eventually immigrated permanently to the United States in 1997. Needless to say, this research was an intellectual endeavor as much as it was personal, and my goals were not neutral. As a Chicana researcher, my desire was to be an agent of knowledge and produce transformative research in what I still consider my community. Hence, I was strongly guided by my own cultural intuition (Delgado Bernal, 2001), which draws on the researcher's personal, professional, and collective experiences, community memory, and existing literature, as a legitimate epistemic framework in the entire inquiry and analysis process of Chicanas' research goals. As the ethnographer, I was a partial insider whose insight is substantially informed by my experiences growing up in Ciudad Juárez and by my work for almost a decade with Mexican families on the border as a bilingual educator and as a critical pedagogue. In addition, I drew from border theories and Chicana feminist thought, which recognize the borderlands as a privileged space not only for the study of multiple and fluid identities, but also as a source of new knowledge and epistemologies (Anzaldúa, 1987; Elenes, 2006; Mignolo, 2000).

The young women narrating their *testimonios* were among the students whom I interviewed or conversed with during my fieldwork. I witnessed the young women share their *testimonios* with friends or peers or with me during interviews. As the ethnographer, I merely serve as the interlocutor through which the narrators seek to bring their situation to the attention of the academic and international audiences. I recorded the narrators' oral accounts, transcribed them, translated them into English, and edited them. I strived to remain as close as possible to the narrators' voices, seeking to affirm the authority of their personal experiences. Thus, some Spanish words remained in their *testimonios*, to maintain the authenticity of their message. I attempted to preserve their individual communication styles by translating some words or phrases in ways that

I considered effective. Simultaneously, I eliminated my own questions, interjections from other students, and significant deviations from the subject to keep the fluidity and cohesiveness of their narratives. While the girls wanted their voices and ideas to be shared, I used pseudonyms to offer some degree of anonymity.

Given the unequal power relations and intrusiveness present even in feminist ethnographic research (Stacey, 1988), a greater effort to decolonize it should employ practices that center the participants' concerns and knowledge and result in theory based on the participants' own point of view and for their own goals (Smith, 2005). Smith underscores that *testimonios* with indigenous peoples can have a decolonizing effect in that there is an inherent "notion that truth is being revealed" (p. 144). As I offer the *testimonios* of young Juárez women, I seek to situate their lives and voices as knowledge and truth that comes from experience and that deserves a protected space and serious attention. The young women offering their *testimonios*, do so courageously as organic intellectuals (in Gramsci's [1971/2000] sense), aiming to intervene in the academic world and seeking solidarity and coalition (Beverley, 2000). But the ideas that these girls express through their *testimonios* are also organic in the sense that they were grown in a soil that they know well, rather than imported from academic circles (Levins Morales, 2001).

> [T]he intellectual traditions [they] come from create theory out of shared lives instead of sending away for it . . . [They] grew directly out of listening to [their] own discomforts, finding out who shared them, who validated them, and in exchanging stories about common experiences, finding patterns, systems, explanations of how and why things happened. (p. 28)

BACKGROUND

To provide a clearer context from which the girls have testified, I briefly describe two of the realms that inevitably helped shape their views, ability, and purposes to talk back. Although a more detailed and extensive discussion is outside the scope of this article, my goal is to reveal through their *testimonios* the girls' agency in negotiating their identities and the contrasting messages inherent in these contexts.

Ciudad Juárez in Times of Dystopia

Anzaldúa (1987) referred to the U.S.-Mexican border as "*una herida abierta* (an open wound) where the Third World grates against the first and bleeds. And before a scab forms it hemorrhages again, the lifeblood of two worlds merging to form a third country—a border culture" (p. 3). Her description applies to Ciudad Juárez today, more than as a metaphor for a literal reality. Located on the U.S.-México border, across El Paso, Texas, and with a population of over 1,332,000 residents (Instituto Nacional de Estadistica y Geografia [INEGI], 2011), Juárez is one of the largest industrialized border cities in the world. In 2008, Juárez became the epicenter of the war on drugs initiated in México by President Felipe Calderón, making it the most violent city in North America, despite the thousands of troops patrolling its streets. More than 11,000 drug-related homicides have been reported in Juárez since 2008 (Goodman, 2011). The impunity that reigns in the city also has given way to an exponential proliferation of additional crimes not related to the cartels, ranging from armed robberies and assaults to extortions and kidnappings (INEGI, 2011) that victimize people from all walks of life.

Border Women

Since the 1990s, Juárez has been known as a killing field for women, with hundreds of feminicides committed and still unresolved; violence against women continues as a normalized phenomenon in everyday life (Staudt, 2008). The young, poor women of today were born into the era of the feminicides; many have witnessed violence in the home, have been directly affected by the rise in crime and impunity in the city, and have experienced a perpetual sense of insecurity and risk throughout their lives (Monárrez Fregoso, 2005; Moreno Acosta, 2008; Schmidt Camacho, 2005). Part of this insecurity comes from a general distrust of the authorities, especially on the part of women, who have witnessed a continuous discursive tradition of blaming the victim (Castillo & Tabuenca Córdoba, 2002; Fregoso, 2003; Lugo, 2008; Staudt, 2008; Wright, 2001). Furthermore, these young women and their families represent the sources of cheap labor in the arrangements of a predatory capitalist globalization and the dispossessed sector of the population in the obscene economic inequalities characterizing this border city since the 1970s (Fernández-Kelly, 1983; Lugo, 2008).

According to Leadbeater and Way (1996), urban girls are typically perceived as both potential victims of domestic violence and as pathological threats to society by their propensity for school dropout, teen pregnancy, and addictions. Young poor women of color in Juárez experience additional layers of oppression and stigma. The old colonialist narrative that continues today about the border as a zone of sexual excess, degeneration, illicit drug dealing, and violence (Martínez, 2006) has typically portrayed Juárez women as hyperfeminine, prostitutes, and bound to sexual chaos that requires patriarchal control (Fregoso, 2003). In this way, young Juárez women, have historically had to deal with dichotomous depictions and to adjust to contradictory expectations: seductive but virgin, breadwinners but submissive housewives. While popular culture has objectified and consumed Juárez violence in the form of movies, video games, and makeup (Beck, 2010), more alarming is the patronizing gaze in much of the media and journalistic literature about Juárez that reproduces stereotypes and even portrays poor Juárez women of color as a fetish—as sexual objects of desire (Monárrez Fregoso, 2010; for examples see Bowden, 1998, 1999).

Mohanty (2003) argues that women in the Third World have been pervasively considered victims rather than agents of their own destiny by Western feminist scholarship. Indeed, reports about the violence against women in Juárez often position them as victims, but the young women in this study do no see themselves as such. Activists are constantly threatened, have been harshly repressed and unprotected by the State, and in several cases have been silenced by death (for examples see, Amnesty International, 2010; Ellingwood, 2010; Fregoso & Bejarano, 2010; Frontera Norte Sur, 2011; Hernández Navarro, 2010; King, 2011). Nonetheless, the subjectivities of the young women whose voices are presented here have also been influenced by the political consciousness emerging from women's and student grassroots movements that have denounced police impunity and violent repressions against poor women, activists, and youth.

15

Preparatoria Esperanza: Cultivating Subaltern Voices and Knowledge

Despite the dystopic landscape that the city offers its youth, the young women in this study attend a public high school that maintains a strong critical and social justice orientation and promotes the development of their own critical consciousness and agency, as well as the use of students' lived experiences and counter-narratives as pedagogical instruments.

With approximately 350 students, Preparatoria Esperanza is the only public high school serving low-income youth from the northwestern zone of the city, one of the most marginalized areas in Juárez. Esperanza's students come from the barrios, characterized by shantytowns, *picaderos* (clandestine houses or small establishments where a variety of illicit drugs are sold and used), gangs, and high crime rates. Thus, the students are constantly criminalized by the police, the military, and other state authorities, as well as stigmatized in the Juárez community at large, due to their working-class background. In my ethnographic conversations with people in the city and the discourses propagated by some of the media and local authorities, many of those unfamiliar with the school, including educators from other schools, often depicted Esperanza students as lazy, mediocre, rebellious, and as drug addicts and gang members. Some believe that the teachers frequently cancel classes, have low expectations, and are there only to make a few pesos.

But Preparatoria Esperanza is quite the opposite of these stereotypes. Despite being overwhelmingly underfunded, it stands as an example of collective activism and revolutionary education that prevails even in the direst conditions of Ciudad Juárez. Esperanza's teachers are highly educated—many having master's degrees and Ph.D.s, have been involved in numerous social movements at the local and national levels, and are extremely committed to their vision as critical educators—sometimes to the point of sacrificing their personal lives and working without pay. Most of them come from the barrios, as the students do, and often take the role of organic intellectuals by remaining grounded in the community and by building reciprocal relationships of trust with students. Activists and researchers in the city who know the school are often eager to partner with Esperanza students and teachers.

The goal of Esperanza, is to foster *autogestión*[3] or what I define as the students' ability to self-author their identities and become critical and active initiators and agents of change. When asked about the vision of the school, the principal stated, "We are not interested in creating objects of production, but rather, in developing critical thinking subjects." The school's cultural and pedagogical practices are characterized by offering to their students an environment of freedom and autonomy, authentic and caring teacher-student relationships, and critical discourse and activism.

One way in which Esperanza teachers deliberately promote the legitimization of students' voices is through critical dialogue (Freire, 1970) and sharing narratives. Because of their scarce resources and lack of access to textbooks, both teachers' and students' narratives of lived experiences become part of the everyday curriculum and are considered a legitimate and valuable knowledge for critically applying and analyzing theory, much like Chicana feminist thought and the practices of *testimonio*.

In contrast to most public *preparatorias* in México where students wear uniforms and abide by strict rules and a rigid curriculum, at Esperanza, students are able to express themselves freely verbally and through dress, music, and art. They are also encouraged to take charge of their own learning inside and outside of the classroom by selecting and initiating their own activities and forms of collective activism. Thus, students have initiated and organized numerous marches for social action, a radio station, school-wide forums, committees, class seminars, and research projects to discuss topics of interest, such as economic inequalities, gendered violence, homophobia, social movements, neoliberalism, environmental issues, and the city's violence. It is not surprising that when Subcomandante Marcos[4] visited Juárez in 2006, Preparatoria Esperanza was his main host. While not all students and teachers promote or engage in all of these activities, this type of discourse appears to be privileged by the school community in general.

In light of this context, I present the *testimonios* of two different girls. These are only two examples out of many that constitute the type of politicized and pedagogical girl discourse that often takes place among some groups at Esperanza. I chose these particular narratives because they exemplify the type of powerful testimonial discourse prevalent among many girls as counter-narratives, confessions, and *consejos* based on their own life experiences and shared among friends, sisters, and peers.

TESTIMONIOS AS COUNTER-NARRATIVES

Diana

Diana was an extremely high achieving and vocal 11th grader who identified as a feminist and was the leading organizer of an ecology committee at school. Diana was eager to share her *testimonios* during interviews, seeing it as part of her political activity.

My name is Diana Blanco Corona [pseudonym]. I am 16 years old, and I am a student at Preparatoria Esperanza. I am open and sincere, and I don't have any taboos. I am a perfectionist, energetic, and sometimes impatient. But I like how I am. I am a leader.

I have changed a lot in the past couple of years and in the past months. In middle school my peers didn't like me because I would answer every question and would not let anyone silence me. After I finished middle school, I wasn't interested in school very much. It bored me. But when I started attending this school I began to experience the freedom that it offered. I loved the educational system here because it is up to you to learn. I think that's the reason why I went from a 75 average grade to a 94. That's how much I love school now; yes, I love it. Let me tell you that I am not that fond of studying all the time, but I am very inquisitive. Whenever I don't understand something, I ask questions. I like to research things, especially when they are of interest to me, and I like to converse with teachers and learn from them. The teachers here are open to you. You can talk with them about anything you want. An example that I can give you is the way in which my interest in Cuba was born. I used to talk to my reading teacher every day after class. He would tell me about his experiences and trips to Cuba and I began to do my own research. Then my friends started asking me questions about that, and that made me further my research. So now, I have essays, syntheses, and summaries all about Cuba. In the past, I used to say that school was not for me, and I would put minimal effort in just trying to get by. But when I entered this school, my focus changed completely because it was not about having to do it anymore, but because I was interested in doing it.

But, since December 14, other things have happened that have also changed me. On that day, I went with my mother to the veterinary clinic and we got assaulted, and the man who assaulted us raped me. The veterinary clinic is on a corner of a major avenue where the military are patrolling every five minutes. But, what good does that do anyway, right?

The man did not beat me, but I realized how people can manipulate your mind. Before the man raped me, he told me, "Don't say anything, and don't do anything because I'll kill your mother."

We went to take our cat and were waiting for our turn. A man then arrived with a dog. I remember thinking how odd it was that it looked like a stray dog wearing a new leash. The clinic was about to close. "Open the door," he demanded. "Yes, let's open," said the vet, "he will be the last one." As soon as he got in, he ordered my mother to close the door, pulled out his gun, and said, "This is an assault." And that's where everything started. We didn't know . . . well, I had no idea of how long it all lasted because from that moment I lost any notion of time.

He made me take off my shoelaces and tie up the vet, and then sent me to a little room in the back ordering me to look for I don't know what. He then went to the room with me and told me, "Look, don't freak out, right now I'm going to kill the vet, but if you don't want anything to happen to your mother, don't say anything." He said, "Pull down your pants," but I wasn't registering anything, I was in a nervous shock, gone. Then as he began to take off his pants, he put his gun on the table. I tell my mother that I wouldn't have hesitated to grab it, but he saw me looking at it, and he took it back.

And then that was it. He raped me and then sent me back to the main room. I just sat on the floor and put my face between my knees. I bowed my head so that my mother would do the same and wouldn't look at the scene if he ended up killing the vet. What enrages me is that he thinks that he did us a favor for not having killed us. He would refer to us as "señora" and "señorita"[5] and would say "excuse me" and I don't know what. You see? Like if he was doing us a favor by treating us like that. Then he said, "They're picking me up. Don't leave the clinic in the next 15 minutes." He then told the vet, "I'm going to say that I beat you up, and that I didn't kill you because there were two women." Again, as if we should thank him, you know what I mean?

My mother asked me if I wanted to report him to the authorities, and I said, "Yes." He had the appearance of a soldier, 100%. He was wearing military boots, was dark skinned, had a birthmark on his face, sounded like a Veracruzano[6], and seemed southern. I reported him, and it was very denigrating having to declare 25 times and being examined in front of I don't know how many people. It was very traumatic. They asked me for my undergarments to get the DNA, but I know they won't do anything, as usual they won't do anything. And I am sure there was DNA everywhere.

I also got several infections, and the homeopathic experts that I know did some tests and found that there is a probability that I was infected with HIV. I was devastated. Before, I used to tell the story and cry, but the therapy from a civil association has helped me, and I'm following a rigorous homeopathic therapy to heal my body. Although sometimes I get attacks of rage, not fear, but rage, I hope to transform this rage into boldness. That's why I'm getting involved in all these marches against violence. This experience changed my perspective completely. But from then on, only good things have happened. I got a job and, and my friends here at Esperanza, and all the new people I have met have helped me heal.

Clearly, Diana's life on the border is not one of excesses, reckless rebellion, or naïve victimization. Her *testimonio* disrupts the images of young border women as being too loose, silent, or passive. Despite her early dislike for school, she was able to gain back her love for authentic learning at Esperanza. She had become a purposeful and self-directed young woman. As such, she was able to self-author her identity beyond her violent and traumatic experience by choosing to re-channel her rage into forms of activism. Rather than a victim, Diana sees herself as a fighter and survivor who despite any situation will rise again full of life, strength, and courage. She has accepted the healing that comes from being in community with others. Her hope is not in the hands of the authorities, which she views as useless. Instead, her healing comes from the support of her friends at Esperanza, civic agencies, and women healers, as well as from her own ability to fight back, which was not born the day she was attacked. For example, even before this experience, Diana has been writing poetry about the violence against women and has read her poems at women's conventions. Her school also contributes to this healing by offering opportunities for collective agency through various forms of activism, such as marches and forums. Her *testimonio* speaks of the layers of patriarchy and impunity that reign in the city, but it is also a counter-narrative that underscores the significance of the agency she gained back at Esperanza, as well as the collective action and knowledge among many Juárez residents who work tirelessly to heal the wounds and reclaim the humanity of those suffering injustice.

Gabriela

Gabriela was in the 12th grade, and she was perhaps the most popular girl in the school. Based on my observations and conversations with teachers and students, what made her popular were her friendly, open, and peaceful demeanor, as well as her activism, eloquence, intelligence, and unapologetic counter-hegemonic forms of expression through dress, music, and art. She dressed in a "hippie" kind of style, wore her hair in dreadlocks, and spent much of her free time reading, playing the guitar, and writing raps and poetry, as well as initiating various forms of activism—from painting murals to organizing marches and events, and working on research projects related to social justice issues. She did very well in her classes and was one of the most inquisitive and participative students. Gabriela was clearly a girl whose consciousness and identity were shaped by growing up in the barrio. The police and others who did not know her well saw her with suspicion and contempt, and she had suffered multiple aggressions and discrimination by the local and federal authorities and institutions.

I am only 17 years old, but despite my young age, I could say that I have lived through things that most kids my age haven't. I live with my mother and my 16-year-old sister. My mother is a supervisor at a local supermarket where she works very long hours and makes about $1,700 pesos [about 150 dollars] a month. Some days, we don't even get to see each other at all, due to her schedule. As a child, I saw how my father would abuse my mother. She divorced him, but then she got a new partner who brought a lot of problems to our home. I really disliked him, but he was murdered last year by accident.

I am passionate about music and art. That's how I try to make a few pesos, selling crafts on the streets and boulevards while my boyfriend does his torch juggling routines. Other times I sell candy or homemade burritos. I have looked for jobs, but employers usually reject me because of the way I look. They don't like my dreadlocks, and they probably want me to wear a miniskirt. You know how it is—they care more about your appearance than about your intellect.

Since I was about 11 years old, I have been involved in activism. Ever since I was a little girl I would hear about the murders and the things they did to women. In fact, that was the first issue that I undertook. Ever since I had use of reason, I would be working on campaigns with my sister, Paty. We did marches and organized the International Day for the Elimination of Violence Against Women on March 28 and other dates commemorating all those Mexican women who were raped or murdered. So from the beginning I was involved in those things and that shaped my perspective of Juárez.

Have you heard of Géminis Ochoa? He was the leader of the flea market, a real activist, and so was his wife. One morning last year he invited my boyfriend and me to sell our crafts at the flea market. But by the afternoon they had already killed him. They killed him because he was the leader of the street vendors, and since he was making too many waves, the soldiers killed him right there in downtown in the midst of all the people. It was all over the news. I went to support his wife because they had always helped the people. It was a struggle for the people, and they killed him for being a revolutionary.

The police are always after us. When we went to the last march a couple of police officers told us, "We know who you are. You better watch out because we're going to hunt you until we get each one of you." And yeah, you'll see them roaming in the barrio threatening us. Like the other day the police had been chasing one of my friends and a few minutes later he was found dead on the ground. All my friends were crying and, yes, I cried a lot too, but I tell you, I have to be strong.

So I do feel stressed, to think that we have not gotten out of this, out of this violence. And to think that Juárez is not just any place because this is a border. A kilometer north from where I stand there's a whole other world. We are so close and so far away. I sit on top of the hill and look down and can see that line that divides two very different worlds. Yet you can see the influence of the United States, on TV, everywhere. Even in the violence. Juárez is where all kinds of people end up, those escaping the law in the United States, those who are deported, people from southern México, and suddenly you have a combination of Americans, Mexicanos, and Chicanos living here. Some see this border as a place of hope. That's what my friends from the South tell me; it is their dream to come here. And here we are, trying to get out. I feel so sad to see how paranoia has overwhelmed people. I tell one of my teachers that I like to gather people and help them clarify things because people today are very confused. That's why we need to keep people informed, not through the mainstream media because that is mere manipulation, but amongst ourselves. That is why I helped organize the march with other students because it is where we can speak up.

Gabriela's *testimonio* speaks of the struggles and loneliness of growing up in the barrio where patriarchy, violence, and poverty strike. It reveals the stigma that poor youth carry for not following normative ways of dress and behavior. It also offers evidence of institutional oppression through a policing system that criminalizes poor youth and silences activists. However, like Diana, Gabriela's *testimonio* demonstrates a strong spirit of survival and critical agency. Growing up in a context and discourse of violence toward women has made her a fighter and organizer. At her early age, she is also able to analyze the various layers of power and oppression that produce violence on the border. There is no fatalistic passivity in her. It is clear that Gabriela talks back as a witness of oppression, who has acquired knowledge from lived experiences.

Both Gabriela and Diana speak to a collectivity—they stand alongside others who have experienced trauma and in many cases, death, wishing to bring healing while pointing to the power dimensions that create these realities. Their goal in sharing these experiences was to counter the narratives propagated in the media and in middle- and upper-class circles about poor youth being ambitionless, drug addicts, or criminals, as well as discourses about women being loose or passive victims, which erases not only the suffering, but also the knowledge and activism that exist in the barrio. They also wanted to raise consciousness among those who maintained naïve views about the realities in their community, including their girlfriends, class peers, family members, and other people from the barrio, by pointing to the oppression caused by neoliberal agendas, patriarchy, and cycles of corruption. Their activism was in part what brought them healing, as they engaged in a collective effort to re-invent themselves and their communities beyond tragedy.

TESTIMONIOS AS CONFESSIONS

In addition to *testimonios* as counter-narratives of what it means to be a young working-class woman in the border, *testimonios* took a pedagogical role in shaping the identities of girls at Esperanza. These often came in the form of confessions as they talked with their friends or in the poetry and songs that some of the girls wrote. This type of discourse involved making themselves vulnerable by sharing stories about intimate or difficult experiences, or even what they considered shameful behaviors, and the reflections that they provoked. One afternoon as we "hung out" in the school courtyard Gabriela shared the following *testimonio* with two other girls and me. Margarita, one of the girls, had told us about how she became bitter and aggressive after she had felt too repressed at home and marginalized in middle school by various girl cliques. To that, Gabriela responded:

Listen, I used to be real crazy. But I began to change because I got into a lot of trouble. When I was in middle school, I had very curly and kinky hair, and I would put it up in a pony tail, and it would get all puffy, so they would pull me aside and ask me to fix it. I would tell them that my hair was naturally like that, Afro, and I could not style it any other way. So they made me cut it very short and straighten it every day with the flat iron for a whole year. My mother has an Afro, too, because my whole family is very dark and has African features. Her hair was her inheritance to us, "How are you going to take off my curls that I'm giving you?" she would say. I think that really injured me.

At that middle school, they would also make us stand up to chorally greet every adult that entered the classroom. I thought it was so ridiculous, so I began messing with them by standing whenever one of my classmates who was 18 years old walked in. The teachers would get annoyed, and I would respond, "He's an adult, too, isn't he? You said you wanted me to do that with every adult." Of course, I was being sarcastic, but it seemed to me that they just wanted to keep us students down and blindly obedient.

In fact, I had just gotten out of detention for wearing makeup and the wrong stockings the day that Armida [the principal of Esperanza] showed up at my middle school for a recruitment visit. As soon as she said that Esperanza didn't require uniforms like the rest of the schools, I thought, "That's the best school." But I also became interested in it when I learned about how critical the teachers were and that Subcomandante Marcos had been here.

But when I first enrolled at Esperanza, I was different. I used to listen to hard-core rock and punk music, and I dressed in that same style. I wore dark eye makeup, tight dark clothes, and chains. I didn't talk to anyone, I didn't like anyone, and I would treat everyone badly. Everyone was afraid of talking to me.

Since in my mind I was superior, I thought I could do anything, and I didn't give a shit about what anyone thought. I would get all drunk and high. I got into punk culture, and that really messed me up. I used to hang out with guys who trained me to be aggressive. This one guy would hit me, and I would punch him in the face with all my strength, like a *vato* [guy]! Sometimes I didn't want to be like that, but I was too prideful, and I didn't want to get rid of that image that I had made for my self. I didn't want to appear weak.

I behaved like a *chola* [female gang member], and I was an anarchist, *so la chota* [the police] meant nothing to me. Once, I even started a fight with this one *chota* at a bar. I beat the crap out of her, and she was real skinny, so I was stronger. It was awful; I had never beat up someone like that. But you don't know how many times I've seen *chotas* come to the bars to sell cocaine, pot, heroine, and all kinds of stuff. Most people don't know about that, and if I told them, they wouldn't believe me. But I ended up in prison after beating her up, and I drove my mother sick and tired of having to get me out of jail.

But after being here for some time, I started to think that that attitude didn't match the real me, so I began to change. I still like the same music, but I left that life behind. I changed because I saw how it was affecting my family, especially my sister. I was always fighting with her, and she couldn't defend herself because she was younger than me. I would pull her hair and hit her, and with a lot of anger, but I didn't know where that anger came from. And I was making my mother ill. I realized that I couldn't keep living like that. My head hurt for being high all the time. I saw myself in the mirror, how skinny I was getting and I thought, "If I continue on this path, I'm gonna die."

I guess it did affect me in some way how they treated me in middle school because they wouldn't let me be who I was. But I have changed. When I saw the freedom here at Esperanza, I knew that nobody would repress me anymore, so I started by dread-locking my burnt hair. I have liberated myself, as some would call it. I have felt more free because I can wear my hair any way I want and dress any way I want, and I can now think what I want to think. I realized that I didn't belong to the cliques I used to hang out with before, because they are aggressive and like to fight. And I like to fight too, but for the right reasons and with real arguments. It's better to fight with the mind than with fists.

The exchange between Margarita and Gabriela demonstrates the confessional nature of their *testimonios*. Through them the girls shared truths from their own experiences and taught and learned from each other lessons about self-authorship, agency, and critical reflection. The girls who were present listened attentively and respected the confession, while negotiating their identities by affirming similarities or differences. Margarita, for example, said, "I am not the way I used to be anymore either. I dress the same way, but I don't fight anymore." Gabriela's *testimonio* encouraged Margarita to self-author her identity as a changed person as well.

These confessions also pointed to issues of oppression and resistance. In her *testimonio*, it is clear that Gabriela's negative behavior was originally affected, in part, by the way her middle school teachers and principal controlled and repressed her body based on racist and authoritarian ideas. While not excusing her own negative behavior, Gabriela exposes the unjust treatment that she received. Consequently, when sharing her confession, the girls who listened appeared to gain knowledge and admiration for her honesty and strength, rather than judging her negatively by focusing solely on her faults or mistakes. For instance, Marsella, one of the students who struggled with issues of self-esteem, expressed to me that if she had to pick a role model, it would not be a famous person or a historical figure; it would be Gabriela, a girl with whom she could identify and who demonstrated how to love herself regardless of what the world thought.

Gabriela's *testimonio* also demonstrates the role of the school in allowing her to experience theory in the flesh through her own transformation and self-authoring of her identity as an intellectual fighter. Her school provided her a space where she could be herself, reflect on her behavior and feelings, and redirect her anger toward furthering social justice goals. With her body no longer being policed, Gabriela's need to fight with peers and loved ones gradually began to decrease, as she was able to accept her own body and freely negotiate new ways of being. For example, she began to explore aspects of the Rastafari movement that helped her embrace her African roots and physical features, as well as create a new identity that sought inspiration through spirituality and music. While Gabriela did not explicitly identify herself as a Rasta, she did adopt some of the ideologies of the movement as well as the dress style, music, and language. For example, she does not abide by Rasta religious ideas, nor does she follow any other specific religion despite her family's long tradition of Catholicism, but instead believes in a higher power or god, who she calls Jah. What is important to note is the freedom and space that the school offered her to weave her exploration and bodily expressions of the Rasta ideology with her critical and social justice orientation, as this clearly helped Gabriela heal and develop her own theories and new forms of agency.

TESTIMONIOS AS CONSEJOS

Girls at Esperanza also shared *testimonios* often with the goal of providing advice to others. These *consejos* were sometimes implicit in their confessional narratives. Other times, they were explicit and deliberate. The following *testimonio* was one of the many raps that Gabriela wrote spontaneously during her free time as one of her hobbies and that illustrates this idea. This particular excerpt speaks of her experiences and those of her friends in the barrio, with which many other youth can identify. It concludes with a *consejo*, urging the listener to reject the life of drug dealing and addictions and find spiritual peace.

> I was 15 years old when cocaine got to my hands
> What's the situation here in the barrio?
> There're no more basketball or soccer games
> We all saw how Carlitos was devoured by the barrio
> When a shooting burst out in the middle of the crowd
> And Carlitos remained dead on the ground . . .
> I know you're tired, I can see it in your eyes
> It's been a while since the coke won't do it anymore
> The effect fades away and the sorrow continues
>
> You look weary and old
> Listen to these words
> They bring a message of peace for your soul
> It's not a bunch of lies,
> Jah points at my mouth, and I speak the truth
> Listen to the words of life. This is the only way out
> This one will forgive you and heal your hurt,
> Will erase the pain, fill in the void,
> The memory of your friend broken on the ground
> Or the time when you had to tell your girl goodbye . . .
> Did you listen, my friend? Do you know I'm with you?
> I don't force you, but I give you these words
> So you can think of your decision
> To choose between life or remain between the blocks

Gabriela explained that Carlitos is an interpretation of the boy who used to enjoy sports and create barrio hip-hop, but fell in the trap of drug dealing and addictions. She also indicated that her MC friends like to use this character as well as that of God in their raps. Finally, she explained to me that in her conclusion, the choice between life or the blocks, represents not only a personal decision to improve one's lifestyle, but the choice to take a stand or continue being a puppet of world powers like the United States, who continue to fuel the drug business. Her *consejo* thus incorporates not only her own experiences and knowledge of the barrio but also a necessary understanding of power dimensions and the role of spirituality in the search for healing.

These *consejos* illustrate the pedagogical nature of *testimonios*, particularly when one considers their close relationship to the culturally situated meaning of *educación*. Not limited to formal academic preparation, the Spanish term often refers to the inculcation of morals, ethics, respect, and social and personal responsibility that serve as a basis for all other learning (Delgado-Gaitán, 1992; Valdés, 1996; Valenzuela, 1999). But beyond the inculcation of cultural values, the *consejos* inherent in these young women's *testimonios* embody *mujerista* pedagogies that involve the interrogation and critique of social practices and power, while offering a language of hope and agency validated by the wisdom gained from their own life experiences (Elenes, González, Delgado Bernal, & Villenas, 2001; Hernández, 1997).

DISCUSSION

These *testimonios* offer a window into young women's definitions of their lives beyond the feminicides, the violence, and the fear, as well as their desire to reclaim their humanity and seek solidarity. Considering the harsh and violent context in which these girls' lives unfold, textbook or traditional school learning is not only insufficient, but is also irrelevant. The challenges that these urban girls experienced on a daily basis, have caused them to not only develop a keen awareness of power dimensions and strategies to defend themselves (Pastor, McCormick, & Fine, 1996), but have also led them to acquire identities embedded in critical consciousness (hooks, 1991). In this way, *testimonios* become a necessary way of knowing, a pedagogical tool based on the truths from which they can speak back and learn the lessons that help them survive and resist oppression in such a contested space.

These *testimonios* also bear witness of the importance of Preparatoria Esperanza in decolonizing both curriculum and instruction by privileging and legitimizing subaltern and critical discourse where "the voice of a witness is accorded space and protection . . . silencing certain types of questions and formalizing others" (Smith, 2005, p. 144), and thus giving way to grater student agency. In this type of environment, *testimonios* naturally emerged and became part of the cultural and pedagogical practices inside and outside the classroom.

It is important to note that while these *testimonios* occurred in the school setting, they often transpired from spaces outside the classroom, during conversations with friends, or came in the form of poetry or raps that girls wrote in their personal journals and shared during their free time. I listened to and observed girls participate in this type of testimonial discourse to highlight the challenges of growing up female and poor in Juárez. Their testimonial conversations involved issues of self-esteem and imposed body images, gendered repression and violence, abuses from the authorities and other public institutions, and discrimination in their access to college and employment to name a few, but they also included stories of victory, strength, activism, honor, and resilience in which the girls or other women in their lives were the protagonists.

Furthermore, these were not simply stories, but rather, a politicized discourse that situated the girls' experiences in the context of power dimensions and systemic oppression. This discourse sheds light on the powerful *mujerista* pedagogical spaces that were a natural part of these girls' lives on the border and through which they individually and collectively self-authored their identities as Juárez women (F. González, 2001; Trinidad Galvan, 2001; Villenas, 2006). It also highlights the possibility for schools to expand the notion of education and develop a more relevant and empowering curriculum by validating the wisdom, agency, and ways of knowing of subaltern young women embedded in ordinary and intimate spaces, even in some of the most dystopic and contested contexts, such as Ciudad Juárez. Neither the status quo, nor educational reforms imposed from above and motivated by neoliberal goals have been able to bring healing and hope to a generation of Juarez youth profoundly immersed in sorrow, fear, poverty, and desperation. In a space where women's bodies are positioned as docile objects and abused by patriarchy and voracious capitalism, young women's reclamation of voice and knowledge requires more than a Cartesian approach to learning and schooling. It requires epistemological tools that take students' everyday life and suffering seriously. Through the use of *testimonios*, this school was able to nurture the development of theory in the flesh—a theory where the realities of their lives, including the physical, mental, spiritual, and emotional struggles of navigating a predatory and precarious territory, and the very injuries, longings, and healing felt and experienced in their bodies "all fuse to create a politic born out of necessity" (Moraga & Anzaldúa, 1981, p. 23). This type of transcendental knowledge has the potential of changing lives and, in some cases, breathing life back in the midst of death. As Diana said, pointing to a dry tree after sharing her *testimonio* in the middle of the most devastating winter in her life, "Just like that tree, my roots are strong, and I will be green and alive again."

CONCLUSION

The complex conditions that poor youth experience in Juárez today are unique, yet marginalized communities and suffering exist everywhere. In the United States, for example, Chicanas, as well as other students of color and low socioeconomic background have and continue to experience political violence and marginalization in schools and in society in general due to racism, classism, patriarchy, and linguistic discrimination among many other things. They often face deficit views due to their cultural background and a subtractive schooling context (Valenzuela, 1999), and in many cases they are forbidden from exploring their own histories (as in the case of Arizona today). The intelligences and knowledge developed and weaved in their daily border-crossing experiences as they negotiate their identities and navigate multiple and, in many cases, opposing cultural worlds are often unrecognized and neglected in schools (Carrillo, 2010; Godinez, 2006). As the standardization of curriculum becomes more prevalent and yet more disconnected from the daily lives of marginalized communities in Juárez (as well as in the United States and in the world), the recognition and use of *testimonios* as an epistemological and pedagogical tool would reflect an emphasis on the urgency to seek new theories and knowledge beyond the ones that continue to fail the disenfranchised. The use of *testimonios* would enable students and educators to interrogate current schooling rituals (McLaren, 1986) and to create new truths and theory felt and produced in their own flesh and situated in their daily material realities. *Testimonios* as a pedagogical practice fosters humanizing knowledge stemming from students' and teachers' own narratives of survival and resistance, and promotes theory that offers both a language of critique and a language of hope through the reclamation, transformation, and emancipation of their own lives and communities. While practicing this type of pedagogy in the highly controlled contexts of U.S. schools may involve looking for or fostering liminal spaces, the current conditions of minority students in schools and the possibilities for creating empowering learning spaces should be compelling enough to take on the challenge.

The *testimonios* that Diana and Gabriela shared, while painful, demonstrate their agency and strength. But a look into their lives today offers even more hope of the possibilities for a renewed future despite tragic experiences and ever-present obstacles. Both Gabriela and Diana completed high school successfully and have continued their process of *autogestión.* Diana persisted in her efforts to improve her health and focused on renewing her spirit by supporting the healing of others, working as a *masseuse* at a local spa. After graduation, she spent a year at an institute in Guadalajara that specializes in holistic healing. Upon her return she continued to be actively involved in a non-governmental organization (NGO) that focuses on coaching youth to support their personal development through life experiences, research, reflection, and personal and collective consciousness. She is currently attending a local university to become a physical therapist.

Gabriela has persisted in her activist goals and identifies herself as a promoter of urban art and community work. Among many other activities, she completed a one-year internship at an NGO led by feminist leaders in her community through which she helped found El Instituto Paulo Freire, a community-based school that draws from the talents of urban youth to offer extracurricular activities and teach arts, crafts, literacy, and musical skills to young children from the barrio. Through her internship, she also attended various conferences nationally and in the United States, building coalitions for social justice. Today, Gabriela is an education major at the Universidad Autónoma de Ciudad Juárez.

Clearly, the successes and triumphs over tragedy evident in these young women's lives today are not the result of a standards-based curriculum or a strong accountability system. Instead, they stem from the knowledge and wisdom that they learned through their own life experiences. Needless to say, recognizing and legitimizing this embodied theory by incorporating it in the daily practices of teaching and learning has the potential to impact students in powerful ways.

NOTES

1. I utilize the term "feminicide" over "femicide," following Fregoso and Bejarano's (2010) conceptualization of the term which interrupts essentialist constructs of female identity by underscoring how gender norms, inequalities and power relationships, rather than the biological notion of the female sex, increase women's vulnerability to violence.

2. *Consejos* are spontaneous homilies utilized to give advice or to instill behaviors and attitudes and relate closely to the concept of educacioán (Valdeás, 1996; Valencia & Black, 2002).

3. While the translation of the word *autogestión* is usually found in dictionaries as *self-management*, this English term does not fully encompass the meaning of this word at Preparatoria Esperanza. Elsewhere, I (Cervantes-Soon, 2011) have provided a nuanced analysis of the way this term was used and what it represented to both students and teachers at Esperanza. Suffice it to say that, to them, *autogestión* involved not only self-management skills, but also, and more importantly, the ability to "read the world" (Freire, 1970) and the power dimensions of their context in order to be critical self-makers and agents of change. For this reason, I chose to maintain the Spanish term and the definition above.

4. Subcomandante Marcos is a public intellectual and the spokesperson for the Zapatista Army of National Liberation (EZLN), a Mexican guerrilla movement demanding rights for indigenous peoples.

5. "Señora" and "señorita" are formal ways to refer to women, Mrs. and Miss respectively.

6. A person from the Mexican state of Veracruz, a state from which many of the soldiers in Juárez are recruited.

REFERENCES

Amnesty International. (2010). Mexico urged to protect activists after campaigner shot dead. Retrieved from http://www.amnesty.org/en/news-and-updates/news/mexico-urged-protect-activists-after-campaigner-shot-dead-20100106

Anzaldúa, G. (1987). *Borderlands/la frontera: The new mestiza.* San Francisco, CA: Aunt Lute Books.

Anzaldúa, G. (2002). Now let us shift … the path of conocimiento … inner work, public acts. In G. E. Anzaldúa & A. Keating (Eds.), *This bridge we call home: Radical visions for transformation* (pp. 540–578). New York, NY: Routledge.

Beck, L. (2010). Mac kisses off Juárez-inspired product names: Company changes plans for MAC Rodarte collection after explosion of customer outcry. NBC-DFW. Retrieved from http://www.nbcdfw.com/the-scene/fashion/MAC-Kisses-Off-Juarez-Inspired-Product-Names-98799069.html

Beverley, J. (2000). Testimonio, subalternity, and narrative authority. In N. K. Denzin & Y. S. Lincoln (Eds.), *The Sage handbook of qualitative research* (3rd ed., pp. 547–558). Thousand Oaks, CA: Sage.

Bowden, C. (1998). *Juárez: The laboratory of our future.* New York, NY: Aperture.

Bowden, C. (1999, September). "I wanna dance with the strawberry girl." *Talk Magazine,* 114–118.

Carrillo, J. F. (2010). So far from home: Portraits of Mexican-origin scholarship boys. Unpublished dissertation. University of Texas, Austin, TX.

Castillo, D. A., & Tabuenca Córdoba, M. S. (2002). *Border women: Writing from la frontera.* Minneapolis, MN: University of Minnesota Press.

Cervantes-Soon, C. G. (2011). Schooling in times of dystopia: Empowering education for Juárez women. Unpublished dissertation. University of Texas, Austin, TX.

Cruz, C. (2001). Toward an epistemology of a brown body. *International Journal of Qualitative Studies in Education, 14*(5), 657–669.

Delgado Bernal, D. (2001). Using a Chicana feminist epistemology in educational research. *Harvard Educational Review, 68*(4), 555–582.

Delgado-Gaitán, C. (1992). School matters in the Mexican-American home: Socializing children to education. *American Educational Research Journal, 29*(3), 495–513.

Elenes, C. A. (2006). Borderlands, pedagogies, and epistemologies. In D. Delgado Bernal, C. A. Elenes, F. E. Godinez, & S. Villenas (Eds.), *Chicana/Latina education in everyday life: Feminist perspectives on pedagogy and epistemology* (pp. 215–217). Albany, NY: State University of New York Press.

Elenes, C. A. (2000). Chicana feminist narratives and the politics of the self. *Frontiers, 21*(3), 105–123.

Elenes, C. A., Gonzalez, F. E., Delgado Bernal, D., & Villenas, S. (2001). Introduction: Chicana/Mexicana feminist pedagogies: Consejos, respeto, y educación in everyday life. *International Journal of Qualitative Studies in Education, 14*(5), 595–602.

Ellingwood, K. (2010, December 18). Mexico under siege: Mother shot dead at anti-crime vigil in Chihuahua. *Los Angeles Times.* Retrieved from http://articles.latimes.com/2010/dec/18/world/la-fg-mexico-mom-20101218

Fernández-Kelly, M. P. (1983). *For we are sold, I and my people: Women and industry in Mexico's frontier.* Albany. NY: State of New York University Press.

Foley, D. E. (2002). Critical ethnography: The reflexive turn. *International Journal of Qualitative Studies in Education, 15*(4), 469–490.

Foley, D., & Valenzuela, A. (2000). Critical ethnography: The politics of collaboration. In N. Denzin & Y. S. Lincoln (Eds.), *The Sage handbook of qualitative research* (3rd ed., pp. 217–234). Thousand Oaks, CA: Sage.

Fregoso, R. L. (2003). *MeXicana encounters: The making of social identities on the borderlands.* Berkeley, CA: University of California Press.

Fregoso, R. L., & Bejarano, C. (2010). Introduction: A cartography of feminicide in the Americas. In R. L. Fregoso, C. Bejarano, & M. Lagarde y de los Rios (Eds.), *Terrorizing women: Feminicide in the Americas* (pp. 59–69). Durham, NC: Duke University Press.

Freire, P. (1970). *Pedagogy of the oppressed.* New York, NY: Continuum.

Frontera Norte Sur. (2011, March 11). The silencing of women's voices. La Prensa de San Diego. Retrieved from http://laprensa-sandiego.org/stories/the-silencing-of-women%E2%80%99s-voices/

Godinez, F. E. (2006). Haciendo que hacer. In D. Delgado Bernal, C. A. Elenes, F. E. Godinez, & S. Villenas (Eds.), *Chicana/Latina education in everyday life: Feminist perspectives on pedagogy and epistemology* (pp. 25–38). Albany, NY: State University of New York Press.

González, F. E. (2001). Haciendo que hacer—Cultivating a mestiza worldview and academic achievement: Braiding cultural knowledge into educational research, policy, and practice. *International Journal of Qualitative Studies in Education, 14*(5), 641–656.

González, N. (2006).Testimonios of border identities: "Una mujer acomedida donde quiera cabe." In D. Delgado Bernal, C. A. Elenes, F. E. Godinez, & S. Villenas (Eds.), *Chicana/Latina education in everyday life: Feminist perspectives on pedagogy and epistemology* (pp. 197–214). Albany, NY: State University of New York Press.

Goodman, S. (2011). Mexico drug war a lost cause as presently fought. *Huffpost World*. Retrieved from http://www. huffingtonpost.com/sandy-goodman/mexico-drug-war-a-lost-ca_b_833097.html

Gramsci, A. (1971/2000). *Selections from the Prison Notebooks*. New York, NY: International Publishers.

Hernández, A. (1997). *Pedagogy, democracy, and feminism: Rethinking the public sphere*. New York, NY: State University of New York Press.

Hernández Navarro, L. (2010). Ciudad Juárez, Mexico's nameless dead: As Mexico's drugs war goes on, the government is breaching the rights of citizens innocent of any involvement with the cartels. *Guardian*. Retrieved from http: //www.guardian.co.uk/commentisfree/2010/nov/09/ciudad-juarez-mexico-drugs-war

hooks, b. (1991) *Yearning: race, gender, and cultural politics*. Boston, MA: South End Press.

Instituto Nacional de Estadística y Geografía. (2011). Información Nacional por Entidad Federativa y Municipios: Juárez. Retrieved from http://www.inegi.org.mx/sistemas/mexicocifras/default.aspx?ent=08

King, J. (2011). Poet Susana Chavez's death sparks outrage in Juárez. *Colorlines*. Retrieved from http://colorlines.com/ archives/2011/01/poet_susana_chavez_fought_femicide_in_juarez_becomes_latest_victim.html

The Latina Feminist Group. (2001). *Telling to live: Latina feminist testimonios*. Durham, NC: Duke University Press.

Leadbeater, B. J. R., & Way, N. (Eds.). (1996). *Urban girls: Resisting stereotypes, creating identities*. New York, NY: New York University Press.

Levins Morales, A. (2001). Certified organic intellectual. In Latina Feminist Group (Eds.), *Telling to live: Latina feminist testimonios* (pp. 27–32). Durham, NC: Duke University Press.

Lugo, A. (2008). *Fragmented lives, assembled parts: Culture, capitalism, and conquest at the U.S.-Mexico border*. Austin, TX: University of Texas Press.

Martínez, O. J. (2006). *Troublesome border*. Tucson, AZ: The University of Arizona Press.

McLaren, P. (1986). *Schooling as a ritual performance: Towards a political economy of educational symbols and gestures*. Boston, MA: Routledge & Kegan Paul.

Menchú, R. (1984). *I, Rigoberta Menchú. An Indian woman in Guatemala* (E. Burgos-Debray, Ed., A. Wright, Trans.). London, England: Verso.

Mignolo, W. (2000). *Local histories/global designs: Coloniality, subaltern knowledges, and border thinking*. Princeton, NJ: Princeton University Press.

Mohanty, C. T. (2003) *Feminism without borders: Decolonizing theory, practicing solidarity*. Durham, NC: Duke University Press.

Monárrez Fregoso, J. E. (2005). Violencia e (in)seguridad ciudadana en Ciudad Juárez. In L .E. Cervera Gómez (Ed.), *Diagnóstico geo-socioeconómico de Ciudad Juárez y su sociedad* (pp. 273–314). Juárez, Mexico: El Colegio de la FronteraNorte/Instituto Nacional de las Mujeres.

Monárrez Fregoso, J. E. (2010). The victims of the Ciudad Juárez feminicide: Sexually fetishized commodities. In R. L. Fregoso, C. Bejarano, & M. Lagarde y de los Rios (Eds.), *Terrorizing women: Feminicide in the Americas* (pp. 59–69). Durham, NC: Duke University Press.

Moraga, C. (1993). *The last generation: Prose and poetry*. Boston, MA: South End Press.

Moraga, C., & Anzaldúa, G. (Eds.). (1981). *This bridge called my back: Writings by radical women of color*. San Francisco, CA: Aunt Lute Books.

Moreno Acosta, H. A. (2008). Situación de la Seguridad. In C. Jusidman (Ed.), *La realidad social de Ciudad Juárez* (pp. 241–279). Ciudad Juárez, Mexico: Universidad Autónoma de Ciudad Juárez.

Pastor, J., McCormick, J., & Fine, M. (1996). Makin' homes: An urban girl thing. In B. J. Leadbeater & N. Way (Eds.), *Urban girls: Resisting stereotypes, creating identities* (pp. 75–96). New York, NY: New York University Press.

Schmidt Camacho, A. (2005). Ciudadana X: Gender violence and the denationalization of women's rights in Ciudad Juarez, Mexico. *The New Centennial Review, 5*(1), 255–292.

Smith, L. T. (2005). *Decolonizing methodologies: Research and indigenous peoples (8th impr.)*. New York, NY: Zed Books.

Stacey, J. (1988). Can there be a feminist ethnography? *Women Studies International Forum, 11*(1), 21–27.

Staudt, K. A. (2008). *Violence and activism at the border: Gender, fear and everyday life in Ciudad Juárez.* Austin, TX: University of Texas Press.

Trinidad Galvan, R. (2001). Portraits of mujeres desjuiciadas: Womanist pedagogies of the everyday, the mundane, and the ordinary. *International Journal of Qualitative Studies in Education, 14*(5), 603–621.

Valdés, G. (1996). *Con respeto: Bridging the differences between culturally diverse families and schools.* New York, NY: Teachers College Press.

Valencia, R. R., & Black, M. S. (2002). "Mexican Americans don't value education!" On the basis of the myth, mythmaking, and debunking. *Journal of Latinos and Education, 1*(2), 81–103.

Valenzuela, A. (1999). *Subtractive schooling: U.S.-Mexican youth and the politics of caring.* Albany, NY: State University of New York Press.

Villenas, S. (2006). Pedagogical moments in the borderlands: Latina mothers teaching and learning. In D. Delgado Bernal, C. A. Elenes, F. E. Godinez, & S. Villenas (Eds.), *Chicana/Latina education in everyday life: Feminist perspectives on pedagogy and epistemology* (pp. 147–160). Albany, NY: State University of New York Press.

Villenas, S., Godinez, F. E., Delgado Bernal, D., & Elenes, C. A. (2006). Chicanas/Latinas building bridges: An introduction. In D. Delgado Bernal, C. A. Elenes, F. E. Godinez, & S. Villenas (Eds.), *Chicana/Latina education in everyday life: Feminist perspectives on pedagogy and epistemology* (pp. 1–9). Albany, NY: State University of New York Press.

Wright, M. W. (2001). A manifesto against femicide. *Antipode, 33*(3), 550–566.

Chicana/Latina *Testimonios* on Effects and Responses to Microaggressions

Lindsay Pérez Huber

California State University, Long Beach

Bert María Cueva

University of California, Los Angeles

Testimonio in educational research can reveal both the oppression that exists within educational institutions and the powerful efforts in which students of color[1] engage to challenge and transform those spaces. We utilize *testimonio* as a methodological approach to understand how undocumented and U.S.-born Chicana/Latina students experience the effects of and responses to a systemic, subtle, and cumulative form of racism, racist nativist microaggressions. We draw from critical race and Chicana feminist frameworks to understand the effects of microaggressions as embodied systemic oppression (Cruz, 2006; Moraga & Anzaldúa, 2002b). Our analysis reveals that the students engaged and created counterspaces within K-12 institutions that challenged oppression and sought to transform the educational spaces that marginalized them. Throughout these findings, we explore the process of *conocimiento* (Anzaldúa, 2002) that allowed the women to engage in reflection, healing, and celebration of their resiliency.

> *Testimonio* has been critical in movements for liberation in Latin America, offering an artistic form and methodology to create politicized understandings of identity and community. . . . Similarly, many Latinas participated in the important political praxis of feminist consciousness-raising. . . . Drawing from these various experiences, *testimonio* can be a powerful method for feminist research and praxis. (Latina Feminist Group, 2001, p. 3)

Within the field of education, *testimonio* continues to develop as a powerful methodological approach that uncovers systemic subordination of Chicanas/Latinas. *Testimonio* also serves as a feminist research method that repositions Chicanas/Latinas as central to the analysis and reassigns agency to the oppressed (Latina Feminist Group, 2001). At the same time, *testimonio* reveals the resistance, resilience, and hope we engage in our research to challenge and transform that subordination to collectively move toward social justice (Burciaga, 2007; Burciaga & Tavares, 2006; Cruz, 2006; Delgado Bernal, Flores Carmona, Alemán, Galas, & Garza, 2009; Espino, Muñoz, & Marquez Kiyama, 2010; Flores Carmona, 2010; N. González, 2006; Gutiérrez, 2008; Pérez Huber, 2009a, 2009b). *Testimonio* is used in our research as a collective strategy that deconstructs the apartheid of knowledge that exists in the academy and allows Chicana/Latina researchers and participants to enter ourselves—our knowledge, positionalitities, and experiences—into the process of theorizing, researching, teaching, and reflecting.[2] Additionally, *testimonio* allows Chicana/Latina researchers to document and inscribe into existence a social witness account reflective of collective experiences, political injustices, and human struggles that are often erased by dominant discourses.

Chicana/Latina feminists have built on Latin American social movements like Freire's (2001) process of *conscientização* (a critical consciousness, *conscientización*) where oppressed communities construct self-reflective movements to mobilize through critical pedagogies of empowerment and praxis. Through this process, the subaltern assumes agency by engaging a shared knowledge of oppression to resist and humanize our experiences. For example, Delgado Bernal (2002) asserts that "If we believe in the 'wisdom of our ancient knowledge,' as Ana Castillo suggests, then the knowledge that is passed from one generation to the next can help us survive in everyday life" (p. 113, citations omitted). Documenting *testimonios*, then, becomes a part of this process—passing down knowledge from one generation of scholars to the next.

In this study, we utilize *testimonio* as a methodological approach to understand how undocumented and U.S.-born Chicana/Latina[3] students experience the effects of and responses to a systemic, subtle and cumulative form of racism, racist nativist microaggressions.[4] We draw from critical race and Chicana feminist frameworks to understand the effects of systematic oppression on the Chicana/Latina body and analyze how the women respond to this oppression to heal, to resist, and to become empowered.

We first outline the overarching theoretical frameworks that guide this work—LatCrit and Chicana feminisms. We then explain the conceptual tools that have emerged from each of these theories that help us understand the experiences of the Chicana/Latina students in this study. These include racist nativism and racist nativist microaggressions as conceptual tools developed from a LatCrit framework, and theory in the flesh and *conocimiento* (critical awakenings)—tools located within Chicana feminisms. Following the theoretical discussion, we explain *testimonio* as our methodological approach, and finally, we present the findings on the effects and responses to racist nativist microaggressions.

THEORETICAL FRAMEWORKS: LATINA/O CRITICAL THEORY (LATCRIT) AND CHICANA FEMINISMS

Latina/o Critical Theory

One of the overarching theoretical frameworks for this study is Latina/o critical theory (LatCrit), a branch of critical race theory (CRT) in education. CRT draws from multiple disciplines to challenge dominant ideologies embedded in educational theory and practice, which shapes the way researchers understand the educational experiences, conditions, and outcomes of people of color (Smith-Maddox & Solórzano, 2002; Yosso, 2006). CRT builds from the knowledge of communities of color to reveal the ways that race, class, gender, and other forms of oppression mediate educational trajectories. Moreover, it is committed to deconstructing these oppressive conditions and empowering communities of color to work toward social and racial justice (Solórzano & Yosso, 2001). LatCrit evolved as a challenge to the black-white binary that often guides racial discourse, providing a more focused lens for researchers to examine the experiences of Latina/o communities. LatCrit extends the efforts of CRT and acknowledges issues specific to the ways

Latinas/os are confronted with subordination due to immigration status, language, culture, ethnicity, and phenotype (Solórzano & Delgado Bernal, 2001).

Racist Nativism

CRT allows us to focus the research lens on communities of color; LatCrit narrows that lens to focus on Latina/o communities. Refining our focus even further, racist nativism has emerged from LatCrit as a conceptual tool to examine the specific intersection of race and immigration status in the lives of Latinas/os (Pérez Huber, Benavides López, Malagon, Velez, & Solórzano, 2008). The concept of racist nativism helps researchers understand how race and immigration status are intricately tied in a historical and contemporary process of racialization and colonialism of Latinas/os. For example, scholarship on nativism has examined how various groups of immigrants have been excluded from the white "American" national identity and how that national identity has constructed a fear and acute animosity of the racialized "foreigner." In turn, immigrants of color and those racialized as immigrant (regardless of actual nativity) are perceived as non-native and thus not belonging in the U.S. (Higham, 1955; Saito, 1997). Racist nativism is thus a form of racism that (a) occurs within a historical and contemporary context, (b) intersects with other forms of oppression, and (c) is based on real and perceived immigration status.[5]

Racist nativism provides a lens to examine how perceived racial differences construct Latinas/os as "non-native" to the U.S. and, thus, not belonging to an "American" identity that has historically been tied to social constructions of whiteness (De Genova, 2005; Johnson, 1997; Ngai, 2004; Pérez Huber et al., 2008; Roberts, 1997; Saito; 1997; Sánchez, 1997). Racist nativism allows us to see how the ideological beliefs of Latina/o inferiority manifest in education (Galindo & Vigil, 2006; Pérez Huber, 2009a, 2010; Velez, 2008).

Racist Nativist Microaggressions

Yet another important conceptual tool that has been further developed from CRT is racial microaggressions. According to Solórzano (2010) racial microaggressions are one form of a systemic everyday racism that are subtle, layered, and cumulative verbal and non-verbal assaults directed toward people of color that are committed automatically and unconsciously. Solórzano describes a model for understanding racial microaggressions that includes:

1. Types of racial microaggressions—how one is targeted by microaggressions, which can be based on race, gender, class, language, sexuality, immigration status, phenotype, accent, or surname
2. Context of racial microaggressions—how and where the microaggressions occur
3. Effects of racial microaggressions—the physical, emotional, and psychological consequences of microaggressions
4. Responses to racial microaggressions—how the individual responds to inter-personal and institutional racist acts and behaviors

This model provides researchers with a tool to expose, understand, and challenge subtle forms of racism that occur in education and can have negative, lasting impacts on students.[6] A study conducted by Pérez Huber (2011) found racist nativist microaggressions are a type of racial microaggression experienced by undocumented and U.S.-born Chicana/Latina students within the context of public K-12 education in California. Thus, racist nativist microaggressions are systemic, everyday forms of racist nativism that take the form of subtle, layered, and cumulative verbal and non-verbal assaults directed toward people of color that are committed automatically and unconsciously (Pérez Huber, 2011).

As described earlier, racist nativism inserts a discussion of immigration status and colonialism into racial discourses to acknowledge a history of subordination that informs how Latinas/os experience contemporary racism.[7] Furthermore, this form of racism can intersect with other forms of oppression (e.g., sexism, classism). Thus, racist nativist microaggressions help identify the subtle, everyday acts of larger systemic oppression faced by Latinas/os. Specifically, our work here provides findings on the latter elements of Solórzano's (2010) model—the effects of these racist nativist microaggressions on the women who experienced them, and the responses they had to them.

Chicana Feminisms

Chicana feminisms have developed from stages of historical specificity, including the Chicano Movement, the Women's Movement, and the Civil Rights Movement that challenged such issues as racism, sexism, patriarchy, socioeconomic inequities, and power (de la Torre & Pesquera, 1993). Additionally, from this body of work, a critical feminist analysis of racialized intersectionalities, pedagogies of praxis, and empowerment emerged. Chicana feminisms have transformed over time and inscribe into history counternarratives, *testimonios*, and *autohistorias* (autobiographies) that preserve and document experiential knowledge of Chicanas/Latinas that have been erased by imperial, colonial, and hegemonic feminist discourses (Latina Feminist Group, 2001). Chicana feminist scholars theorize from lived experience as a knowledge base to understand, critique, and challenge systemic oppression and theorize identity, sexuality, the body, resistance, healing, transformation, and empowerment (Castillo, 1994; Fregoso, 2003; Hurtado, 1998; Pérez, 1999; Sandoval, 2000). Moreover, Chicana feminist scholars assert that it is important to create feminist-oriented research practices that critique oppression within a history of colonialism, patriarchy, and white privilege (Alarcón, 1990; Anzaldúa, 1999; Moraga & Anzaldúa, 2002a, 2002b).

Theory in the Flesh

Chicana feminist scholars Moraga and Anzaldúa (2002a) offer theory in the flesh as a conceptual tool that allows for an explicitly racialized feminist approach to constructing knowledge from the body, lived experience, and Chicana subjectivities. Theory in the flesh refers to how "the physical realities of our lives—our skin color, the land or concrete we grew up on, our sexual longings—all fuse to create a politic born out of necessity" (p. 21). It is a tool that allows us to theorize from our intersectionalities or, the "physical realities" we inhabit, our experiential knowledge, and our bodies as discursive sites of knowledge construction that is created from a need to challenge and inscribe ourselves into dominant discourses (Moraga & Anzaldúa, 2002a).

Theory in the flesh asserts that knowledge is produced through our bodies, as trauma and pain are imbedded within us through memories. This concept allows us, as Chicana scholars, to recognize the role of our own body, mind, and spirit in the creation of a unique knowledge base from which we theorize and use to guide our work (Lara, 2002). Theory in the flesh, then, serves as a foundation for a larger body of Chicana feminist scholarship. Theory in the flesh challenges

Western racialized, patriarchal, heteronormative processes of female subordination by providing a conceptual tool that allows us to strategically theorize from the body and flesh. It allows us to inscribe into history and preserve the voices of racialized women by documenting our *testimonios*. From these *testimonios*, we are able to reflect, analyze, and theorize discursive assaults on the body, such as microaggressions. Theory in the flesh provides a lens to understand the psychological and physiological effects of oppression, as we explore in this study. Additionally, theory in the flesh allows us to understand the coping mechanisms Chicanas/Latinas develop to respond to microaggressions, such as the social and academic counterspaces we will also explore.

Conocimiento

Chicana feminisms offer an additional conceptual tool that helps us understand how Chicana/Latina students respond to the systemic oppression they encounter within schooling institutions. *Conocimiento*, developed by Anzaldúa (2002), outlines seven interconnected stages that invoke our ancestral wisdom, lived experiences, cultural knowledge, and resilience in a process that allows us to heal from the effects of race-based trauma and other forms of oppression as we strategically navigate within and outside of hostile educational environments. Thus, *conocimiento* is intricately tied to theory in the flesh as a tool that allows us to engage in a process of theorizing from our bodily knowledge. These conceptual tools urge us to recognize the vital connections between the body, mind, and spirit in understanding the psychological and physiological effects of the race-based trauma we experience as a result of systemic oppression (Lara, 2002). *Conocimiento* extends this understanding by allowing us to theorize healing from microaggressions in a holistic (body, mind, and spirit) way through a process of critical reflection that emphasizes social advocacy and well-being (Anzaldúa, 2002).

Collectively, these frameworks and conceptual tools allow us to name the forms of oppression encountered by the Chicana/Latina students included in this study and how they respond to them. LatCrit, racist nativism, and microaggressions provide the tools to understand how we experience systemic forms of racism and how that racism can manifest within our daily experiences. Chicana feminisms, theory in the flesh, and *conocimiento* allow us to understand how we respond and heal from those oppressive experiences, by calling attention to the complex processes we encounter as we engage our agency in resistance. These theories and tools provide the theoretical scaffolding to build knowledge from an explicitly critical race-gendered epistemological stance, grounded in our lived realities as Chicanas/Latinas (Delgado Bernal, 2002). Moreover, they allow for a more explicit, holistic analysis of microaggressions as an embodied experience that must be theorized from a process of critical reflection. Thus, *testimonio* plays a critical role in this process as a methodological tool that supports critical reflection, healing, and collective memory through the act of *testimoniando* (providing one's *testimonio*, to testify).

TESTIMONIO AS METHODOLOGY

Testimonio as a methodological approach was employed to provide the participants with a space to reveal and reflect on their educational experiences as mediated by race, immigration status, class, and gender. This methodological approach builds from the work of academics—namely women of color scholars—in and outside of education who use *testimonio* to document experiences of struggle, survival, and resistance within the context of oppressive institutional structures and interpersonal events (Benmayor, 1988, 2008; Brabeck, 2001, 2003; Burciaga, 2007; Burciaga & Tavares, 2006; Cruz, 2006; Delgado Bernal et al., 2009; Espino et al., 2010; Flores Carmona, 2010; N. González, 2006; Gutiérrez, 2008; Latina Feminist Group 2001; Pérez Huber, 2009b). We use *testimonio* as a methodological tool that allows us to tell a collective narrative that reveals these complex relationships as they emerge in education. Moreover, Anzaldúa (1990) reminds us that *testimonio* is used as a collective, political act of resistance. Thus, it is a methodology informed by a Chicana feminist stance, used by us and for us.

Contemporary Chicana feminist scholars like Cruz (2006), Delgado Bernal and co-authors (2009), and the Latina Feminist Group (2001) utilize *testimonios* to theorize from the intersections of Chicana subjectivities that are linked to a Freirian process of *concientización* (a critical consciousness of oppression). Such scholars utilize this method to shift discursive power to Chicanas/Latinas in constructing knowledge from our lived realities, positioned within a decolonial framework that challenges larger social inequities. Furthermore, the Latina Feminist Group explains that *testimonios* re-assign agency to Chicana/Latina scholars through the telling of one's history as part of a larger collective memory.

In this study, *testimonios* serve as important counternarratives that challenge deficit educational discourse about Chicana/Latina students. Furthermore, *testimonio* allows us to theorize and document these experiences from an explicitly Chicana/Latina feminist perspective. Finally, *testimonio* is connected to *conocimiento*, as it allows one to enter the process of healing through reflecting, recounting, and remembering the past. In our research, we engage *testimonio* as a methodological process by drawing from our Chicana/Latina feminist epistemological positions and, specifically, the forms of knowledge we have gained from our personal, professional, and academic experiences—what Delgado Bernal (1998) terms cultural intuition.

Cultural intuition informed the analysis process of this study by allowing for an open and reiterative process of bridging and building theory from lived experiences of our participants and ourselves. Engaging our own cultural intuition, we were able to draw from our experiences with microaggressions as Chicana students in the educational pipeline. We reflected on the ways that our minds, bodies, and spirits have been and continue to be affected by low expectations, doubts in our academic and professional abilities, and the consistent challenges we face as scholars who position our work in critical race-gendered epistemologies. In her work on an epistemology of a brown body, Cruz (2006) describes how we have embodied the systematic oppression we have faced through a range of psychological and physiological consequences. However, also similar to our participants, we have found and have created collective spaces of resistance and healing to recover and move forward in our work and in our lives.

We drew from 40 *testimonios* conducted with 20 students (each participant provided a series of two *testimonios*). Ten of these students were undocumented and ten were U.S.-born. At the time of data collection, each of the participants was attending one University of California (UC) campus. Using a network sampling method, participants were identified who met several criteria to participate in the study. Each of these students at the time of data collection were (a) either undocumented or U.S.-born, (b) female, (c) of Mexican descent, and (d) from a low-income family. The majority of the participants in this study self-identified as either Chicana or Latina. In addition to the *testimonios*, we also drew from data collected in two focus groups with these participants, each consisting of six to eight students.[8] Although we use the term "focus group" to describe these interviews, the purpose of these groups was to provide a space for participants to engage in collaborative data analysis through reflection and theorizing their experiences.

For this study, *testimonio* was a continuous process of reflection. We shared our experiences and engaged in discussions about how to better understand them. The focus groups played a critical role in this reflection. During these meetings, the women were asked to reflect on excerpts from their *testimonios*. From these reflections, we engaged in discussions about representation, contradictions, similarities, and differences in our experiences. These discussions were used to build our analysis and theorize from our lived realities. We also discussed the women's reflections on engaging in *testimonio* for this study and offer some of their descriptions in our conclusion.

In the following sections, we provide the findings that emerged from this methodology. Within each section, we present representative examples of our major themes—effects of and responses to racist nativist microaggressions. Following these examples, we provide a context to understand better how these effects and responses occurred in the participants' educational experiences. Finally, we provide an analysis informed by our theoretical frameworks and conceptual tools.

FINDINGS: EFFECTS OF RACIST NATIVIST MICROAGGRESSIONS

The findings extend previous work that examined how the same Chicana/Latina students were subordinated by teacher practices of English dominance in public California K-12 schools (Pérez Huber, 2011). For example, teachers held perceived deficiencies and academic inferiority of participants based on their status as English Learner (EL) students. These practices were supported by restrictive language policies in the state that enforce English immersion for EL students in public schools.[9] The findings provided here reveal how these students were affected by these microaggressions.

Throughout their *testimonios,* the women described a sense of academic self-doubt; they questioned their own abilities. For example, Silvia was an undocumented student born in Jalisco, México and arrived to the U.S. when she was seven years old. In elementary school, she was bussed to a predominately white public school a few miles away from her home where she was placed in an English Language Learner (ELL) program. In middle school, she was placed in English-only instruction classes. She described the transition from her elementary school as an ELL student, to her first year of middle school.

> Sixth grade was just really hard for me. I just hated it. I didn't want to be there, and I was doing really bad in science. I think I got a C . . . I think in English too. I just felt like, "I hope nobody notices I'm at a disadvantage here." I had one-year experience in English language grammar, so I did feel like . . . "I can't handle this. I shouldn't be here." I felt like I wasn't gonna measure up to other kids . . . They were all really smart.

Silvia explained that unlike her predominately Latina/o classes in elementary school, her middle school peers were now predominately white and Asian students. She described being self-conscious, hoping that other students did not notice that she was bilingual. As a result, she felt that she would not perform on the same level as her peers, who she perceived were "smarter" than her. Silvia felt that she was at a "disadvantage" having had less exposure to reading and writing in English. However, neither her teacher nor the classroom environment allowed Silvia to see her own strengths as a fluently bilingual speaker, reader, and writer.

Lourdes shared a similar experience in her transition from her ELL program to English instruction classes. Lourdes was an undocumented student born in Jalisco, México and arrived in California at the age of two. She attended her local public schools from kindergarten through

12th grade. Her elementary school was predominately Latina/o, and her middle and high schools were more racially diverse. She explained that by third grade, she developed enough language skills to be in English-only instruction classes. She made the transition in the middle of the third grade.

> I was in third grade. In the first trimester I was in the bilingual class. In the second [trimester] I was in all-English, and then the third [trimester], they put me in all-English too . . . I remember Mr. Roberts[10] was the bilingual teacher, and then Ms. Olsen, that was the all-English [teacher] . . . I remember I was really excited when they put me in Ms. Olsen's class . . . and then they were like, "Oh you're not good enough to be here." I guess it also brought down my self-esteem a little bit because I had always considered myself smart . . . I was a straight-A student, and always getting awards . . . since kindergarten. So once they put me [back], it kind of brought down my self-esteem a little bit. So I was just like, "Ok, maybe I'm just working hard, but I'm not really smart," and like, "Maybe I don't belong here." I don't know, I guess at that point I doubted myself . . . so then I remember I was going down like, in my grades.

Lourdes explained that she was placed in the English instruction class for several months (with Ms. Olsen) then removed and re-placed in the ELL class. When asked why Lourdes thought she was removed from Ms. Olsen's class, she responded, "The teacher thought I had no place in that class." As a third grader, Lourdes sensed the perceptions of academic inferiority held by her teacher. She explained how this experience negatively affected her self-esteem and made her feel like she was not intelligent, even though she had always done well in school.

Similar to Silvia, Lourdes internalized the perceptions that English-dominant students were more intelligent than Spanish-dominant students like her. Other students described the cumulative effects of the racist nativist microaggressions that followed them into their higher education. For example, Lorena was born in the U.S., grew up in South Los Angeles, and was a monolingual Spanish speaker until she entered school. She was in ELL classes throughout her elementary and middle school years and described the same feeling of "not being smart enough" as Silvia and Lorena. Lorena explained how racist nativist microaggressions in early K-12 affected her as a college student.[11]

In high school, Lorena's top college choice was Pacific University,[12] an elite, private, research institution in California. She applied but was not accepted. Instead of choosing to attend another university where she was accepted, she decided to attend community college and later transfer to Pacific. When she applied to transfer, she was denied admittance again. Lorena had to wait another year to apply to other schools because she had only applied to Pacific. The following year, she explained how her own self-doubt caused her nearly to miss the opportunity to apply to other UC campuses because she felt she was not a competitive candidate. She described completing the online applications for transfer:

> To be honest, I wasn't going to pick [the UC campus in which she is currently enrolled]. I don't know if it was because I just felt, I didn't feel confident after [Pacific University] said no twice . . . I felt, "Wow, am I not good enough? Am I not smart enough, or what's going on?" It really depressed me a little not getting accepted after two years at community college. One counselor said, "Just go to a [state college] and you'll finish there." And I was like, "Okay, I'll just do that." And then I met another counselor who was Latino. His name was Mr. Laso. He said, "Just apply . . . you never know." And I said, "Eh, I don't know," and he said, "You don't have to do anything extra, it's the same package, everything, *nada mas que* [nothing but], one little click extra." So he made me feel like, "Ok, that's

true." So I clicked it. So if it wasn't for him, I don't think I would have clicked it. He pushed me a lot, because I had given up hope, like, "Oh my god, I'm not good enough."

Lorena explained how she became discouraged by not being accepted to the university that she had such high hopes to attend. Instead of questioning the schooling process that did not prepare her to be a successful applicant, she blamed herself for not being "smart enough," a feeling she has held since she entered public school as an ELL student.

Consequently, Lorena felt academically inferior, which deterred her from applying to highly competitive UC campuses. She explained that one community college counselor advised her to attend the less-competitive public state universities. However, with the encouragement of another Latino counselor, she applied and was later accepted to a top UC institution. Lorena's experience demonstrates how she developed internalized beliefs that she was not "smart enough" and how those internalizations mediated her college choice process. A critical (and fortunate) moment with a supportive counselor changed that choice process, which could have ultimately altered her educational trajectory and life opportunities.

Similarly, Alicia shared feelings of academic inferiority as a college student. Alicia was an undocumented student who experienced multiple racist nativist microaggressions throughout K-12 as an ELL student. The accumulation of those experiences led Alicia to feel a deep sadness.

> Poli sci classes can be intimidating sometimes because I would say 90 percent are white students, like male, white students. It's really intimidating when the professor asks you a question, and you're expected to know, and you're supposed to be really articulate. For me, I was actually a little bit sad this week because I don't feel like I'm very, I don't know, it's kinda sad to say, but I think I have problems with my speech. Sometimes [the professor] wants us to argue in class and make good points and like this girl that was sitting in back of me ... and she was bringing some good arguments, I mean, words I never even heard of, like from a Poli Sci dictionary. And I was like, "Damn, why can't I do that?" I can't be argumentative like that and articulate. And I got really sad ... like, "Why can't I have good speech like that?" I don't know if you understand [what] I'm trying to tell you ... They bring out these smart words in like every sentence, and I'm like, "Wow! I don't even know what that word was." So I feel intimidated a lot.

Alicia told this story with great pain in her voice. She explained that she felt she was not able to articulate herself as well as her white peers, and this made her feel "intimidated." Additionally, she felt that there was something psychologically "wrong" with her. Throughout K-12, Alicia described experiences with racist nativist microaggressions that resulted in her feelings of academic inferiority. Alicia's experience reflects the long-term, cumulative effects of racist nativist microaggressions over time in which she has internalized that inferiority and believed she suffered from "speech impairment," as a form of disability.

Cruz (2006) articulates the process of embodiment from theory in the flesh. Cruz poses the question, "How does a regime in a given society become inscribed into the bodies of our youth?" (p. 68). She explains how the body becomes a discursive site of oppression and colonialism where the racism that Chicanas/os (and other people of color) encounter becomes inscribed upon the brown body.[13] Alicia and Lorena gave us examples of this embodiment when, in their *testimonios,* they described the deep sadness and depression they experienced. Cruz's articulation of the process of embodiment illustrates how the microaggressions that the students encounter remain deeply embedded in the bodies, minds, and spirits of Chicanas/Latinas navigating through the educational pipeline. In the process of critical reflection afforded by *conocimiento* and the process of *testimonio*, we see how the Chicana/Latina body becomes a discursive site where effects of racist nativist microaggressions emerge.

Anzaldúa's (2002) concept of *conocimiento* teaches us that these painful and traumatic experiences are part of a process that leads us to reflect, heal, and transcend the oppression we encounter. The *testimonios* presented here illustrate several stages of *conocimiento*. In these excerpts, the women describe their transitions into English-dominant spaces where their sense of not-belonging or not being "good enough" leads them to internalize such negative perceptions. Anzaldúa may describe this experience as the first stage of *conocimiento*, "*el arrebato* ... [the] rupture, fragmentation" of our reality where racism manifests to show that 'something is lacking'" (p. 546). As a result, we feel a painful vulnerability as we are removed from the spaces that were once familiar to us. Moreover, these new classroom environments can be described by the second stage of *conocimiento*, what Anzaldúa calls "*nepantla*," the "liminal space" where we become caught in "*remolinos*"(whirlwinds) between the world we know—our families, our homes, our communities, and the unfamiliar (p. 548). Their examples also manifest the third stage of *conocimiento*, the "*Coatlicue* state," where our internalized oppression emerges in what Anzaldúa calls our "shadow-beasts" (p. 553). However, the "*Coatlicue* state" is also a stage of *conocimiento* that leads us to resist our shadow-beasts and the systemic oppression we have internalized as a result, moving us toward healing and transformation. In the following section, we provide further examples and discussion of this resistance.

The findings clearly support that the effects of racist nativist microaggressions have resulted in negative consequences to the body, mind, and spirit that theory in the flesh and *conocimiento* have helped us understand. The women's internalized feelings of academic inferiority, their "shadow-beasts," resulted in feelings of deep sadness and depression they experienced in the "*Coatlicue* state*" of *conocimiento* (Anzaldúa, 2002). Theory in the flesh reveals how the body remembers the pain and trauma of racist nativist microaggressions over time. Thus, the findings also highlight the *cumulative* aspect of microaggressions at the K-12 level that shape higher education trajectories and experiences.[14]

Chicana feminist scholars suggest that research is needed to identify the strategies Chicanas/Latinas use to navigate racialized and gendered experiences; forming our own categories, methods, and theories created from the inequities we uncover (Alarcón, 1990; Anzaldúa, 2002). In the following section we explore some of the strategies the participants in this study used to navigate through educational institutions and respond to the microaggressions they encountered. Through the women's *testimonios*, these strategies emerged as counterspaces.

RESPONSES TO RACIST NATIVIST MICROAGGRESSIONS: K-12 COUNTERSPACES

A final component to Solórzano's (2010) model of racial microaggressions is how students respond to them. This next component highlights the ways that students counter, challenge, and heal from these experiences. Past research has identified social and academic counterspaces as places inside and outside of the classroom where students find healing, empowerment, and sense of community (Grier-Reed, 2010; Solórzano, Ceja, & Yosso, 2000; Solórzano & Villalpando, 1998; Yosso, 2006; Yosso, Smith, Ceja, & Solórzano, 2009). Yosso et al. describe counterspaces as places that "enable Latina/o students to develop skills of critical navigation through multiple worlds (e.g., home and school communities) and ultimately to survive and succeed in the face of racism" (p. 678). While counterspaces have mostly been explored in higher education, the students in this study describe engaging in counterspaces in their K-12 education. Beginning in middle school, participants described acknowledging spaces where they found a sense of community, empowerment, and healing from their daily experiences with racist nativist microaggressions.

Earlier, Lourdes described the effects of the English dominance that she experienced as an elementary school student. Throughout her K-12 education, she shared many instances of racist nativist microaggressions. In middle school, Lourdes participated in a college preparation program open to all students in high academic standing. Lourdes described the program as a place where she found encouragement and validation in her academic pursuits, despite experiences with teachers and peers who perceived her to be academically inferior. Lourdes described the program, called EXCEED[15] and one of her program teachers in particular:

> I remember Ms. Chavez . . . I would say she's one of the greatest teachers I've ever had. She was just very motivating . . . she saw everything in everybody. She saw the people that were stronger in areas, and then she would help out others, and she . . . motivated me. I remember when I told you that they didn't want to take us to the competitions and then I was kind of like, "Well, maybe I shouldn't be in EXCEED," and she was like, "No! You have the knowledge. You should be part of it. You should be recognized as one of those [EXCEED] students! . . . EXCEED was divided into two classes, two groups. I [was] in the group with Ms. Chavez, and then the ones that would travel more, the ones that go to more competitions, they were in Mr. Howard's group . . . It was predominantly white and Asian . . . and then in my class with Ms. Chavez, all of us were Latinos.

Lourdes explained that the EXCEED program was composed of two eighth grade cohorts, each assigned one teacher. One cohort was mostly white and Asian students, led by a white male teacher, Mr. Howard. Lourdes's cohort was mostly Latina/o students, led by a Latina teacher, Ms. Chavez. Even though both cohorts of students were in equal academic standing, Lourdes explained that Mr. Howard's cohort would be given more opportunities to travel and participate in school competitions and that her (mostly Latina/o) cohort were perceived as less capable than their white and Asian EXCEED peers. Lourdes remained in the program because of the support and encouragement she felt from her teacher and peers. This program was a place where Lourdes felt encouraged and that her college aspirations were attainable. Lourdes suggests that the EXCEED program was a counterspace where she challenged the perceptions of her teachers and peers and continued to work toward preparing for higher education.

Yadira, was a first-year, undeclared major and undocumented student who emigrated to the U.S. when she was 12 years old. Yadira entered seventh grade in a Los Angeles middle school where her first experiences with racist nativist microaggressions began. In her *testimonio,* she described her "ESL" (English as a Second Language, same as ELL) classroom as a place where she felt a sense of community, something she did not feel outside of this space.

> My class, it was ESL 1 . . . my teacher . . . she never wanted to speak Spanish unless you *really* didn't understand. She always wanted us to use dictionaries and write whatever we wanted to say in Spanish, and then translate it word by word in English . . . What many [students] did was that they already knew how to translate, so they would, like, learn how to pronounce [the words] and then just give the information to the new students. Many other students enrolled in the class after I got there, so when I learned how to say, "Can I go to the restroom?" or "May I use a pencil?" I would share the information with other students that didn't know because I was in that situation too. It was

a very emotional learning experience because it wasn't just Mexicans. It was a whole bunch of us, mostly girls, from other Mexican states, and Central America. That's when I first met students from Honduras, El Salvador, Guatemala, Colombia. It was so cool because they spoke different, you know, a different accent, so I learned so much! I learned how to dance *punta*, how to dance *merengue*, how to cook Salvadorian dishes. It was so emotional for me because I was so happy. It was one of the few times I felt that I really belonged! We would share our stories . . . There was a lot of experiences that we shared, and we felt that we belonged there.

In this excerpt, Yadira explained that her seventh grade ESL class was a space where she connected with other Latina/o immigrant students who had shared similar experiences coming to the U.S. as young adolescent women. They would help each other learn the English language and taught each other about their unique cultural customs. They shared their stories of emigrating, of their home countries, and of their difficult experiences living in an unfamiliar place. This was a counterspace, in a new country where she was constantly reminded that she was an outsider, where Yadira felt like she belonged.

Beatriz was a fourth-year sociology major and undocumented student who arrived in the U.S. when she was nine years old. She entered fourth grade as a monolingual Spanish speaker at a public elementary school in Anaheim, California. Beatriz shared a similar account of a counterspace. In seventh grade, Beatriz began participating in a *baile folklórico* dance class. In this class, students were taught traditional Mexican dances from various regions in México. Several times a year, the class would perform at school events.

I was in *baile folklórico,* I started when I was 13 years old and . . . it was just so great. The teacher, she's one woman I admire so much because not only did she want us to be good dancers, but she wanted us to know and appreciate the culture of México. The class was in Spanish. She once told us, "People are going to say a lot of things [about] you, but remember that wherever you go, you represent yourself, you represent your family, and you represent your culture, where you come from." I think that always stayed with me. She really wanted us to be great dancers but also great students. It was just great to go after school every Thursday and have my dance classes . . . It just gave me a sense of love [for] my culture. It really allowed me to . . . escape for one hour, to not be at home, not to be in school and not doing homework. It was *my* hour to do something fun just for me. And so I really liked that . . . to be in front of the whole school . . . and just be very proud . . . people think México is just one little thing, but it's so complex, and it's so many beautiful things.

Beatriz explained that in this *baile folklórico* program, she could be proud of who she was. Her dance teacher was well aware of the subordination her students experienced as Latina/o immigrant students. As a result, the teacher encouraged a form of resiliency and resistance through dance. Thus, the *folklórico* class was a counterspace where Beatriz and her peers learned strategies of resilience, and challenged racist nativist perceptions of themselves and their home country through an empowering form of artistic performance.

Each of these counterspaces provided a sense of belonging and empowerment where students demonstrated resilience to the subordination they faced in schools. By collectively engaging in these spaces, they found encouragement to continue to hold on to their high aspirations. The academic counterspaces Lourdes and Yadira described provided them with "critical navigational skills" that allowed them to persist and succeed in school (Yosso et al., 2009). Social counterspaces—such as Beatriz's *folklórico* class—are places where students represent the community cultural wealth (cultural resources and assets) of their home communities (Yosso et al., 2009). Indeed, the K-12 counterspaces the students described were sites of resistance and resilience to the subordination they encountered in public school as Spanish-dominant Chicana/Latina students.

Conocimiento further sheds light on how students engaged in these counterspaces. In Beatriz's *folklórico* class as counterspace, we see the fifth stage of *conocimiento*, a stage of (re)creating ourselves and co-constructing a collective discourse that locates our lived realities. Anzaldúa (2002) explains this stage is one where we "examine the description of the world, picking holes in the paradigms currently constructing reality" (p. 560). Beatriz and Yadira both explained that they utilized their counterspaces to challenge dominant deficit perspectives of immigrant Chicana/Latina students and to create a collective counternarrative of themselves and each other where their academic and cultural strengths could be reinforced and celebrated. Counterspaces served as sites to engage in a process of reflection as Chicanas/Latinas, students, immigrants, daughters, and other identities they held. It was also a site to engage in healing through building collective networks of support and community.

We see the final stage of *conocimiento*, transformation, in these counterspaces as well. For example, Yadira mentions that her ESL peers were "mostly girls," and that the class served as an important gender-specific space of support and community. In this space, they developed counter-strategies to engage in a dialogical process of teaching and learning language skills to use when the teacher refused to assist. Yadira and her peers transformed the very space (schools) that marginalized them to create a space (ELL classroom) of resistance to move forward in their educational trajectories. Students developed strategies in this counterspace, to support each other and found a place to (re)connect the spirit through empowerment. In turn, they became more resilient to challenge injustice they faced as young Chicana/Latina immigrant girls. Through sharing their unique cultural practices, stories of migration, and experiences as immigrant students, they developed a broader understanding of their educational journeys as connected to a collective struggle of Chicana/Latina immigrant communities.

CONCLUSION

In this article, we have used a model of racial microaggressions (Solórzano, 2010) to explore the effects of and responses to racist nativist microaggressions in the educational experiences of Chicana/Latina students. We presented multiple frameworks and conceptual tools that bridge critical race and Chicana feminist scholarship that revealed the complexities of these experiences and allowed us to incorporate an analysis of the body in relation to oppression. While CRT allowed us to identify microaggressions, theory in the flesh provided a framework to further theorize the process of embodiment and healing from them. We considered Anzaldúa's (2002) process of *conocimiento* as a pathway to understanding and healing from microaggressions and other forms of race-based trauma Chicana/Latina students experience in education. It allows us to consider a process of critical reflection and healing from painful and traumatic experiences caused by oppression that have the ability to impair our health and lives. Moreover, *conocimiento* enables us to confront what Anzaldúa (2002) calls the *remolinos*, or "whirlwinds," we experience as a result of subordination—the psychological and physiological effects on our bodies, minds, and spirits (p. 548). In turn, the process of *conocimiento* is also transformative—enabling us to heal from traumatic experiences caused by oppression through empowerment and social advocacy. Anzaldúa argues that this advocacy challenges us to seek social justice for others, moving us toward dismantling the institutional systems of power that causes oppression and injustice—central goals of LatCrit and Chicana feminist frameworks.

As Chicana feminist scholars in education have argued before us, the bridging of these bodies of work provides a powerful "looking prism" (F. González, 2001, p. 643) to analyze and further theorize those complexities we discover in Chicana/o and Latina/o student experiences (Cueva, 2010; Delgado Bernal, 2002; F. González, 2001; Malagon, 2010; Malagon & Alvarez, 2010). Through our "looking prism" the *testimonios* revealed the serious and negative physiological effects of racist nativist microaggressions on the women's overall well-being. Our analysis highlights the importance and connection of microaggressions to the Chicana/Latina body, mind, and spirit in education. Further, our prism sheds light on the academic and social counterspaces that served as collective sites of empowerment, resistance, and *conocimiento* as the students sought to combat hostile K-12 academic spaces. A clear relationship emerged between structural oppression as manifested in educational policy and students' experiences with microaggressions that have serious consequences on their overall health and well-being.[16] However, despite these experiences they engaged in resilient counter-strategies to navigate, resist, reflect, and transform spaces of structural oppression. While past research on counterspaces in education have focused on college students, these findings provide important insight into the powerful ways young Chicana/Latina students identify and respond to racist nativism through K-12 counterspaces. Finally, our study illustrates the cumulative aspect of microaggressions as these students continued to struggle with its traumatic effects.

The process of *testimonio* played a critical role in developing our "looking prism" and our findings. Hearing the ways the students described the process of *testimonio* prompted us to consider the connection with theory in the flesh and *conocimiento*. We provide the following examples from the focus groups conducted with the women, where they were asked to reflect on the process of *testimonio* in this study. Lourdes explains that her *testimonio* allowed her to critically reflect on her experiences:[17]

> I saw it [the *testimonio*] as kind of a reflection; because I know things that I lived through. I ignored them at the moment, but then thinking about them, like when I told you everything, I was just like, "Wow! I have been through a lot!" And it hadn't hit me because I just keep thinking, ok, another day, another day, another day, but then if you think back on all of it, it's like wow! I'm sure it's like that for all of us ... because we go through so many things daily and we don't think about [it] ... And it's like, "Wow! And I'm still here!" So it gets me thinking about stuff.

Lourdes explained how engaging in the process of *testimonio* allowed her to reflect and come to a realization about her own resiliency to the multiple forms of racism she experienced, which she shared in her *testimonio*. Beatriz also shared her thoughts on the process.

> Just to have a space where I could start from the beginning [laughs]. Not everyone has ... many hours to do both interviews. A lot of my close friends know a lot about me and my own history ... my hopes and my faith and they know the struggle, but I think having this type of step where you let enough space for us to say our stories, I feel like I was not rushed so it gave me freedom to say much more. I think in a way it also scratched *heridas que* [pause] I guess I have to say ... because sometimes I was not able to say everything with such detail, so it hurt at the end. It was healing as well, because ... just to be able to say everything with detail and not holding back, it's just like, having someone having enough time [to listen].

Here, Beatriz explains that her *testimonio* allowed her the space and time to fully explain her experiences in ways that she had not been able to previously, "to start from the beginning." She explained feeling "hurt" when she was not able to tell her story completely—perhaps from the telling of her story without time to reflect. She explained that sharing her experiences "scatched *heridas*" (scratched wounds), a feeling that prompted her to share her story more fully.[18] In this description, Beatriz alludes to an embodiment that takes place for her in the telling of her experiences with subordination as an undocumented Chicana/Latina immigrant student—an experience theory in the flesh allows us to understand. However, in both descriptions we also see stages of *conocimiento* present, particularly in how they describe *testimonio* as reflective and healing. Indeed, these examples illustrate the powerfully positive impact that *testimonio* has on those who engage in them.

We argue that the process of *testimonio* allowed us to see a more complete picture of the systemic oppression the women experienced in schools. They described the *remolinos* caused by these experiences—the psychological and physiological effects caused to their bodies, minds, and spirits. The students also challenged that oppression by engaging in counterspaces. Our analysis demonstrates that in collectively sharing *testimonios* we engage in a process of *conocimiento*. One student explained that the *testimonios* she and other participants gave were important "because other people are gonna read this and see what we have to go through." Their stories spoke to a collective struggle to which readers would bear witness. *Testimonio* provided a means to reflect, engage, and theorize. It allowed us a space to be vulnerable—to share the pain of oppression and to rejoice in our struggles to overcome. Through this work, we engage in social advocacy by revealing the effects of and responses to racist nativist microaggressions to disrupt the educational practices and policies that enable such oppression. In this process of *conocimiento*, we become active agents of social change, freeing ourselves from the effects of microaggressions to heal and celebrate our empowerment, hope, and resiliency in education.

NOTES

1. Typically in our work, we intentionally capitalize the term "Students of Color" to reject the standard grammatical norm. Capitalization is used as a means of empowerment and represents a grammatical move toward social justice. We typically use this rule to apply to "People, Immigrants, Women and Communities of Color" in our writing. However, we understand the policies this journal has established to maintain consistency in the use of capitalization and the potential to exclude other oppressed groups in this grammatical practice (i.e., Queer, Persons with Disabilities, etc.).

2. Delgado Bernal and Villalpando (2002) argue that an apartheid of knowledge exists in academia where racial divisions are created between Eurocentric epistemologies and other epistemological stances, producing an ideological divide between "legitimate" and "illegitimate" forms of knowledge. This apartheid maintains white superiority through a narrowly defined knowledge production process that devalues and delegitimizes the forms of knowledge that exists within communities of color.

3. The majority of women in this study self-identified as either Chicana or Latina. Thus, we use the term Chicana/Latina to describe this group of participants. All ten of the undocumented participants were born in México. In addition, all ten of the U.S.-born participants' parents were born in México. The salience of racial identification varied in the lives of the participants. Some women were very committed to the political dimensions of a Chicana/Latina identity, while others explained using the term Latina because it was more of a collective identity. Others used terms like Mexican American, American Mexican, Mexican, and Hispanic to describe themselves.

4. This work extends a previous study that explored how the women experienced racist nativist microaggressions in California public K-12 schools (Pérez Huber, 2011).

5. The original definition of racist nativism can be found in Pérez Huber et al. (2008). We would like to acknowledge the assistance of Dr. Daniel Solórzano in crafting a brief version of this definition as provided here.

6. The concept of racial microaggression was first developed by psychiatrist Dr. Chester Pierce (1969) to explain the subtle, yet powerfully harmful "offensive mechanisms" directed by Whites toward African Americans (p. 303). CRT scholars have built upon this conceptual tool within critical race scholarship in education and have found that this concept can be used to explain how Latina/o and African American students are targeted by low expectations, racist and sexist stereotypes, and racially hostile college campus environments (Greir-Reed, 2010; Smith, Allen, & Danley, 2007; Solórzano, 1998; Solórzano, Ceja, & Yosso, 2000; Yosso, 2006; Yosso, Smith, Ceja, Solórzano, 2009). Racist nativist microaggressions as a type of racial microaggression have been theorized from a LatCrit lens that has allowed researchers to examine the role of immigration status in the way microaggressions are experienced (Pérez Huber, 2011).

7. See Pérez Huber et al. (2008) for a discussion of the historical subordination of Latinas/os in the U.S., specifically through immigration and educational policies.

8. These focus groups included undocumented and U.S.-born students.

9. In this previous study, Pérez Huber (2011) discusses the current law guiding language policies in California public K-12 schools, Proposition 227 (Prop 227). Prop 227 restricted bilingual education in schools and mandated EL students into structured English immersion programs. She explains that this law targeted Spanish-speaking Latina/o students who comprised the majority of English Learner students at the time the law was passed in 1998. She argues that such restrictive language policies support and encourage teacher practices of English dominance over Latina/o students in these schools.

10. All names provided in this article are pseudonyms to protect the identities of the students and confidentiality of their *testimonios*.

11. Our analysis of microaggressions uncovers the subordination the women experienced as a result of being labeled English Lanuage Learners in K-12 schools. However, we feel it is also important to acknowledge that being bilingual was also a source of strength that provided the students with a skill-set they utilized to navigate educational institutions. In a previous study, Pérez Huber (2009a) explains how these bilingual skills can be considered a form of linguistic capital within a community cultural wealth framework.

12. Pseudonym

13. Cueva (2012) has found other examples of embodiment. Her data (46 *testimonio* interviews) on Chicana and Native American doctoral students highlights the various types of racialized and gendered microaggressions women encounter in higher education that impair their bodies, health, and overall quality of life. Some of the symptoms include: depression, anxiety, dissociative disorder, posttraumatic stress disorder, insomnia, fatigue, high blood pressure, diabetes, irritable bowel syndrome, anxiety/panic attacks, sweats, weight gain, weight loss, low sugar levels, migraine headaches, chronic pain, contemplation of suicide, as well as reproductive issues (e.g., missed periods, miscarriages, stopped ovulation, heavy bleeding/cramping, extreme PMS, pelvic pain).

14. Both undocumented and U.S.-born students experienced the effects of racist nativist microaggressions in similar ways. However, we feel it is important to highlight the heightened negative effects of microaggressions experienced by the undocumented women in the study, such as Alicia's symptoms of depression. Future research should further theorize the relationship between the body, mind, spirit, and traumatic experiences that undocumented Chicanas/Latinas encounter as a result of racist nativism, sexism, patriarchy, and other forms of oppression.

15. Pseudonym

16. Here, we consider the findings of Pérez Huber (2011) on restrictive language policies as institutional oppression that results in the young women's experiences with microaggressions.

17. The two excerpts provided here have been previously published in a different analysis focused on method to illustrate how the women described the process of *testimonio* as reflective and healing and how participants' descriptions were incorporated into the conceptualization of *testimonio* as a methodological process (see Pérez Huber, 2010).

18. The direct English translation of *herida* is "wound." However, the way Beatriz uses this word is more of an expression that lacks a direct translation. Similar to this expression of *herida,* we see Anzaldúa's (1999) use of the term in her concept of *la herida abierta*, "the open wound" of the social world created by the

oppressive physical and symbolic borders imposed by neocolonialism (e.g., racism, patriarchy, capitalism, heterosexism).

REFERENCES

Alarcón, N. (1990). The theoretical subject(s) of this bridge called my back and Anglo-American feminism. In G. Anzaldúa (Ed.), *Making face, making soul (haciendo caras): Creative and critical perspectives by women of color* (pp. 356–369). San Francisco, CA: Aunt Lute Foundation.

Anzaldúa, G. (1990). Introduction: Haciendo caras una entrada. In G. Anzaldúa (Ed.), *Making face, making soul (haciendo caras): Creative and critical perspectives by women of color* (pp. xv–xxvii). San Francisco, CA: Aunt Lute Foundation.

Anzaldúa, G. (1999). *Borderlands/la frontera: The new mestiza* (2nd ed.). San Francisco, CA: Aunt Lute Books.

Anzaldúa, G. (2002). Now let us shift . . . The path of conocimiento . . . Inner work, public acts. In G. Anzaldúa & A. Keating, (Eds.), *This bridge we call home: Radical visions for transformation.* (pp. 540–578). New York, NY: Routledge.

Benmayor, R. (1988). For every story there is another story which stands before it. *Oral History Review 16*(2), 1–13.

Benmayor, R. (2008). Digital storytelling as signature pedagogy for the new humanities. *Arts and Humanities in Higher Education, 7*(2), 188–204.

Brabeck, K. (2001). *Testimonio: Bridging feminist ethics with activist research to create new spaces of collectivity.* Paper presented at the Feminisms in Participatory Action Research Conference. Newton, MA.

Brabeck, K. (2003). Testimonio: A strategy for collective resistance, cultural survival and building solidarity. *Feminism & Psychology, 13*(2), 252–258.

Burciaga, R. (2007). *Chicana/Latina Ph.D. students living nepantla: Educación and aspirations beyond the doctorate.* Unpublished dissertation. University of California, Los Angeles.

Burciaga, R., & Tavares, A. (2006). Our pedagogy of sisterhood: A testimonio. In D. Delgado Bernal, A. C. Elenes, F. Godinez, & S. Villenas (Eds.), *Chicana/Latina/Latina education in everyday life: Feminista perspectives on pedagogy and epistemology* (pp. 133–142). Albany, NY: State University of New York Press.

Castillo, A. (1994). *Massacre of the dreamers: Essays on Xicanisma.* New York, NY: Plume Book.

Cruz, C. (2006). Toward an epistemology of a brown body. In D. Delgado Bernal, A. C. Elenes, F. Godinez, & S. Villenas (Eds.), *Chicana/Latina/Latina education in everyday life: Feminista perspectives on pedagogy and epistemology* (pp. 59–76). Albany, NY: State University New York Press.

Cueva, B. M. (2010). A testimonial of resistance, survival, and hope: Breaking the silences of racial battle fatigue in academia. *Social Sciences and Comparative Education Newsletter, 2*(2), 3–5.

Cueva, B. M. (2012). Theorizing the impacts of race-based trauma to Chicanas and Native American women in higher education: Testimonios of resilience, survival, and hope. Unpublished dissertation in progress. (copy on file with author).

De Genova, N. (2005). *Working the boundaries: Race, space, and "illegality" in Mexican Chicago.* Durham, NC: Duke University Press.

de la Torre, A., & Pesquera, B. M. (Eds). (1993). *Building with our hands: New directions in Chicana Studies.* Berkeley, CA: University of California Press.

Delgado Bernal, D. (1998). Using a Chicana feminist epistemology in educational research. *Harvard Educational Review, 68*(4), 555–579.

Delgado Bernal, D. (2002). Critical race theory, Latino critical theory and critical raced-gendered epistemologies: Recognizing students of color as holders and creators of knowledge. *International Journal of Qualitative Studies in Education, 8*(1), 105–126.

Delgado Bernal, D., Flores Carmona, J., Alemán, S., Galas, L., & Garza, M.(Latinas Telling Testimonios). (2009). *Unidas we heal: Testimonios of the mind/body/soul.* Salt Lake City, UT: University of Utah.

Delgado Bernal, D., & Villalpando, O. (2002). An apartheid of knowledge in academia: The struggle over the "legitimate" knowledge of faculty of color. *Equity & Excellence in Education, 35*(2), 169–180.

Espino, M. M., Muñoz, S. M., & Marquez Kiyama, J. (2010). Transitioning from doctoral study to the academy: Theorizing trenzas of identity for Latina sister scholars. *Qualitative Inquiry, 16*(10), 804–818.

Flores Carmona, J. (2010). *Transgenerational educación: Latina mothers' everyday pedagogies of cultural citizenship in Salt Lake City, Utah.* Unpublished dissertation. University of Utah, Salt Lake City.

Fregoso, R. L. (2003). *MeXicana encounters: The making of social identities on the borderlands*. Berkeley, CA: University of California Press.

Freire, P. (2001). *Pedagogy of the oppressed* (30th ann. ed., M. B. Ramos, Trans.). New York, NY: Continuum.

Galindo, R., & Vigil, J. (2006). Are anti-immigrant statements racist or nativist? What difference does it make? *Latino Studies, 4*(4), 419–447.

González, F. E. (2001). Haciendo que hacer: Cultivating a mestiza worldview and academic achievement: Braiding cultural knowledge into educational research, policy, practice. *International Journal of Qualitative Studies in Education, 14*(5), 641–656.

González, N. (2006). Testimonios of border identities: Una mujer acomedida donde quiera cabe. In D. Delgado Bernal, A. C. Elenes, F. Godinez, & S. Villenas (Eds.), *Chicana/Latina/Latina education in everyday life: Feminista perspectives on pedagogy and epistemology* (pp. 197–213). Albany, NY: State University of New York Press.

Grier-Reed, T. L. (2010). The African American student network: Creating sancturaries and counterspaces for coping with racial microaggressions in higher education settings. *Journal of Humanistic Counseling, Education, and Development, 49*(2), 181–188.

Gutiérrez, K. D. (2008). Developing a sociocritical literacy in the third space. *Reading Research Quarterly, 43*(2), 148–164.

Higham, J. (1955). *Strangers in the land: Patterns of American nativism 1860–1925*. New Brunswick, NJ: Rutgers University Press.

Hurtado, A. (1998). Sitios y lenguas: Chicanas theorize feminism. *Hypatia, 13*(2), 134–159.

Johnson, K. (1997). The new nativism: Something old, something new, something borrowed, something blue. In J. F. Perea (Ed.), *Immigrants out! The new nativism and the anti-immigrant impulse in the United States* (pp. 165–189). New York, NY: New York University Press.

Lara, I. (2002). Healing sueños for academia. In G. Anzaldúa & A. Keating (Eds.), *This bridge we call home: Radical visions for transformation* (pp. 433–438). New York, NY: Routledge.

Latina Feminist Group. (2001). *Telling to live: Latina feminist testimonios*. Durham, NC: Duke University Press.

Malagon, M. C. (2010). All the losers go there: Challenging the deficit educational discourse of Chicano racialized masculinity in a continuation high school. *Journal of Educational Foundations, 24*(1–2), 59–76.

Malagon, M. C., & Alvarez, C. R. (2010). Scholarship girls aren't the only Chicanas who go to college: Former Chicana continuation high school students disrupting the educational achievement binary. *Harvard Educational Review, 80*(2), 149–173.

Moraga, C., & Anzaldúa, G. (2002a). Entering the lives of others: Theory in the flesh. In C. Moraga & G. Anzaldúa (Eds.), *This bridge called my back: Writing by radical women of color* (3rd ed., pp. 19–21). Berkeley, CA: Third Woman Press.

Moraga, C., & Anzaldúa, G. (Eds.). (2002b). *This bridge called my back: Writing by radical women of color* (3rd ed.). Berkeley, CA: Third Woman Press.

Ngai, M. M. (2004). *Impossible subjects: Illegal aliens and the making of modern America*. Princeton, NJ: Princeton University Press.

Pérez, E. (1999). *The decolonial imaginary: Writing Chicanas into history*. Bloomington, IN: Indiana University Press.

Pérez Huber, L. (2009a). Challenging racist nativist framing: Acknowledging the community cultural wealth of undocumented Chicana college students to reframe the immigration debate. *Harvard Educational Review, 79*(4), 704–729.

Pérez Huber, L. (2009b). Disrupting apartheid of knowledge: Testimonio as methodology in Latina/o critical race research in education. *International Journal of Qualitative Studies in Education, 22*(6), 639–654.

Pérez Huber, L. (2010). Beautifully powerful: A LatCrit reflection on coming to an epistemological consciousness and the power of testimonio. *Journal of Gender, Social Policy and the Law, 18*(3), 339–851.

Pérez Huber, L. (2011). Discourses of racist nativism in California public education: English dominance as racist nativist microaggressions. *Educational Studies, 47*(4), 379–401.

Pérez Huber, L., Benavides Lopez, C., Malagon, M. C., Velez, V., & Solórzano, D. G. (2008). Getting beyond the "symptom," acknowledging the "disease": Theorizing racist nativism. *Contemporary Justice Review, 11*(1), 39–51.

Pierce, C. M. (1969). Is bigotry the basis of the medical problems of the ghetto? In J. C. Norman (Ed.), *Medicine in the ghetto* (pp. 301–312). New York, NY: Meredith.

Roberts, D. (1997). Who may give birth to citizens? Reproduction, eugenics and immigration. In J. F. Perea (Ed.), *Immigrants out! The new nativism and the anti-immigrant impulse in the United States* (pp. 205–219). New York, NY: New York University Press.

Saito, N. T. (1997). Alien and non-alien alike: Citizenship, "foreignness," and racial hierarchy in American law. 76 *Oregon Law Review* 261.

Sánchez, G. J. (1997). Face the nation: Race, immigration, and the rise of nativism in late twentieth century America. *International Migration Review, 31*(4), 1009–1030.

Sandoval, C. (2000). *Methodology of the oppressed.* Minneapolis, MN: University of Minnesota Press.

Smith, W. A., Allen, W. R, & Danley, L. L. (2007). "Assume the position . . . you fit the description": Psychosocial experiences and racial battle fatigue among African American male college students. *American Behavioral Scientist, 51*(4), 551–578.

Smith Maddox, R., & Solórzano, D. G. (2002). Using critical race theory, Freire problem-posing method, and case study research to confront race and racism in education. *Qualitative Inquiry, 8*(1), 66–84.

Solórzano, D. G. (1998). Critical race theory, race and gender microaggressions, and the experiences of Chicana and Chicano scholars. *International Journal of Qualitative Studies in Education, 11*(1), 121–136.

Solórzano, D. G. (2010, March). *Using critical race theory and racial microaggressions to examine everyday racism.* A keynote presentation to the University of California Santa Barbara, Multicultural Center's Race Matters Series. Santa Barbara, CA.

Solórzano, D. G., Ceja, M., & Yosso, T. J. (2000). Critical race theory, racial microaggressions and campus racial climate: The experiences of African American college students. *Journal of Negro Education, 69*(1–2), 60–73.

Solórzano, D. G., & Delgado Bernal, D. (2001). Examining transformational resistance through a critical race and Latcrit theory framework: Chicana and Chicano students in an urban context. *Urban Education, 36*(3), 308–342.

Solórzano, D. G., & Villalpando, O. (1998). Critical race theory, marginality and the experience of students of color in higher education. In T. Mitchell & C. A. Torres (Eds.), *Sociology of education: Emerging perspectives* (pp. 181–210). Albany, NY: State University of New York Press.

Solórzano, D. G., & Yosso, T. J. (2001). Maintaining social justice hopes within academic realities: A Freirean approach to critical race/LatCrit pedagogy. 78 *Denver University Law Review* 595.

Velez, V. N. (2008). Challenging lies LatCrit style: A critical race reflection of an ally to Latina/o immigrant parent leaders. *4 Florida International University Law Review 119.*

Yosso, T. J. (2006). *Critical race counterstories along the Chicana/Chicano educational pipeline.* New York, NY: Routledge.

Yosso, T. J., Smith, W. A., Ceja, M., & Solórzano, D. G. (2009). Critical race theory, racial microaggressions, and campus racial climate for Latina/o undergraduates. *Harvard Educational Review, 79*(4), 659–690.

Pedagogies from *Nepantla*: *Testimonio*, Chicana/Latina Feminisms and Teacher Education Classrooms

Linda Prieto

California Polytechnic State University, San Luis Obispo

Sofia A. Villenas

Cornell University

This article describes a process of testimonial co-creation between two teacher educators. We created *testimonios* in dialogue to examine who we are, how we "know," and how we teach as Chicana/Latina educators of prospective teachers in predominantly white institutions (PWIs). An active exploration of our lived experiences growing up as racialized, gendered, and classed Chicanas/Latinas reveal both "the theory of our practice and the practice of our theory" (Latina Feminist Group, 2001, p. 19). As teacher educators engaged in contradictory and transformative ways of knowing, teaching, and learning, our *testimonios* revealed fruitful tensions for mining the liminal and relational moments across difference and privilege with our prospective teachers. We develop the themes of cultural dissonance, *conciencia con compromiso* (consciousness with commitment) and *cariño* (authentic care) as Chicana feminist pedagogies. We close by sharing how Latina/Chicana feminist *testimonios* articulate *nepantla*—a space of frustration, discomfort, and always improvised visionary modes of teaching and learning.

How do we build caring relationships with our students and together explore *Nepantla*? . . . a Nahuatl word for the space between two bodies of water, the space between two worlds . . . It is very awkward, uncomfortable, and frustrating to be in that *Nepantla* because you are in the midst of transformation. (Ikas, 2002, p. 13)

In the burgeoning literature on multicultural teacher education, there are important conversations and critiques surrounding the preparation of prospective teachers for a diverse world. They speak to institutional barriers that hamper university programmatic attempts to sustain students' intellectual and emotional engagement with difficult issues surrounding difference, power, privilege, and race. The literature also describes the transformational work of multicultural education classrooms where method (pedagogy) is just as important as content knowledge. For example, teacher educators and scholars make the case for students to learn about themselves and uncover their own biases, assumptions, and cultural practices often through autobiographical narratives (Nieto & Bode, 2011). Yet, while the focus in the literature remains on the dynamics of the teacher preparation classroom, there is less interest in the lives of multicultural teacher educators themselves who are expected to engage future teachers in the aforementioned transformative educational experiences. And there is even less knowledge about the teacher educator of color—Latina teacher educators among these. We are inspired by women of color in institutions of higher education who have theorized their pedagogies and identities in teacher education and ethnic studies classrooms (Asher, 2005; Beauboeuf-Lafontaine, 2005; Elenes, 2001; hooks, 1994; Rendón, 2009; Reyes & Ríos, 2005; Rodriguez, 2006). These scholars develop borderlands pedagogies (Elenes, 2001), womanist of color pedagogies (Asher, 2005), critical race feminist epistemologies (Delgado Bernal, 2002; Rodriguez, 2006), and describe the challenges of women of color in predominantly white institutions (Flores & Garcia, 2009; Vargas, 2002). Our aim here is to call attention to the power of *testimonio* as a method and political tool for naming and claiming Chicana/Latina feminist pedagogies in multicultural teacher preparation classrooms.

This article describes a process of testimonial co-creation between two teacher educators. We created *testimonios* in dialogue to examine who we are, how we "know," and how we teach as Chicana/Latina educators of prospective teachers in predominantly white institutions (PWIs). The Latina Feminist Group (2001) posed an important question for us: "How can *testimonio* as self-construction and contestation of power, help us build the theory of our practice, and the practice of our theory?" (p. 19). Through an active exploration of our lived experiences growing up as racialized, gendered, and classed Chicanas/Latinas we create both the theory of our practice and the practice of our theory. As teacher educators we are engaged in contradictory and transformative ways of knowing, teaching, and learning as articulations of Chicana feminist pedagogies (see Delgado Bernal, Elenes, Godinez, & Villenas, 2006). We have often experienced the university classroom space in terms of personal hurt and deep frustration in relation to our collective and individual life stories. Yet our urgent *testimonios* also revealed fruitful tensions for mining the liminal and dialogic moments of connection and caring as we relate across difference and privilege with our prospective teachers.

We begin by situating our conversation within current scholarship addressing the experiences of women of color faculty in PWIs and Latina public school teachers. These studies confirm our own experiences and reveal hopeful pedagogies; they also point to the lack of attention to the specific lives and work of teacher educators of color in Colleges and Schools of Education. Next, we discuss our *testimonios* as methodology and data co-created with Chicana feminist sensibilities and perspectives. Through our dialogues, we created urgent *testimonios* of our lived experiences as a resource for apprehending our collective work as educators of prospective teachers. Finally, in analyzing how we are situated to know what we know, and to know how and what we teach via our *testimonios*, we uncover the themes of dissonance, *conciencia con compromiso* (consciousness with commitment), and *cariño* (authentic care) (see Prieto, 2009a). We close by sharing how Latina educators' *testimonios* and Latina/Chicana feminist perspectives can rearticulate pedagogies of *nepantla*—a space of frustration, discomfort, and always improvised visionary modes of teaching and learning.

EDUCATORS OF COLOR AND CRITICAL MULTICULTURAL ENDEAVORS IN UNIVERSITY AND K-12 CLASSROOMS

Women Faculty of Color in PWIs

For those of us who were ever students of women faculty of color, we might remember the feelings and the experiences of their university classrooms. In our own memories, we were deeply touched by their passionate attempts to make the teaching and learning experience different—more humane, collaborative, and urgently critical. Critique and resilience were lessons embodied by these women faculty of color who were far and few between for Villenas (the second author) in the mid 1980s, and even for Prieto (the first author) in her undergraduate years in the mid 1990s. The theme of critique and resilience follows an edited collection of powerful voices theorizing the experiences of women of color teaching and learning in PWIs. Vargas (2002) draws important lessons from the diverse group of authors who contributed to her edited collection. Vargas and contributors emphasize the impact of the institutional context on the teaching-learning experience of women faculty and instructors of color. For example, they highlight teacher anger and the pressure from academia to assimilate into academe's culture of niceness where restraint from passion and emotion is valued. In our own experiences, fears of being labeled and dismissed as "hot-headed Latinas" by our peers and our students make engaging the very real emotions of injury from racism, classism, sexism, heteronormativity, and other oppressions difficult.

Vargas (2002) also helps us consider our experiences in relation to the structural features of a teacher preparation program. In our experiences across several universities and in conversations with other teacher educators, the multicultural or diversity course is often a required course set apart from the literacy methods, math methods, or social studies courses (see Villegas & Lucas, 2002). Multiculturalism is often framed as an "extra" or "add-on" issue—a structural feature which can negatively impact students' and faculty members' attitudes toward the subject matter and the instructor (Villegas & Lucas, 2002). In addition, a cursory hand-raising survey every year in Villenas' classroom reveals that very few aspiring teachers have taken courses in Ethnic Studies and American Indian Studies. In the absence of ethnic studies prerequisites, students approach the study of multicultural issues in education with little knowledge of the history of non-dominant groups. We are often hard pressed to find even one person in our classes with some knowledge of the experiences of American Indian children in federal boarding schools. This structural devaluation of the knowledge and histories of communities of color, along with a lack of attention to critical multiculturalism, forms the backdrop to our work as women educators of color in higher education.

At the same time, Vargas (2002) and the contributors to her volume expose how the fluid nature of our power, prestige, and knowledge constructs our authority as teachers or instructors of multicultural education and ethnic studies courses. However, this authority is most often not afforded to women of color when they teach core or mainstream courses in the disciplines. Vargas (2002) highlights the difficulty of transformative relationships and pedagogies when institutional barriers and contexts impact classroom and instructional dynamics. Yet, the writings by women of color faculty in PWIs also help us draw strength from the spaces of marginalization. They highlight processes of self-healing, resilience, and transformation that result in pedagogical transformations (see Asher, 2005; Berry & Mizelle, 2006; Elenes, 2001; Vargas, 2002). Our teaching practices, which emerge from our diverse cultural experiences and memory, are invaluable to the university classroom.

Latina Teachers in Public Schools

Recent studies on Latina teachers flesh out their stories in relation to their culturally relevant practices and their Latina feminist philosophies of *respeto, cariño,* and *conciencia* for social justice (Guardia Jackson, 2010; Ochoa, 2007; Prieto, 2009a). While the context of public school classrooms is different from the university context, these studies contribute to a picture of the diverse and common ways in which Latina educators, in many educational settings, articulate *testimonios* that link their "theory of practice and their practice of theory" (Latina Feminist Group, 2001, p. 19). Guardia Jackson's (2010) person-centered ethnography of an exemplary veteran, Mexican American, bilingual educator traces the conscious development of an activist identity in relation to her teaching and leadership practices. This teacher's *testimonios* involve a critical awareness of the historical legacy, lived experiences, and the communities and contexts in which she has taught. Likewise, the novice Latina bilingual education teachers in Prieto's (2009a) study, though very early in their careers, already bore witness to the connections between their life stories-in-the-making and that of their Latino students. This critical awareness informed their teaching practices. Finally, studies by Reyes and Rios (2005) and Ochoa (2007) emphasize the importance of dialogue and story among Chicana/Latina university faculty and Latina public school teachers respectively. These stories illuminate how reductive and deficit-oriented policies and classroom practices negatively impact the Latina/o educational pipeline and the influence of these experiences on Latina teachers' work and relationships in the classroom. Like Latina teachers, veteran and novice, we too connect our politically urgent stories—our *testimonios*—to our work as educators. Alarcón, Cruz, Guardia Jackson, Prieto, and Rodriguez-Arroyo (2011) poignantly emphasize how "the telling of our personal histories and testimonios as Chicanas and Latinas in the academy becomes nothing less than transformational" (p. 370).

TESTIMONIO AS METHODOLOGY: BUILDING THE THEORY OF OUR PRACTICE

> Through *testimonio,* we learned to translate ourselves for each other. (The Latina Feminist Group, 2001, p. 11)

Women of color have long made the case that theory and the production of knowledge cannot be disassociated from people's lived experiences (Gonzales, 1997; Hurtado, 2003; Latina Feminist Group, 2001; Martínez, 1996). This exploratory study examines our stories as two Chicana/Latina feminists wanting to theorize our practice as educators. We employed a narrative approach and dialogical research methods (Padilla, 1992; Reyes & Ríos, 2005) conducted over the course of two years. Our dialogues—translating ourselves for each other—functioned in a reformulated tradition of *testimonio.* Emerging from Latin America, *testimonios* consist of life stories usually told by a person from a marginalized group in society, to an interlocutor who can write down and disseminate them. The *testimonio* has an overtly political intent, which Haig-Brown (2003) explains, "is to inform people outside a community/country of the circumstances and conditions of people's lives" (p. 419) and to impel others to take some form of action. *Testimoniantes* (the narrators of the text) bear witness to injustice and violence inflicted on their communities. Their call for change is urgent. For this reason, Haig-Brown continues, "the life story presented is not simply a personal matter; rather, it is the story of an individual who is also a part of a community. A *testimonio* presents the life of a person whose experiences, while unique, extend beyond her/him to represent the group of which she/he is a member" (p. 420).

As professionals in academia, Latinas are hardly economically marginalized members of society. What does *testimonio* have to do with Latinas who are professionally privileged as instructors and professors in prestigious universities in the United States? Delgado Bernal and Elenes (2011) posit that, "A group identity and group marginalization continues to exist in academia even when we have attained a relatively privileged status" (p. 111). The Latina Feminist Group (2001) argues that this collective experience of achievement often involves negating our diverse modes of being and knowing:

> For racialized ethnic women of subjugated peoples, achievement is always a double-edged sword. In becoming women of accomplishment, we have had to construct and perform academic personas that require "professionalism," "objectivity," and respectability in ways that often negate our humanity (p. 14).

Testimonio then, names the workings and abuses of institutional power, the human costs, and our collective *sobrevivencia* (survival and beyond). Latina and women of color creative writers, artists, intellectuals, and scholar/activists make the case for the intensely political nature of our creative and professional work. Through our stories, we bear witness to our unique and collective experiences as racialized/ethnicized women in the United States. Different from the traditional genre of *testimonio*, Latina/Chicana feminist *testimoniantes* bear witness to each other as interlocutors through our own voice and authoring. Klahn (2003) writes, "It is from this culturally or politically rooted position that the narrator becomes the voice, her own, of a self who recollects her memories and those of others in her community" (p. 120).

Chicana feminist and borderlands writings have provided the *testimonios* and *feminista* legacies upon which to ground our own teaching selves. With Latina/Chicana feminist perspectives, we interpret structural conditions, our social locations and life options (Pesquera & Segura, 1997), and our stories of schooling and community work. These ways of knowing, or Chicana feminist epistemologies, position Latinas/Chicanas as central subjects and *pensadoras* (knowers/thinkers). In this article, the *pensadoras* included Prieto, who at the time of the study was a doctoral student in the College of Education at a large southwestern and predominantly white research institution. Villenas was a newly arrived faculty member at the same university during the years 2003–2005.

We began to get to know one another through a class Villenas was teaching and as colleagues when Villenas invited Prieto to co-teach the required multicultural education course for prospective teachers. We continued to teach our own sections of the course in following semesters. As we began to share our teaching joys and struggles, we developed an urgent need to bear witness to our lives in our teaching. We wanted to theorize our pedagogy in our predominantly white teacher education classrooms. Why do we teach the way we do? How do Chicana/Latina feminist perspectives inform our teaching? How do we mine those spaces of *nepantla*—of turmoil and transformation—as we engage our prospective teachers in the classroom? We decided to study our own *testimonios* as political narratives that, while unique, connected us to our foremothers and to Latinas and women of color in the academy. We carried out our "*testimonio* narratives" (Alarcón et al., 2011) as a method of bearing witness to each other. Over the course of two years, we recorded our narratives and reflected upon them together and in individual transcriptions and writing. In the process, we noticed our differences and commonalities. We both experienced immigration raids, translating for our parents as children, and race, ethnic, gender, and class awareness at an early age. We both were products of public education, and we both became teachers and, later, teacher educators. In addition to these shared experiences, we also experienced differences growing up in California. Prieto comes from a rural poor community and grew up in a farm worker family, while Villenas grew up in a majority Latino suburban barrio, and later in an ethnically diverse middle-class neighborhood. The analysis of our *testimonios* focused on comparison of experiences, events, and emotions that emerged as significant and impactful. From there, we developed three themes that are elaborated upon in the remaining sections.

TESTIMONIOS OF DISSONANCE, *CONCIENCIA CON COMPROMISO,* AND *CARIÑO*

Our *testimonios* revealed tensions, challenges, and opportunities as Chicana/Latina teacher educators. From the analysis of our *testimonios*, three themes emerged that informed the theories of our practice—cultural dissonance, *conciencia con compromiso* (consciousness with commitment), and *cariño* (authentic care) (see Prieto, 2009a).

Cultural Dissonance: *Me Retumba la Cabeza* (My Head Resounds)

The theme of cultural dissonance emerged continually in our stories. Cultural dissonance highlights the contradictions we experienced in the institutions of family and education, particularly along markers of race/ethnicity, class, gender, sexuality, immigration status and experience, and language. It also emphasizes the profound learning and consciousness we were developing as children about power and justice in society, even if we did not have the language to express and sort out the contradictions we experienced on a daily basis. For example, as child translators, we were placed in adult roles to negotiate business, health, family, and school transactions. Villenas recounts such experiences:

> As a daughter of Latina/o immigrant parents from Ecuador, I was always the broker at home and everywhere. Like so many other kids of immigrants, I was a child translator; I always translated for my mother. I remember coming home from school and having to translate a bill, or call a department store, a utility company, or a real estate agent, or having to always go along with my mom to translate at hospitals, banks, and grocery stores.

From these language-brokering experiences, we came to an early awareness of power relations in the adult world—how money and value were distributed, who mattered, and what knowledge counted. We became keenly aware of how our parents were, or would be, treated as Latina/o immigrants, hoping with all our might that the store clerk, the doctor, or the teacher would treat our parents *con respeto* (with respect) as we translated. We quickly learned that not knowing English and only speaking Spanish was viewed as a deficit. We shared how we responded differently to our translating roles. Prieto felt honored to translate, as it provided her with an important and valued role in her family (see also Orellana, 2009). Villenas, on the other hand, felt very burdened as a child and sometimes ashamed.

The deficit view of the Spanish language can be juxtaposed with the value Spanish held in our homes, at church for Prieto, and with our ability to maintain ties with *familia* in the U.S. and our heritage countries (Mexico and Ecuador for Prieto and Villenas, respectively). Here our individual *testimonios* about language are part of a collective experience shared by many Latina/o bilingual children growing up in the United States. Our bilingual and bicultural talents were not recognized or valued in the classroom. Our linguistic capital, which includes the intellectual and social skills attained through our bilingual communication experiences (Yosso, 2005), was not validated in the learning experience. The inconsistency between what we learned in the home and what we experienced in school created a dissonance that opened up pain but also awareness.

In the following passage, Prieto recalls a conflicting incident as a child in the first grade, reiterating the theme of cultural dissonance.

> In the first grade my class took a field trip to a Sun Maid factory in one of our neighboring towns. As we began our tour of the facility, our guide, an older white woman asked if we had any questions. One of my white classmates raised her hand. The guide called on her, and she asked, "How are raisins made?" I quickly raised my hand. Since I had firsthand experience working in the grape vineyards with my family, I knew all about the initial production of grapes. My teacher turns to me and sees my hand in the air. She motions for me to put my hand down (see Prieto, 2009b for other parts of her life story).

This illustrates the "banking" concept of education that Prieto experienced as a public school student which did not allow for her cultural knowledge to enter the learning space. As Freire (1971/2002) writes, oppressors view knowledge as "a gift bestowed by those who consider themselves knowledgeable upon those whom they consider to know nothing" (p. 58). The guide proceeded to give the class the story of how a grape becomes a raisin, but this version did not include Prieto's experience. Her version skipped over the fact that Mexicans and Filipinos worked in the fields and spoke only of the cleaning and packaging process that took place in the factory. Prieto's funds of knowledge went unnoticed and remained untapped. The teacher and guide missed an opportunity for culturally responsive teaching and learning.

The lack of acknowledgment of our funds of knowledge (González, Moll, & Amanti, 2005) and community cultural wealth (Yosso, 2005) contrasts with the values, beliefs, and cultural practices of our families. The following excerpt reveals Prieto's parents' belief in education and their desire for increased opportunities for their children.

> I remember my parents' words on those days when our bodies and spirits were burdened with exhaustion. "*¿Qué piensan? ¿Quieren seguir quebrandose la espalda como burros por el resto de sus vidas, o quieren darle duro al estudio y salir adelante?*" [What do you think? Do you want to continue breaking your backs like mules for the rest of your lives, or do you want to hit the books to get a head?] The question seemed unnecessary. Of course, we didn't want to work in the fields for the rest of our lives. If all it took was doing well in school, then we'd give it our best.

Prieto's parents provided real life experiences of hard work out of economic necessity, which translated into aspirational capital. Yosso defines aspirational capital as "the ability to maintain hopes and dreams for the future, even in the face of real and perceived barriers. This resiliency is evidenced in those who allow themselves and their children to dream of possibilities beyond their present circumstances, often without the objective means to attain those goals" (Yosso, 2005, pp. 77–78). These experiences served to motivate Prieto to pursue academic success. Prieto shared these stories as a *testimonio* to the wealth of knowledge in her home and the dissonance she felt with the school curriculum and pedagogy. Unfortunately, working hard is not enough for all children, even in the same family.

Advancing this theme, Villenas describes how teachers who did not make connections between the students' culture and the school curriculum negatively impacted her brother's interest and success in school.

> My brother had some trouble in school, and my parents always brought me to school with them when they had to meet with his teachers. So my parents didn't really get to communicate well with the teachers, and even though we lived in a Latino neighborhood, the schools didn't use translators. But I always remember my parents working very hard with my brother, but not connecting with teachers. I know he didn't speak English very well when he entered kindergarten, and there weren't bilingual teachers.

Our *testimonios* express our dissatisfaction with the unrelieved tension between the educational system and our home cultures. As we continued with our formal schooling, the saliency of these notions of cultural dissonance did not diminish.

We also experienced other kinds of dissonance within our families that have to do with gender roles and expectations, and our budding feminist understandings. Prieto's story reveals this common experience between the two of us. She explains that her introduction to gender roles within the family did not encompass and, at times, directly countered those she envisioned for herself.

> Even though my mother encouraged us to continue to do well in school and pursue our dreams, she also fell victim to my father's beliefs about the role of women in the home, so that I was suppose to reproduce those roles too. But having an older sister to serve as my trailblazer opened doors for me—other experiences I would not have otherwise known existed. Outside of my immediate family, my mother was also faced with family members who preached, "*Cualquier mujer que se va de su casa y no viste de blanco es una perdida.*" [Any woman who leaves her home and is not dressed in white is lost.]

Prieto also experienced sexist notions that equated leaving her home, not to get married but instead to go to college, with becoming a whore. At the same time, her mother encouraged her to soar. These contradictions emerge from the intersections of gender and heteronormativity experienced in racialized and classed ways (Villenas & Moreno, 2001).

The dissonance we experienced within the family, and between schooling and family life is part of a larger racist nativism we experienced in our everyday lives. Pérez Huber (2009) explains that racist nativism constructs Latina/o immigrants as non-natives who are assigned to a subordinate or second-class citizen position in the United States. Our *testimonios* reveal how racist nativism in the form of racial inequities and discrimination permeated our earliest memories. Prieto illustrates how at an early age, state and federal policies informed her of her lower status in society:

> I remember the immigration raids in the fields, my parents running into the nearby orchards and fields as they sent us to hide in the tall grass until the *migra* [immigration] van disappeared taking other young *Mexicano* immigrants. I reflect back that in these fields we were reminded of our lower status

in society. I was afraid and disgusted. Why would anyone want to take our parents from us? Didn't they see we weren't doing anything wrong? We were simply working, trying to make a living.

Echoing this theme, Villenas expressed similar fears of immigration raids and the potential of being separated from her parents.

I can remember with such clarity the fear I felt every time we turned on the *noticiero* [news hour] to hear the nightly news of immigration raids in the Los Angeles *fabricas* [sweatshops] where my father worked. I remember being so afraid that one day he wouldn't come home, that he'd be picked up. Because even though he was a legal resident, I knew he could be picked up and sent back to Ecuador with no questions asked. And I was very little then, no more than seven or eight years old. And I remember this being the big secret that I thought other kids didn't have. Or maybe they did, but we didn't discuss this in the schools.

Further illustrating racist nativism, Prieto recounts the use of epithets as violence upon the body and the counter-narratives she received at home:

I can recall the first time I was called a "wetback," and at times those emotions seem to rest just below the surface. I was in second grade and had never heard this word before, and I didn't even know what it meant. But just by the scornful delivery from our white peers on the school bus, my older brother, sister, and I understood it was intended to both hurt and insult us. We went home that day after school and asked my father what this word meant. His stern brown eyes began to well up, something we didn't see too often as children. So he proceeded to *aconsejarnos* [give us advice] that we should not let such words hurt us as they did not apply to us. That yes, perhaps this word could be used against our mother and him because they had crossed the Rio Grande [dividing *México* and the U.S.] but that we were born here, and no one should use this word to refer to us.

Macedo (2000) emphasizes the power and ideology of words: "Language such as 'border rats,' 'wetbacks,' 'aliens,' 'illegals,' 'welfare queens,' and 'non-White hordes,' used by the popular press not only dehumanizes other cultural beings, but also serves to justify the violence perpetrated against subordinated groups" (p. 15). Prieto recalls how her heart ached as she witnessed her father's tears, "I felt a separation being drawn between us, the U.S.-born children, and our immigrant parents."

As college students in predominantly white institutions, Villenas and Prieto continued to experience racist nativism as the following conversation about their involvement with MEChA [*Movimiento Estudiantil Chicana/o de Aztlán*], a Chicano/a student organization, illustrates.

Villenas: In college, I learned the hard lessons about racial politics. There was so much racial conflict, especially with members of the Greek fraternities ... I remember the Mexican themed parties of some of the fraternities, and then our protesting. I remember them [Greek fraternity and sororities] driving by and throwing tortillas at protestors.

Prieto: When I was at Stanford, I was also in MEChA, and my freshman year we had a hunger strike where we presented four demands to the university. We wanted the university to issue a campus-wide ban on grapes in support of the UFW and our *familias* who worked in the fields. We also wanted to take part in developing a community center in East Palo Alto, which was selfishly used for research by many scholars at the university without reciprocity. Our third demand was that the university offer a formal apology to our highest-ranking Chicana administrator, Cecilia Burciaga, which they had fired that spring under the guise of budget cuts. And our fourth demand called for the creation of a

Chican@ Studies major and academic department. As we camped out in front of Memorial Church protesting, white fraternity guys would come by eating grapes, pizza, and they'd barbeque.

Villenas: These were cultural experiences that were so meaningful for us through MEChA and other organizations of color. It's interesting how racial wars were similar in different college settings even in two different decades. We had the same questions. And we experienced the same kind of political, racial, and cultural turmoil.

The racial campus climate or "racial wars" of California universities during the 1980s and 1990s demanded, as Rosaldo (1993) explains, both "a civil rights agenda for institutional change and an intellectual agenda for testing ideas and projects against a more demanding and diverse range of perspectives" (p. xv). Our *testimonios* speak to how critical, culturally responsive, and anti-racist pedagogies were, and continue to be, essential in university classrooms.

Perhaps noticing the emotion in our voices as we recalled such painful incidents and the blatant disregard and disrespect displayed by white students toward us, our issues and our *gente* (people), Villenas asked Prieto to share how this made her feel about her relationships with white people and the conversation continued:

Prieto: I became very embittered with Whites. I came to feel like they need to prove themselves to me. I think it comes from my lived experiences. Most people who were white provided such a terrible experience. I've tried to share this in classes, but it gets used against me. Peers tend to think that I hate Whites. And then when you try to share that with people they call you racist.

Villenas: So how do you do that in the classroom?

Prieto: I want to tell them, "I want you to experience some emotion because I've experienced such deep emotions in being poor and not being part of the mainstream." But people want to be comfortable; they don't want to show any emotions.

Prieto was speaking to the actions and embodiment of institutionalized white dominance, not about Whites as individuals. Her peers in graduate school often misunderstood her words and emotions as reverse racism or "hating white people."

Perhaps this naming of the cumulative nature of what has been documented in the literature as racial microaggressions—the subtle and not so subtle acts of racism supported through the curriculum, and the implicit rules and organization of student and school life (see Yosso, Smith, Ceja, & Solórzano, 2009)—shapes our understandings and approach to schooling and education. These understandings are often different from that of our predominantly white prospective teachers in our university classrooms. What then might be the implications for sharing our stories with students from more privileged backgrounds? *Testimonios* of dissonance demand an audience, an invitation to witness, to *estar con el hablante* (to be with the speaker), and to be in solidarity (Sommer, 1991). As we will later explore, the necessary contradictions, discomfort, tumultuousness, and in-between-ness that being with the speaker demands, precisely animate our pedagogies of *nepantla*.

Conciencia con Compromiso (Consciousness with Responsibility/Commitment)

Our *testimonios* of dissonance created much emotion; they also revealed our negotiations, our resilience, and the ways in which we developed our commitments as educators. Our second theme, *conciencia con compromiso*, speaks to the urgency we experienced to address issues of inequality via social engagement. *Conciencia con compromiso,* developed by Prieto (2009a) articulates our conviction to enact our beliefs in pursuit of a transformative pedagogy. At an early age we developed a sense of social consciousness. We learned it was our responsibility to use any acquired privilege to help others. For example, pursuing graduate studies represents a means to increased access to quality education for all students in the U.S. Prieto shares the following excerpt from a 2009 journal entry, which highlights the theme of *conciencia con compromiso.*

> As my body struggles with my health, and I battle fatigue and stress brought on by my experiences as a racialized, gendered, and classed Chicana, I discover daily the strengths within these lived tensions. I reflect back on these experiences as they are layered upon my childhood familial and academic experiences to remind me of the need to challenge the status quo. I also learn to view this narrative of struggle as a site for the conception and cultivation of hope. These sites lead to my enduring interest in education as a means by which I can continue to *cosechar* [to cultivate, to harvest] success within me and with others.

As daughters of immigrants, we grew up in households that taught us the importance of hard work, respect for education, and responsibility to others. Through our dialogues we reflected on a number of experiences that served to inform our *conciencia con compromiso*. Prieto recounts family stories that were passed down about the advocacy work of her maternal grandmother. These histories contributed to her familial capital, "those cultural knowledges nurtured among *familia* (kin) that carry a sense of community history, memory, and cultural intuition" (Yosso, 2005, p. 79).

> I have only known my maternal grandmother through stories, family *pláticas*—a woman who traveled from her *pueblito* in *México* to the state capitol, demanding the much needed school supplies for her children. She rode the bus back to her *pueblito* with a box full of *útiles*—paper, pencils, and pens that she shared with the neighborhood children, not just her own.

Prieto reflects on her grandma's ability to stand up for herself and others and to make things *rendir* (go a long way)—these lessons are not wasted on her granddaughter. Yosso's (2005) explanation of familial cultural wealth aptly fits Prieto's story: "This form of cultural wealth engages a commitment to community well being and expands the concept of family to include a more broad understanding of kinship" (p. 79). Our *conciencia con compromiso* was shaped by early family narratives like the one above and played out early in life as well. For both authors, not only were we expected to negotiate the English-speaking world by translating for our parents but to come to understand our privilege as English speakers and to use it to benefit others. Prieto explains, "We were also expected to jump in and translate for others around us, whether we knew them or not."

In addition to our families, we both recount our undergraduate experiences as a formative time in our life. We developed a stronger cultural identity impacted by what we learned in the classroom, the relationships with peers outside the classroom, and our ties to the larger community beyond the university walls. Friends, peers, and mentors who provided us with knowledge and resources and expanded our social networks supported our sense of responsibility. Prieto continues:

> My involvement in community organizations in college helped me understand that my liberation is directly tied to the liberation of others and the importance of building bridges across difference [i.e., gender, racial, ethnic, sexual orientation or preference, socioeconomic class lines]. Along the way, I

was being tested again on my ability to contribute to the intellectual environment and being labeled as "beaners" and "wetbacks" during the viewing of a pro-UFW [United Farm Workers] video at Stanford's Memorial Auditorium. I took courses and had conversations with Chicana/o professors and peers. They allowed me to assert my alternative knowledge as valid. In the classroom and with Chicana/o role models in and outside of the classroom, I was convinced that I had a lot to offer and to learn.

Developing a critical perspective and expanding her worldview was also important for Villenas. She narrates the absence of *conciencia con compromiso* during her K-12 experience but also the positive impact of diverse friendship groups:

> Growing up we were never taught these tools, to think critically. By the end of high school I just wanted to get out. It's interesting how some people make sense of the world through their high school years. But in high school I did meet people from different backgrounds. My best friend in college was Filipina, and I had other good Filipino friends. So in college as a freshman I joined the Filipino club on campus. It was important for me to do that . . . I had Korean American friends and many Latina friends, too.

In addition to developing social networks and friendships of various backgrounds, during college we learned the tools for thinking about global politics. Villenas recalls a Latin American class taught during the years of the Reagan administration and the civil wars in Central America that influenced her political perspectives and activist work.

> I started protesting against the wars. I had a great radical education. I was getting exposed to Marxism and class struggle very early on. It was the same with my literature classes in Latin American Studies. We read authors who were very, very critical of US interventions in Latin America. I also met activists who were doing interesting but also dangerous work in Central America.

The presence of *conciencia con compromiso* took shape formally inside the university classroom as well as informally through newly formed friendships.

> I also developed a very important friendship with an older white student from a background of privilege. He was getting his master's degree . . . and had worked with people who were homeless, and with women residing in shelters for battered women. He had dedicated his life to trying to understand women's lives. I was introduced to feminist theory and perspectives through him, a privileged, white male! He was also a Latin American studies major and worked on issues of immigration; that was a very important friendship. I remember him asking me why I used "girl" instead of "woman."

These supportive and critical friendships were formed with women and men of similar and different backgrounds, experiences, and walks of life, but they all had lasting impacts on her development of *conciencia con compromiso*.

> I was in college taking courses from a Chicano Studies professor and with fellow students who continue to be close friends to this day. It was during the time of IRCA [Immigration, Reform and Control Act] or the amnesty law of 1986. We volunteered at a local community organization for immigration and education. At that time, English as a second language certification for adults applying for amnesty education was being funded through the federal government. That's when I first experienced Freire's theory of education in our practice. You can teach for social change! I was teaching Latina/o immigrants like my parents. The revelation: You can choose how and what you teach. You could teach *Dick and Jane* or about family reunification and the politics of human rights.

The example above illustrates the integration and application of theory and practice, which influenced the shaping of Villenas' *conciencia con compromiso* via praxis. This led to her first formal teaching experiences with Latina/o immigrant adults.

> Some of my best teaching experiences took place there [in the community based organization]. The students were so passionate ... Once we drove to a protest and the students, mothers, and *abuelitas* [grandmothers] showed up to protest with us. We had busloads. We drove to Sacramento from Los Angeles, got there at 8 AM, protested all-day, and came back. I was still a college student, but classes didn't mean anything after that.

Our interest in helping identify and develop programs, classroom settings, and resources that can serve as successful educational interventions for public schools and teacher preparation programs originates from a desire to give back to the environments that raised us. Our *conciencia con compromiso* developed from dissonance and was nurtured by anger, frustration, joy, and always, deep feelings of *cariño*.

Cariño (Authentic Care)

The third theme of *cariño* refers to an authentic notion of caring. Valenzuela (1999) explains, "Caring theory addresses the need for pedagogy to follow from and flow through relationships cultivated between teacher and student" (p. 21). Such caring relationships, understood as the basis of all learning, require critical explorations and interrogations of our social locations. We embrace *cariño* similar to the notion of caring identified by Beauboeuf-Lafontant (2005), as a key force for social activism. In this brief section, we bear witness to our stories of *cariño*—snapshots that illustrate the impact of *cariño* on our sense of self as we journeyed through the Latina/o educational pipeline. These *testimonios* of *cariño* do not imply idyllic, happy family lives, as our experiences of *cariño* are certainly intertwined with gendered and other contradictions.

Prieto's earliest memories of her mother provide clear examples of the connections between *cariño* and a strong self-concept.

> And from my mother, I learned the importance of *cariño* and responsibility to others. I remember those long cold nights when *mi amá* [my mother] made us *avena o una tacita de chocolate caliente* [oatmeal or a little cup of hot chocolate] to nourish us as we finished our homework. And in the mornings when we woke up to the *tlac, tlac* of the rolling pin shaping perfectly round *tortillas de harina* [corn tortillas] on the kitchen counter. I remember the smell going down the trailer corridor and with the smell of *frijoles con chorizo* [beans with chorizo].

Prieto remarks that these are ways in which she has come to know the role of *cariño* in *sembrando* (cultivating) success.

Villenas' parents also displayed *cariño* for school success. The following scenario describes her mom's involvement in a class assignment, albeit one uncritical of Spanish mission history for indigenous people in California.

> My parents didn't go to the schools a whole lot, but they did care very much. My mom would get into it with our school projects. I remember in fourth grade we studied California history, and we had to construct a Mission. My mom helped my brother and I build our mission. She bought real

bells for it and some artificial plants. Both of my parents supported school in that way, in those small ways.

Similarly, Prieto's parents supported school in those small, but significant, ways. The value of education that Prieto's parents employed is displayed in the following account.

> My parents cared a lot about us doing well in school. They always went to teacher conferences and signed up for the last slot available to make it easier to leave their work in the fields. I believe my elementary teachers noticed that they cared, too. My parents were also always at Open House. It was easy to identify us, "the Prieto kids." We were respectful, clean, played together, and got along. I remember how my mom always made our Halloween costumes, and we'd win the best costume prizes, so we always stood out. Days before Halloween our principal talked about how he looked forward to my mom's creative costumes. And my mom always cooked for the end-of-year potlucks. Her cooking was very popular.

Our urgent *testimonios* of teaching in elementary and secondary classrooms helped us articulate our love and commitment to marginalized children and families as praxis. These permeated Villenas' teaching experiences with Latina/o adults in East Los Angeles—the *cariño* that permeated the *cafecito con donas* (coffee with donuts) break time, the protests, the baby showers, the graduation *fiestas* for ESL certification. It extended to both Villenas' and Prieto's teaching with elementary and secondary children. And it permeated Prieto's education and advocacy work in farmworker communities in upstate New York. In our praxis, *cariño* pays attention to the whole person, including the historical and political struggles in which we are embedded. It concerns appreciating and embracing shared and diverse histories. The dissonance created by the intense contradictions we described helped nurture *conciencia con compromiso*, and the recognition of *cariño* in our lives as an impetus for school achievement, as well as a form of praxis in Latino communities. Our intentional *testimonios* describe the theory of our practice. But how do we mine dissonance and activate *conciencia con compromiso* and *cariño* in a predominantly white university? In other words, what is the practice of our theory?

TOWARD PEDAGOGIES OF *NEPANTLA*: CREATING THE PRACTICE OF OUR THEORY

> The Aztec word *nepantla* ... is the place where transformation is possible, but more important it is the magic and the potential for magic within that place. Because of this potential, the concept of nepantla ... has agency ... Once something has agency (activated by ritual or action) the results of that agency can be unpredictable (Cortez, 2001, p. 367).

Resonating with political urgency, our *testimonios* speak through *nepantla* with Chicana/Latina feminist perspectives. They capture symbolically the dialectical tension between our lives and the ideological configurations of education (Pesquera & Segura, cited in Garcia, 1997); they capture how we embrace ambiguity and fragmentation through our *mestiza* consciousness (Anzaldúa, 1987). *Nepantla* speaks to and informs the difficult and often overlapping spaces of cultural dissonance, *conciencia con compromiso*, and *cariño*. They are unpredictable spaces but full of possibility for magic, for agency (Cortez, 2001). *Nepantla* in our classrooms signal uncertain terrain, crossings, moving between identities, and confronting and contesting power—precisely the agency of our everyday lives. Pedagogies within/from *nepantla* reveal fruitful tensions for exploring how we might experience transformative teaching and learning.

Earlier, we discussed our experiences in classrooms within PWIs in conversation with Vargas (2002) and her colleagues who describe dilemmas for women of color faculty. We described structural challenges (i.e., placement and marginalization of the multicultural education course in teacher education programs), preconceived views of our "ethnic" authenticity and academic credentials, and the deep emotions when our embodied histories meet practices of whiteness in our classrooms. At the same time, our prospective teachers also are entering *nepantla* as they encounter their instructors' histories and diverse students' voices in our dialogic classrooms. Uncertainty and alterities activate our classrooms' agency and possibility for new relationships and identities, even if not here and now. So how might this happen?

Dissonance

Naming, cultivating, and staying in the moment of dissonance are at the heart of pedagogies of *nepantla*. As Latina/Chicana teacher educators, we have shared with our students our *testimonios* of dissonance, including those experiences of being child translators, experiencing racist nativism and racial name-calling, and struggles with normative gender roles in our families. We also share our stories of coping, healing, and resilience. In sharing our *testimonios*, we call on students to be with us, which generates its own fruitful dissonance. But cultivating dissonance requires discussions of our interdependency, of our intertwined destinies. *My stories of race-gendered and class oppression and privilege are intertwined with your stories. What are your stories?* In this way, Asher (2005) emphasizes that students and instructors recognize self/other and work the spaces/interstices at which we are all located. We draw on and create hybrid identities to examine intersectionality and how we are implicated in social relations of power. Dwelling in dissonance is a process that activates basic tenets of culturally responsive teaching that call for an active exploration of self and other. Finally, modeling and allowing students to dwell in moments of dissonance requires protocols that let students (and us) freeze, name, and reflect on those moments, though sometimes they may have no words to describe them. All students have knowledge and can derive knowledge from reflection on uncomfortable dissonance.

Conciencia con compromiso

Our own *testimonios* of *conciencia con compromiso* are important to share but not as heroine stories, for they certainly are not. Rather, they are urgent life stories that compel action in authentic relationships with commitment and responsibility. Pedagogies of *nepantla* call on prospective teachers to embark on a journey of their cultural self-awareness, but only with responsibility and commitment to each other and to their instructor as they develop their commitments toward children and families from non-dominant communities. The process of *conciencia con compromiso* in the classroom requires explicit acknowledgment of how dominant ideologies that are supposed to be heard in a "dialogue" classroom are painful. Elenes (2001) draws on Anzaldúa's *mestiza* consciousness as method to think about the importance of breaking down dualistic thinking in the classroom and to resist polarization. She recommends elevating the conversation into the philosophical realm—that is, not debating opinions but instead engaging where such opinions come from. Finally, we cannot forget classroom pedagogies that connect prospective teachers to local families and community members of different backgrounds, including white activist role models. Interview projects with community members that focus on their experiences and stories of talking about race (and its intersections) with friends, family members and co-workers are invaluable. In addition, developing activities of action that allow students to reflect on their peer interactions on campus, and to respectively and with humility enter into other borderland spaces may foster *conciencia con compromiso*.

Cariño

Our urgent *testimonios* revealed fruitful tensions for mining the liminal and dialogic moments of connection and *cariño* as we relate across difference and privilege with our prospective teachers. In reflecting on our *testimonios* of *cariño*, we think of the nourishment we received with loving care and that supported us in our educational achievement—the *chocolate en leche* (hot chocolate milk), the homemade tortillas, the handmade Halloween costumes, the nourishing *cenas* (suppers) that we could always count on every night. It was not these foods per se, but the feelings of caring that came with loving, serving, giving, and connecting, while providing us with the real life experiences of hard work out of economic necessity. These acts of authentic care took care of our whole selves, our spirit, and our spirituality and prepared us to deal with the outside world. In our *testimonios*, they also became the basis for connection and compassion, not only in Latino communities but also, currently, in our predominantly white, teacher education classrooms. Enacting and fostering *cariño*, involves cultivating students' wholeness and inner selves and not disconnecting the intellectual from the emotional (Rendón, 2009). Contemplative activities (Rendón, 2009), including walks, art, reflective journaling, sharing of personal stories and events in students' lives, and even the sharing of food or snacks lay the foundation of *cariño* where students may take chances, stretch, and build bridges to care with courage about the diverse families and children in our public schools.

Finally, *cariño* is required in the hard work of relating to each other as individuals who are also members of collectives and cultural communities with specific histories. Pedagogies of *nepantla* rooted in *cariño* engage students who enact racism, classism, sexism, homophobia, or anti-immigrant sentiments, not as individual racists, sexists, or nativists, but as cultural beings who are tapping into vast epistemological systems that support hierarchies of dominance. *Cariño* animates discussions of our shared global, hemispheric, and national tragedies, as well as hope, possibility, and emancipatory action.

CONCLUDING REMARKS

Nurturing and negotiating dissonance, *conciencia con compromiso*, and *cariño* activate the possibility and "potential for magic" (Cortez, 2001, p. 367) in the tumultuous and often painful spaces of *nepantla*. In this article, our *testimonios* involved giving witness to each other and were born out of the urgent need to name who we are in relation to how we teach. They allowed us to theorize our practice and to think about how we did, and could, practice our Chicana/Latina feminist theories and understandings. Our *testimonios* revealed the difficulties of putting forth stories that implicate white dominance and privilege in our university classrooms. There is no sugar-coating the pain from the always possible fierce backlash and contempt as the literature on women of color faculty in PWIs reveals. But how do we theorize possibility, transformation, healing, and subversive agency in the tradition of Latina/Chicana intellectual thought? How do we transform aggressions into our own strengths? Insofar as *testimonios* are inherently intersubjective, turning all participants, listeners, and storytellers into witnesses as Cindy Cruz (2012) explains, multiple positionings and identities for mutual learning are simultaneously made possible. As we move forward, embracing ambiguity and dissonance, refusing dichotomies, listening well, and letting go to see what happens will contribute to new *testimonios* of teaching and learning. Our *testimonios* are about building bridges to our collective power as the basis for compassionate pedagogy in teacher education classrooms.

REFERENCES

Alarcón, W., Cruz, C., Guardia Jackson, L., Prieto, L., & Rodriguez-Arroyo, S. (2011). Compartiendo nuestras historias. Five testimonios of schooling and survival. *Journal of Latinos and Education, 10*(4), 369–381.

Anzaldúa, G. (1987). *Borderlands/La frontera: The new mestiza.* San Francisco, CA: Aunt Lute Books.

Asher, N. (2005). At the interstices: Engaging postcolonial and feminist perspectives for a multicultural education pedagogy in the South. *Teachers College Record, 107*(5), 1079–1106.

Beauboeuf-Lafontant, T. (2005). Womanist lessons for reinventing teaching. *Journal of Teacher Education, 56*(5), 436–445.

Berry, T. R., & Mizelle, M. (Eds.). (2006). *From oppression to grace: Women of color and their dilemmas within the academy.* Sterling, VA: Stylus.

Cortez, C. (2001). The new Aztlan: Nepantla and other sites of transmogrification. In V. M. Fields & V. Zamudio-Taylor (Eds.), *The road to Aztlan: Art from a mythic homeland* (pp. 358–373). Los Angeles, CA: Museum Associates, Los Angeles County Museum of Art.

Cruz, C. (2012). Making curriculum from scratch: Testimonios in an urban classroom. *Equity & Excellence in Education, 45*(3), this issue.

Delgado Bernal, D. (2002). Critical race theory, Latina critical theory and critical race-gendered epistemologies: Recognizing students of color as holders and creators of knowledge. *Qualitative Inquiry, 8*(1), 105–126.

Delgado Bernal, D., & Elenes, C. A. (2011). Chicana feminist theorizing: Methodologies, pedagogies, and practices. In R. R. Valencia (Ed.), *Chicano school failure and success: Present, past, and future* (3rd ed.). New York, NY: Routledge.

Delgado Bernal, D., Elenes, C. A., Godinez, F. E., & Villenas, S. (2006) (Eds.). *Chicana/Latina education in everyday life: Feminista perspectives on pedagogy and epistemology.* Albany, NY: State University of New York Press.

Elenes, C. A. (2001). Transformando fronteras: Chicana feminist transformative pedagogies. *International Journal of Qualitative Studies in Education, 14*(5), 689–702.

Freire, P. (1971/2002). *Pedagogy of the oppressed* (30th Anniv. ed.). New York, NY: The Continuum.

García, A. M. (Ed.). (1997). *Chicana feminist thought: The basic historical writings.* New York, NY: Routledge.

Gonzales, S. (1997). The Latina feminist: Where we've been, where we're going. In A. M. García (Ed.), *Chicana feminist thought: The basic historical writings* (pp. 250–253). New York, NY: Routledge.

González, N., Moll, L. C., & Amanti, C. (Eds.). (2005). *Funds of knowledge: Theorizing practices in households, communities, and classrooms.* Mahwah, NJ: Erlbaum.

Guardia Jackson, L. (2010). Becoming an activist Chicana teacher: A story of identity making of a Mexican American bilingual educator in Texas. Unpublished dissertation. The University of Texas, Austin.

Haig-Brown, C. (2003). Creating spaces: Testimonio, impossible knowledge and academe. *Qualitative Studies in Education*, *16*(3), 415–433.

hooks, b. (1994). *Teaching to transgress: Education as the practice of freedom*. New York, NY: Routledge.

Hurtado, A. (2003). *Voicing Chicana feminisms: Young women speak out on sexuality and identity*. New York, NY: New York University Press.

Ikas, K. R. (2002). *Chicana ways: Conversations with ten Chicana writers*. Reno, NV: University of Nevada Press.

Klahn, N. (2003). Literary (re)mappings: Autobiographical (dis)placements by Chicana writers. In G. F. Arredondo, A. Hurtado, N. Klahn, O. Nájera-Ramírez, & P. Zavella (Eds.), *Chicana feminisms: A critical reader* (pp. 114–145). Durham, NC: Duke University Press.

Latina Feminist Group. (2001). *Telling to live: Latina feminist testimonios*. Durham, NC: Duke University Press.

Macedo, D. (2000). The colonialism of the English only movement. *Educational Researcher*, *29*(3), 15–24.

Martínez, T. A. (1996). Toward a Chicana feminist epistemological standpoint: Theory at the intersection of race, class, and gender. *Race, Gender & Class Journal*, *3*(3), 107–128.

Nieto, S., & Bode, P. (2011). *Affirming diversity: The sociopolitical context of multicultural education* (6th ed.). Boston: Allyn & Bacon.

Ochoa, G. L. (2007). *Learning from Latino teachers*. San Francisco, CA: Wiley.

Orellana, M. F. (2009). *Translating childhoods: Immigrant youth, language and culture*. New Brunswick, NJ: Rutgers University Press.

Flores, J., & García, S. (2009). Latina testimonios: A reflexive, critical analysis of a "Latina space" at a predominantly white campus. *Race, Ethnicity and Education*, *12*(2), 155–172.

Padilla, R. V. (1992). Using dialogical research methods to study Chicano college students. *The Urban Review*, *24*(3), 175–183.

Pérez Huber, L. (2009). Challenging racist nativist framing: Acknowledging the community cultural wealth of Chicana college students to reframe the immigration debate. *Harvard Educational Review*, *79*(4), 704–729.

Pesquera, B. M., & Segura, D. A. (1997). There is no going back: Chicanas and feminism. In A. M. García (Ed.), *Chicana feminist thought: The basic historical writings* (pp. 294–309). New York, NY: Routledge.

Prieto, L. (2009a). Conciencia con compromiso: Maestra perspectives on teaching in bilingual education classrooms. Unpublished dissertation. The University of Texas, Austin.

Prieto, L. (2009b). The stings of social hierarchies: From the central San Joaquin Valley vineyards to the ivy walls. In J. A. Van Galen & V. O. Dempsey (Eds.), *Trajectories: The social and educational mobility of education scholars from poor and working class backgrounds* (pp. 71–81). Rotterdam, The Netherlands: Sense.

Rendón, L. I. (2009). *Sentipensante (sensing/thinking) pedagogy: Educating for wholeness, social justice and liberation*. Sterling, VA: Stylus.

Reyes, X. A., & Ríos, D. I. A. (2005). Dialoguing the Latina experience in higher education. *Journal of Hispanics in Higher Education*, *4*(4), 377–391.

Rodriguez, D. (2006). Un/masking identity: Healing our wounded souls. *Qualitative Inquiry*, *12*(6), 1067–1090.

Rosaldo, R. (1993). *Culture and truth: The remaking of social analysis*. Boston, MA: Beacon Press.

Sommer, D. (1991). No secrets: Rigoberta's guarded truth. *Women's Studies*, *20*(1), 51–72.

Valenzuela, A. (1999). *Subtractive schooling: U.S.-Mexican youth and the politics of caring*. New York, NY: State University of New York Press.

Vargas, L. (Ed.). (2002). *Women faculty of color in the white classroom*. New York, NY: Lang.

Villegas, A. M., & Lucas, T. (2002). Preparing culturally responsive teachers: Rethinking the curriculum. *Journal of Teacher Education*, *53*(1), 20–32.

Villenas, S., & Moreno, M. (2001). To valerse por si misma between race, capitalism, and patriarchy: Latina mother-daughter pedagogies in North Carolina. *International Journal of Qualitative Studies in Education*, *14*(5), 671–687.

Yosso, T. J. (2005). Whose culture has capital? A critical race theory discussion of community cultural wealth. *Race, Ethnicity and Education*, *8*(1), 69–91.

Yosso, T. J., Smith, W. A., Ceja, M., & Solórzano, D. G. (2009). Critical race theory, racial microaggressions, and campus racial climate for Latina/o undergraduates. *Harvard Educational Review*, *79*(4), 659–690.

Chicana and Black Feminisms: *Testimonios* of Theory, Identity, and Multiculturalism

Cinthya M. Saavedra
Utah State University

Michelle Salazar Pérez
University of North Texas

In this article, we examine our own *testimonios* inspired by Chicana and Black feminisms that have not only informed our research and teaching but have also helped us to make sense of our lives. We offer our *testimonios* related to theory, identity negotiations, and pedagogical concerns with teaching multiculturalism as a way to recognize and acknowledge that as academics, researchers, and teachers, we must continue to learn language from, and create new language for, our theoretical spaces that help us to express and navigate the complexity and multiple locations of struggles and resistance. Collectively, *testimonios* facilitate crucial lessons for examining the interconnectedness between Chicana and Black feminisms through the lived experiences of those living in or on the margins. They also provide critical self-reflection that is needed to unlearn oppression that exists within each of us.

Coyolxauhqui personifies the wish to repair and heal, as well as rewrite the stories of loss and recovery, exile and homecoming ... stories that lead out of passivity and into agency, out of devalued into valued lives. (Anzaldúa, 2002b, p. 563)

Black feminist thought can simulate a new consciousness that utilizes black women's every day, taken-for-granted knowledge ... it affirms, rearticulates, and provides a vehicle for expressing in public a consciousness that quite often already exists ... [and] aims to empower African American women and stimulate resistance. (Collins, 2000, p. 32)

The quotes from Anzaldúa and Collins are great reminders of how awareness inspired by *Coyolxauhqui* and the everyday lived experiences of women of color can create spaces that foster both collective healing and critical pedagogy. We offer examples of these spaces through our personal *testimonios* of theory, identity, and multiculturalism that draw from and build upon the work of Chicana and Black feminisms. These theories speak to the struggles of a collective "we" and continue to speak to the individual "I," as we demonstrate with our own *testimonios* the ways in which our individual lives are influenced, challenged, and transformed by collective scholarship.

Chicana and Black feminisms can inform research and teaching while helping those living on or in the margins make sense of and heal fragmented lives. For example, the *testimonios* we present here provide a window into the negotiations many have embarked on, while serving as a methodological tool that can piece together fragmented experiences, bringing one closer to being whole again. Although we share our personal stories that bear witness to injustices and violence in our own lives, we believe that our *testimonios* have the potential to connect our "I" to the collective "we" (Beverly, 2005). *Testimonios* have an overtly political intent and, therefore, often compel others to take some form of action. Furthermore, for women of color in the academy, *testimonios* can provide a space for self-reflection of the internalized ways that one can embody and live out the very oppressions we desire to challenge, change, and decolonize. Collectively, there is an urgency to heal fragmented lives and to illuminate complicity in dominant thinking (hooks, 2010). Elenes (2000) contends that the *testimonio* is a "map of consciousness" (p. 115) and, thus, can be used to look deeply within to change the inner, colonized self while bringing about collective change—transformations that Chicana and Black feminisms capture.

In this article, we take readers through a series of moments in our own lives that speak strongly about the ties between our experiences and what we call our theoretical homes—Chicana and Black feminisms. In sharing our *testimonios*, we (the authors) are in some ways building bridges of understanding that can lead to powerful, collective sisterhoods for subsequent work and support for navigating through internalized oppressive discourses. Theories do not exist solely for analyzing the experiences of others, they coexist within us and through us. Cutri, Delgado Bernal, Powell, and Wiederman (1998) assert:

> The opportunity and support to personalize theory offers a key process that must be further studied. If scholars pursue critical, feminist, and social reconstructionist theories as vehicles to transform society, then they must seek to better understand how these theories can be more effectively taught and learned so that they transform individuals. (p. 113)

We agree with Curti et al. that to teach or facilitate discussions surrounding social change, we must understand how theory can not only transform others but also ourselves.

We provide such a possibility with our own *testimonios*. We first situate our work by revealing who we are, followed by our *metodología*—how we collected our *testimonios y otros pedacitos de memorias* (and other pieces of memories). Then, we offer through our *testimonios* three themes: (1) the ways in which we came to our theoretical homes, (2) our identity negotiations, and (3) our tensions with multicultural education. In our concluding thoughts, we critically reflect on implications for theory and practice.

WHO WE ARE

We are two *amigas* and *colegas* who have maintained a friendship and sisterhood through the years as a tool to foster resistance and strength in our academic and life journeys (Burciagas & Tavares, 2006; Cutri et al., 1998; hooks, 2010). Cinthya is a bilingual *Tejana Nicaragüense* (Nicaraguan Texan) midway through the tenure process. Michelle identifies as Mexican American (although embodies Caucasian and African American heritages) and is a native *Tejana* English speaker who is at the beginning of her career in academia. Our academic journeys initially brought us together through a shared mentor—a critical white feminist professor who introduced us to the field of Reconceptualizing Early Childhood Education (RECE)[1]. Our work in RECE has purposely and politically infused knowledge, experience, and theories from the margins, which has brought us closer as friends and colleagues. After speaking on panels at conferences over the years about Chicana feminism (Cinthya) and Black feminist thought (Michelle), we have decided to document our *experiencias* through *testimonios* in order to connect our *vidas* (lives) to the theoretical homes that we use in our everyday work. We also contend that our respective theoretical homes have many points of affinity worth examining to build bridges of sisterhood and critical self-reflection. Thus, we turn now to our *metodología*.

METHODOLOGY: *TESTIMONIOS,* WRITING *Y OTROS PEDACITOS DE MEMORIAS* (AND OTHER PIECES OF MEMORIES)

We shared our first *testimonios* through online communication about our thoughts and stories framed by our use of Chicana and Black feminisms. The process of writing prompted us to include *otros pedacitos de memoria*. Thus, the *testimonios* shared in this article were pieced together by our original communications and further expanded upon through conversations that generated new *testimonios* (as memories re/surfaced while engaging in the writing process, finding points of affinities with our *testimonios*, and editing). Even our literature review of our theoretical spaces has become a *testimonio*, as it is deeply connected to our individual experiences with Chicana and Black feminisms—the I—while connected to our larger collective experience—the we (Beverley, 2005).

Through a multidimensional process of conversations (in person, on the phone, and through online communication), writing, and (re)membering[2], we constructed points of affinity as a method of grouping our *testimonios*. Through this methodological process, we determined that our affinities encompassed (1) connections to our theoretical homes, (2) recognition of our multiple and shifting identities, and (3) tensions with multicultural education. We struggled initially when attempting to (re)present our *testimonios*, as we wanted to maintain their authenticity while providing the structure necessary to explain the ways in which they connect to Chicana/Black feminisms and to each other. To reconcile these issues, we (re)membered, (re)worked, and (re)visited ideas, lived experiences, and connections. This process might be described as a *rompe cabeza* (puzzle), that is, finding pieces and trying to fit them together in the hope of creating an image that stems from our strong connections to our theoretical homes. In the end, we hope our *testimonios* are about the individual and collective healing, interconnectivity, and the critical pedagogies (or social transformations) that can come from such processes.

The following *testimonios* embody three themes. First, we speak about our theoretical homes, in which we connect our *vidas* to the theories that have given us direction in our lives and in our work in academia. Next, we reveal our multiple and shifting identities and how we have negotiated and become aware of how our identities are fluid and in constant flux. Finally, in our *tesitimonios* about (un)learning multiculturalism, we examine the tensions surrounding multicultural education. After each theme, we provide a brief analysis that shows the connections between Chicana and Black feminisms and their implications for collective healing and agency. The last section examines the lessons provided by our *testimonios* and implications for pedagogy.

OUR THEORETICAL HOMES

Cinthya: Chicana Feminism

As I have shared my *testimonios* with Michelle, I have come to understand how central Chicana feminist theorizing is both in my personal and *profe* (professor) life. Chicana feminism, in many ways, saved me. I found a healing space, a home that is welcoming to an immigrant child, second language learner, and border crosser (Saavedra, 2011). I came to this home via Gloria Anzaldúa's writings in 1995. When I first read her work *Borderlands* (Anzaldúa, 1987), I felt that I finally understood the ambivalence I felt growing up in Texas. Her words and her historical account of Chicana/os helped me to not only confront my prejudices but also accept my own ambiguities, uncertainties, and how to negotiate dis/comforts of embodying multiple identities, *arrebatos* (violent ruptures), and transformations (Anzaldúa, 2002b). When we can experience this space, or what Anzaldúa (2002a) calls *nepantla*, transformation can occur. *Nepantla* is a "place where different perspectives come into conflict . . . the zone between changes where you struggle to find equilibrium" (Anzaldúa, 2002a, pp. 548–549). I see the concept of *nepantla* helping me to undo and challenge the false binaries that I have inherited in my Western upbringing.

Moreover, the work of Chicana feminist educators (Delgado Bernal, 1998; Delgado Bernal, Elenes, Godinez, & Villenas, 2006; Elenes, 2000; Trinidad Galvan, 2001) have been instrumental in helping me see the counter-discourses, the *testimonios*, and the many (her)stories that exist *y las mujeres y estudiantes que sobreviven* (and the women and students who survive) in our society. For example, Delgado Bernal et al. (2006) exemplify such endeavors as they examine the everyday pedagogies of *mujeres* (women) inside and outside of academia. Elenes, González, Delgado Bernal, and Villenas (2001) urge us to "place cultural knowledge at the forefront of educational research to better understand the lessons from the homespace, our communities and schools" (p. 595). Working under a Chicana feminist framework necessitates that we release in our minds the sanctity of academia and that we embrace and ensure a *respeto* (respect) for the theorizing that happens and exists, in complex ways, in the everyday pedagogies and lives of *la gente* (of people). Trinidad Galvan calls these practices and lessons "the pedagogies of the everyday, the mundane and the ordinary" (2001, p. 605). She compels us to excavate the ordinary and mundane in communities because often these everyday pedagogies are ignored or marginalized for not illustrating traditional androcentric models of critical pedagogies (Elenes, 1997). These critical lessons happen in nontraditional spaces and, unfortunately, are not deemed or recognized as theoretical locations. In these ways, Chicana feminist epistemology speaks to my soul—and my soul has no boundaries, no labels—and it moves with much greater ease than I do. Thus in trying to suture my mind-body-spirit split, I allow myself to learn from the spiritual me—*movimiento*—to be borderless, flexible, and fluid.

Michelle: Black Feminisms

When, as a doctoral student, my advisor first introduced me to Collins (2000), I had never encountered an academic reading that I felt so close and connected to. As an undergraduate and master's degree student, I was often exposed to mainly Euro-white, male, philosophical perspectives, so when given the chance to read and engage in conversations about Black feminisms, I felt like I had found a home in academia—something that I was not sure existed until then. Even though I identify as Chicana (while embodying a multiplicity of ethnicities), once I read Collins' (2000) work, I immediately felt close to the struggles and empowerment she expressed. hooks and Mesa-Bains (2006) suggest that feminists and women of color "do have differences but our commonalities are just as strong, and they represent hope for resistance and freedom" (p. 3). I agree with hooks that while differences exist, I have felt strong parallels to Black feminisms.

Prior to being exposed to Black feminisms, I was mainly encouraged to use deficit approaches to examine the circumstances surrounding and impacting on marginalized communities, which as a Chicana, made me feel as if my everyday lived experiences were irrelevant in academic spaces and that my involvement in academia meant embodying dominant and oppressive discourses. Black feminisms have provided ways in which to theorize (and therefore legitimize) the knowledges of women of color, transforming "both theory and practice in higher education across the disciplinary divide, [and] offering a wide range of methodological approaches to the study of multiple, complex social relations" (Dil, McLaughlin, & Nieves, 2007, p. 629). Even with countless acknowledgments of the theoretical contributions of Black feminisms to academia, when attempting to use Collins to inform my coursework during my doctoral studies, it was met with resistance when one of my professors suggested that I choose a more "serious" scholar with whome to become familiar. I ignored his suggestion and continued where I felt most connected. Embracing Black feminisms has been a refusal to use "the master's tools" (Lorde, 1984, p. 112) as my sole source of support. And as such, it has been a powerful form of resistance to the academic apartheid of knowledge (Delgado Bernal & Villalpando, 2002).

Black feminisms attempt to specifically reclaim the knowledge of Black women thinkers (Crenshaw, 1991; Lorde, 1982; Walker, 1983) and to locate and re-center subjugated knowledges (Hull, 1984; Richardson, 1987; Washington, 1975). Brewer (1993) contends that "what is most important conceptually and analytically in this work is the articulation of multiple oppressions ... historically missing from analyses of oppression and exploitation in traditional feminism, Black Studies and mainstream academic disciplines" (p. 13). By bringing the everyday lived experiences of women of color from the margins to the center of thought, the complexities of identity, power, oppression, resistance, and empowerment are revealed as they intersect and relate to the social contexts that we function in, create, and are marginalized from (hooks, 2000a). These complexities have been conceptualized as a "matrix of domination" (Collins, 2000, p. 299) that is always present in the form of structural, disciplinary, hegemonic, and interpersonal power and oppression that are produced and function both systemically and in our everyday lives through our *experiencias*. Feeling a connection with the writings of scholars like hooks and Mesa-Bains (2006) who proclaimed, "When I realized that I was going to have to resist this domination in every form, my feminist resistance began" (p. 14), I, too, have been inspired by Black feminisms as they have allowed me to gain a clearer understanding of complex systems of oppression while encouraging me to look within myself to transform the dominant perspectives I have taken on throughout my life.

FINDING HEALING AND AGENCY IN OUR THEORETICAL HOMES

Even though neither of us come from the particular communities that produce Chicana and Black feminisms, we have found a healing space within them (hooks, 2000b). For us and many who find themselves marginalized within dominant spaces, connecting with the work of feminist scholars of color like Collins and Anzaldúa can help to legitimize the knowledges of lives on the edge. Profoundly resembling every day lived *experiencias* and spaces of dis/comfort, using Chicana and Black feminisms as theoretical homes can open spaces to reconceptualize subaltern lives and identities.

Testimonios inspired by Chicana and Black feminisms can create possibilities for inner and collective healing as well as agency that resists dominant, Western, patriarchal, epistemological frameworks that have historically ignored or made invisible counter-discourses, her-stories, and non-dominant cultural knowledges. Theoretically inspired *testimonios* also provide validation and recognition of community strengths, while encouraging acknowledgment and rethinking of the complicity that can occur when attempting to function within dominant discourses (Collins, 2000; Cutri et al., 1998). Further, Chicana and Black feminisms recognize intersectionalities that we all embody and perform (Anzaldúa, 1987; Crenshaw, 1991; Dill et al., 2007; Latina Feminist Group, 2001), and therefore, in our next *testimonios*, we illuminate how our (the authors) multiple and shifting identities play out in complex ways.

REVEALING MULTIPLE AND SHIFTING IDENTITIES

Cinthya

I was the master at memorizing and that served me well in Nicaragua and in the U.S. I was considered bright there and here. I cannot deny that I had a privileged position in Nicaragua. My dad was a diplomat who did come from a humble and poor background, but he was one of the extreme few who got out of poverty and had an established career with the Central American Bank. Perhaps it was because of this cultural and class capital privilege that I adopted the language and discourse of us/them that is rampant in the U.S. Thus, upon arriving to the U.S., I immediately saw myself different from Mexicans. Overtly disparaging comments were common about *los mexicanos* by my grandparents and later by my parents. Anytime I remember this, I shudder, but now know how easy it is to adopt these dominant discourses that perpetuate the us/them dichotomy. That is, these discourses are readily available in school curriculum, my family, and the media.

We encountered tremendous poverty in the U.S. as my dad struggled to find a job and the discrimination he faced because of his "foreignness" and limited English. My formal schooling exposure and even perhaps the style of teaching in Nicaragua—direct instruction and banking method—were similar to what I encountered in the U.S. I "fit" perfectly in the school system. This fitting in came at a price of hiding my Nicaraguan culture and my Spanish language and assimilating into the dominant Anglo culture. If we had old money privilege in Nicaragua, my dad would have known English and had connections in the U.S.; then perhaps we would have avoided really hard economic times when we immigrated. It is all so complex, attempting to situate cultural and class "privileges" and their varying degrees and show that a first-generation breaking out of poverty is not the same as having inherited privilege. Privileged identities can shift and change depending on contexts, situations, and spaces. I often think about this in my life, that as a woman of color who is light-skinned, I have many privileges. In many ways, this recognition challenges the us/them dichotomy. Maybe I have more in common with my "others" than I think. I am reminded of the concept of "*yo soy tu otro yo*—I am your other I" (Anzaldúa & Keating, 2002, p. x). With this in mind, I am more open and flexible about whom I embody and that my identity can change depending on contexts. Because of my fluid identities, I should be more vigilant of the intersectionalities present, not only in my investigations of my work but inside me as well (Latina Feminist Group, 2001).

Michelle

Why do I have to put myself into so many boxes to define my ethnicity, gender, sexuality, ability, and so forth? But, I realize that others are constructing me and who I am according to the boxes they want to put me in, and therefore, in some ways, I embody and am positioned by what they construct me as. So, I would have to say that my boxes are multi-faceted and indistinct. As an example of this complexity, to identify as one race or ethnicity is difficult, although I can say that I feel most connected to my Mexican American heritage. My mother identifies as Mexican American but also feels connected to her African American heritage because her father (my grandfather) was both Mexican and Black. I also wonder about my *abuela* (my mom's mom) and what indigenous identities she embodies? Then, my biological father is Caucasian. As an abusive partner to my mother and *mi familia* for much of my childhood, it has been a painful reminder of my *both/and* (Collins, 2000) positioning. If someone forced me into other boxes of identity (for which I would argue can never be as static as the language used to label them), I would be constructed as a "woman," "heterosexual," "able-bodied," and "mono-lingual." I have experienced both comfort and unease being placed in these boxes—probably comfort/unease associated with intersecting privilege and oppression, a sense of both/and always happening to me and that I am producing. Collins (2011) reminds me: "Oppression is full of such contradictions" (p. 760).

In elementary and middle school, being around my Chicana friends and family was the norm. However, when I began high school, I learned that to be "successful" in academic spaces I was expected to embrace and emulate White culture and deny any part of me that would exhibit otherwise. As an example, in high school, I was placed in the honors program where all of my classes had a majority of white, heterosexual, able-bodied, middle- to upper-class students. There were only a few students in the program who did not fit or perform this strict identity. In one of my non-honors classes, I was required to sit across the room from one of my best friends from middle school, and since she was not admitted into the honors program, we did not have as many classes together in high school (a stark contrast from middle school where we were practically inseparable). One day, our class was assigned a kite project. The girl sitting next to me said, "Hey, do you want to work together?" and I said, "Sure." Then, later, after class in the hallway, my Chicana friend from middle school said, "What? Do you think you are better than us now?" I felt an emotional and horribly sinking feeling that one of my very best friends was so angry at me, and rightfully so. Why did I jump to say, "Yes," to work with this other person I didn't even know when my friend for so many years was just across the room?

With countless moments like these, and similar to many young women of color, entering the honors program in high school launched me into a different space—one that was shifting, like cement breaking and moving underneath and all around me in unpredictable ways. I would have to learn how to navigate both who I was and the complexities of institutional structural and disciplinary power (Collins, 2000) that I was forced to encounter every day. Hegemony was all around me; it was happening to me, and I was producing it, but it sometimes revealed itself blatantly, like in the instance of hurting my friend. I was pushed and pulled from and within my intertwined identities. On one hand, I was moving into new spaces of privilege (or what dominant society thinks of as privilege and success) by having access to honors courses that would prepare me for college. On the other hand, I was being sent a message by the system and my white peers that I had to choose, and that the right choice was this hegemonic idea of "success" (e.g., honors classes and making those who had access to them my peers), stripping away my Mexican American identity and alienating me from everyone I knew, loved, and grew up with. Being an honors student in high school literally separated me from my Chicana identity and attempted to teach me that "success" meant emulating a white, middle-class culture.

IDENTITY LESSONS FROM CHICANA AND BLACK FEMINISMS

For both of us, our identities have been shaped not only by our families but also by what is expected of us in society and by the complex negotiations we have engaged in throughout our lives. Both Chicana and Black feminist scholarship have helped us to interrogate the source of our own oppression and our complicity in it as well as to help us negotiate and perhaps even transcend how discourses and structures of power intersect in our lives and bodies (Ayala, Herrera, Jimenez, & Lara, 2006; Collins, 2005).

Collectively, theoretically-inspired *testimonios* facilitate a deeper examination of identity, one that disrupts the oversimplified notion of life as neat and marginal. Instead, *testimonios* encourage the understanding of identities as lying somewhere on the *fronteras* of cultural privilege and cultural oppression in complex ways, thereby facilitating the recognition of interconnectedness (Anzaldúa, 1987; Anzaldúa & Keating, 2002). Furthermore, identities of "success" for women of color can come at a high price that leads to some rewards, while causing more devastating isolation (James, 1993). Collective efforts to resist identity as being able to be categorized is a way to speak back to and resist this isolation. Multiple and shifting identities, and the experiences tied to them, embody what Collins (2000) describes as "both/and"—we are all many things that overlap. This recognition comes from being able to (re)member through *testimonios* how many can feel dismembered through lived experiences.

Success is a structure of power, a hegemonic circumstance that is "enjoyed" while it can strip away the strengths of community, language, and culture. This is because, too often, to be successful means that community and a sense of connectedness must be replaced with individualism. In sharing our *testimonios*, it led us to think deeply about how mainstream education obscures our understanding of ourselves and others in profound ways. We contemplate further the content and pedagogy of multicultural education as another contested area in our lives.

(UN)LEARNING MULTICULTURALISM

Michelle

When I was a teenager, I made a new Caucasian friend who had just moved to South Texas and joined our sports team. Prior to her move, she had little experience with communities outside her privileged, white, upper-class family and friends. During the school year, she was required to do a project for class where she had to ask someone from an "other" culture to teach her how to make an *ethnic* cuisine. She picked me and my family to "study." When I approached my mom about it, she seemed reluctant, but then said, "Okay, we can teach her about guacamole since there is no cooking involved." I remember feeling nervous when we all went to the grocery store together because it felt awkward to do anything with this person outside of the predominantly middle- to upper-class and white spaces of our athletic team.

After we finished shopping, we returned to my house, which looked nothing like my friend's house. She lived in a wealthy, gated community on the "new" side of town (a community that was built to keep out our brown bodies—except for "the help"). In stark contrast, I lived in a house with mold on the floors, holes in the walls, and boards on the windows. It was not in a gated community but on a block nestled between several low-income housing communities.

As we made the dish, my friend said, "Oh wow, this is going to be *so great* to take to class!" I truly felt this person had no clue how this made us feel. She had found the ultimate exotic other dish to take to class, with no questions about how the avocados, tomatoes, onions, limes, and garlic got to the store, the answer to which was on the backs of brown bodies working in the fields. Why couldn't my friend's teacher have assigned a lesson to find out about the struggles and empowerment of our family, friends, and communities? Why did they just want to know how to make guacamole?

This story from my childhood came to mind as I was sitting as a first-year assistant professor with two colleagues in a undergraduate student presentation of her teaching internship cumulative project—which happened to be a thematic unit about Mexico. At this time, I lived in a place with a seasonal head start program and service center for migrant workers and their families just 20 minutes away from the university (a place where students had never been given an option to be able to do their internships); this student decided to talk about Mexican food! As she presented, she said, "I had to think of something to do for mathematics, and I remembered my classes at the university when a particular professor told us that we could make mathematics curriculum culturally relevant by making quesadilla fractions." As she continued to present, I politely interrupted and asked if she and her students talked about any political struggles faced by Mexican children, families, and communities, such as with the recent immigration policy enacted in the state of Arizona. She responded with a simple, "No."

As I sat there and watched the presentation continue, I felt sad, angry, and hurt and remembered my experience with the girl who had to study another culture by learning how to make an ethnic cuisine. My colleagues in the room could feel my body clenching, and after the presentation was over and the student left the room, one of them said, "Are you okay, Michelle?" and I said, "Can we say tourist curriculum?" And then one colleague responded, "I know, honey." And that was that. Absolutely nothing had changed in 15 years.

I had hoped that in the years between my childhood and now as an assistant professor, educators might have changed the way in which they approach multiculturalism. I am reminded of hooks' (2010) revelation in that "many of the abuses of power that I had experienced during my education were still commonplace" (p. 3). Therefore, when considering the continued misuse of multicultural education to reify institutional and social oppressions (Collins, 2000), I have realized more than ever that I must engage in conversations with students and colleagues about recognizing, resisting, and reconceptualizing dominant notions of culturally relevant curriculum.

Cinthya

As I began my first tenure track position in northern Utah, fears of teaching multicultural education to all white students resurfaced. The multicultural classes I had taught before, as a visiting assistant *profe* in North Carolina and as a graduate teaching assistant, were full of resistance both on my end and from my students—the us/them mentality, in particular, the teacher/student, Chicana/white, knowing/not knowing binaries were embodied as much by them as they were by me. I, therefore, began to ask different questions about what to do with my class, my readings, and my pedagogy. One approach that I had to problematize was the belief that I was going to change my students. That implicitly denotes that my students are in one space (the wrong one) and need to be in another space (the right one), as if spaces are not ambiguous sometimes and even contradictory at other times. Who am I to think I know the right way to think? I can think about myself and how I can believe wholeheartedly about one thing but, in the next minute, embrace an opposite belief. I also know that I have not completely rid myself of Western epistemology. It is buried deep. I am complex. And all I can hope for is more spaces where I challenge an old belief or an old me, but perhaps getting completely rid of the old me is an illusion at best. What I have learned from Chicana feminists is that we are ambiguous and even contradictory. And besides, is that not what Western research and pedagogy proposes—to intervene and change those who are not like us? There has to be another way—a different way—to approach the teaching of multicultural education that does not necessitate an us/them mentality but instead promotes a connectionist approach (Elenes, 2006; Keating, 2007).

For Keating (2007), "connectionist thinking is visionary, relational and holistic" (p. 2). I love it when she says that this connectionist approach is about "collective healing." If we move beyond Western epistemological ideas of existing in such hierarchical, dichotomous understandings of the world that produce rigid labels such as me, Chicana, and my students, White, what possibilities lay ahead? What deeper connection can we make? Will it be smooth? Probably not. What I learned from reading Keating is that I had to go back and reread Anzaldúa! I also needed to reengage with spiritualism as Keating asserts, "When we talk about spirits, transformation, interconnectedness, or the sacred, we risk the accusations of essentialism, escapism, or other forms of apolitical, irrational, naïve thinking" (p. 2).

Could it be a coincidence that during this time, I was also coming out of an atheist coma? At the same time, I had just moved to Utah, and I was experiencing a different consciousness in spiritualism. My *Papi* had died two months prior. What and who I thought was my rock and foundation were taken from me, creating what Anzaldúa (2002b) calls *arrebato*—rupture and fragmentation that can force us to rethink, re-interpret who we are. Anzaldúa explained that "*Cada arrebatamiento* is an awakening that causes you to question who you are, what the world is about" (p. 547). The person who had my back was gone! For the first time, I needed to find inner strength, needed to know that I was going to be okay. Finding inner strength was a new experience for me, one that my culture nor my family had taught me. This inner search led to a series of spiritual awakenings in my life. For example, seeing myself as interconnected to other human beings, animals, nature, and cosmos. I began to see life in a different way, not a better way, just another way. This change was inner. As I was rereading Anzaldúa in Entrevistas/*Interviews*, *This Bridge We Call Home* and even *Borderlands*, I saw the message differently this time. For the first time, I began to see her connectionist perspective. The new questions I was asking about teaching were intimately tied to my new perspective in life. My own borderlands necessitate bridges for crossing back and forth or for standing in the middle. Maybe I finally understand what the path of the *nepantleras* are, "'in betweeners' those who facilitate passages between worlds (p. 1)" (Anzaldúa, cited in Keating, 2006, p. 9).

Multicultural Education Through Our Eyes (I's)

Our *testimonios* reveal tensions with multiculturalism. Furthermore, they expose the need to radicalize not only multicultural education but also pedagogical approaches with students in teacher education programs (hooks, 2010). Understandings of dominant content and pedagogy, as framed by Chicana and Black feminisms, helps us to uncover their ties to Western epistemological orientations of the world (Collins, 2006). For example, multiculturalism continues to be reified as a notion that can be concretely explained and performed—a check list. However, we teacher educators argue that we are not pushing our students to grasp (with epistemological and ontological questions) what it means to live or be in multicultural spaces. Pedagogy needs to shift to de-center traditional multicultural content, blurring and zigzagging identities on various levels, not just by destabilizing student/teacher binaries but also, for example, right/wrong views (Keating, 2007). This can lead to engaging with broader issues of connectionist/*nepantla* states as a way to release the us/them dichotomies inherent in Western epistemology. Instead, bridges can be built with many and multiple sisterhoods (hooks, 2000b).

CHICANA AND BLACK FEMINIST-INSPIRED *TESTIMONIOS:* IMPLICATIONS FOR THEORY/PEDAGOGY

Our *testimonios* first came about through our conversations surrounding concepts from our theoretical homes in Chicana and Black feminisms that we believe to be central to our work and our lives. By revealing and writing our *testimonios*, we have found affinities that connect our lives and our theoretical spaces with each other—a *puente* between the two of us. Even though our individual experiences are different, they are parallel, yet are intersecting. For example, both of our *testimonios* point to structures of power that are instrumental in reifying oppressions, while embodying strength, empowerment, and healing (Collins, 2000). Both Chicana and Black feminisms, as our theoretical homes, remind us that experiences and everyday pedagogies are complex navigations that entail constant reflections and negotiations (Anzaldúa, 1987; hooks, 2000a). Our *testimonios* about our closeness to Chicana and Black feminisms, shifting and multiple identities, and tensions with multicultural education, create a space for this to occur. Unpacking our stories and connecting them to our theoretical homes, we contend, bring theories alive and give life to theories through our bodies and stories. Curti et al. (1998) assert that we can engage with theories intellectually but in "failing to engage with them on the personal levels of culture and affect, [we] ... bankrupt the transformative powers of critical self and social examination" (p. 101). *Testimonios* can provide these transformative lessons for individual and collective social justice work in classrooms and local or global communities (Dill et al., 2007).

Thus, we offer the following theoretical and pedagogical implications for critical transformation of the self and social examinations.

Chicana and Black feminisms, when explored more deeply through *testimonios*, create *nuevas posibilidades* (new possibilities) for pedagogy and the way that we, women of color in academia, engage with our colleagues, students, and the world. First, we must recognize and acknowledge that as academics, researchers, and teachers, we must continue to learn language from, and create new language for, our theoretical homes that help us to express and navigate the complexity and multiple locations of struggles and resistance in our lives. Further, what we (the authors), have learned is that our stories are unique and yet are shared experiences even though we have come from different theoretical spaces and cultural, racial, and ethnic communities. Connecting our lived experiences provides lessons and pedagogies of sisterhood and solidarity—reminding us that *testimonios* are the "I" connected to the "we" and vice versa (Beverly, 2005). The "we" can be seen in Anzaldúa's concept of *nos/otras* in that the "we" is cross-cultural, cross-ethnic, cross-racial, cross-gender or any division we have inherited from dominant world views (Keating, 2000). *Nos/otras* with the slash literally translates to we/them (or us/other). Anzaldúa has urged us to take notice of how we exist in each other—finding ourselves "in the position of being simultaneously insider/outsider" (Keating, 2000, p. 254). This is similar to Collins' (2000) idea of both/and—that we embody both the oppressor and the oppressed. These ideas of connectivity stemming from Chicana and Black feminisms provoke building bridges of understanding and knowledge for teaching and research in academic spaces. Connectivity is one way that the us/them dichotomy can be challenged and bring about collective healing.

Finally, the most important pedagogical lesson inspired by our Chicana and Black feminist *testimonios* has been the reminder that we all must begin with ourselves (Dillard, 2006). The currents we ride (our agency, resistance, and complicity) are not in direct opposition to oppression and structures of power but are interwoven, messy, and web-like (Collins, 2000). This provides an important lesson, as it urges us all to learn and engage with the language of critique so that oppression can be recognized and resisted. Anzaldúa (1987) posits that "I change myself, I change the world" (p. 92). Similarly, Lorde (1984) suggests that "we must move against not only those forces which dehumanize us from the outside, but also against those oppressive values which we have been forced to take into ourselves" (p. 135). We agree with Anzaldúa and Lorde that one cannot facilitate, teach, and engage others unless one changes and shifts consciousness within.

Many times, when working toward and demanding that society change, some can forget that perhaps society is in many ways a reflection of each of us. Anzaldúa (1987) suggests that "the struggle has always been inner and played out in the outer terrains" (p. 87). Self-work must be done, then, in conjunction with the work performed in academia. As academics, we are not outside of colonization but very much a part and product of it. With these personal transformations we can offer different kinds of critical pedagogies for healing the self—a very different kind of critical pedagogy from the androcentric models we have been taught. Because *testimonios* are a call for political action from the vantage point of subaltern marginalized bodies and voices (Elenes, 2000), our Chicana and Black feminists' *testimonios* serve as a call for one of the most revolutionary acts—the revolution within the self. In this way, we can collectively heal our fragmented selves.

Healing our fragmented "we" and "I" is the type of praxis that theoretically inspired *testimonios* have to potentially reveal about *nos/otras* (we/they and or us/them). *Testimonios* can become "a quest story of ordeal and distress, cyclic life-stages, and identity transformations" (Anzaldúa, 2002b, pp. 562–563). *Testimonios* inspired by Chicana and Black feminisms, then, can serve as an ongoing reflexive activity that allows women of color in academia to connect with each other, in hopes of transforming the "I" in order to impact the "we," the *nos/otras*, and the world around us.

NOTES

1. RECE has brought challenges, concerns, and counter-stories to the field it was birthed from—early childhood education. RECE can be situated within the uncertainties and ambiguities introduced mainly by postmodern and poststructural research as well as other critical perspective scholarship. Because most of the participants are of European descent, we find it imperative to also bring in voices from the margins.
2. We use parentheses to play with language and to point to languages' multiple meanings. For example, to remember can be to recall but to (re)member offers a new way to visualize this act. That is, we are saying that in the process of recalling we also are putting back together what has been dismembered throughout our lives. Furthermore, by segmenting with parentheses, we also mean that the (re) is deeper and more reflexive. It's not just to rework and revisit an issue but to (re)work and (re)visit it with political and critical awareness.

REFERENCES

Anzaldúa, G. (1987). *Borderlands/la frontera*. San Francisco, CA: Aunt Lute Books.

Anzaldúa, G. (2002a). Now let us shift ... the path of conocimiento ... inner work, public acts. In G. Anzaldúa & A. Keating (Eds.), *This bridge we call home: Radical visions for transformation* (pp. 540–578). New York. NY: Routledge.

Anzaldúa, G. (2002b). Preface. In G. Anzaldúa & A. Keating (Eds.), *This bridge we call home: Radical visions for transformation* (pp. 1–5). New York, NY: Routledge.

Anzaldúa, G., & Keating, A. (Eds.). (2002). *This bridge we call home: Radical visions for transformation*, New York, NY: Routledge.

Ayala, J., Herrera, P., Jimenez, L., & Lara, I. (2006). Fiera, guambra & karichina. In D. Delgado Bernal, C. A. Elenes, F. E. Godinez, & S. Villenas (Eds.), *Chicana/Latina education in everyday life: Feminist perspectives on pedagogy and epistemology* (pp. 261–280). Albany, NY: State University of New York Press.

Beverley, J. (2005). Testimonio, subalternity, and narrative authority. In N. K. Denzin & Y. S. Lincoln (Eds.), *Handbook of qualitative research* (3rd ed., pp. 547–556). Thousand Oaks, CA: Sage.

Brewer, R. M. (1993). Theorizing race, class, and gender: The new scholarship of black feminist intellectuals and black women's labor. In S. M. James & P. A. Busia (Eds.), *Theorizing black feminisms: The visionary pragmatism of black women* (pp. 13–30). New York, NY: Routledge.

Burciaga, R., & Tavares, A. (2006). Our pedagogy of sisterhood: A testimonio. In D. Delgado Bernal, C. A. Elenes, F. E. Godinez, & S. Villenas (Eds.), *Chicana/Latina education in everyday life: Feminist perspectives on pedagogy and epistemology* (pp. 133–142). Albany, NY: State University of New York Press.

Collins, P. H. (2000). *Black feminist thought: Knowledge, consciousness, and the politics of empowerment* (2nd ed.). New York, NY: Routledge.

Collins, P. H. (2005). *Black sexual politics: African Americans, gender, and the new racism*. New York, NY: Routledge.

Collins, P. H. (2006). *From black power to hip hop: Racism, nationalism, and feminism*. Philadelphia, PA: Temple University Press.

Collins, P. H. (2011). Toward a new vision: Race, class, and gender as categories of analysis and connection. In T. E. Ore (Ed.), *The social construction of difference and inequality: Race, class, gender, and sexuality* (5th ed., pp. 760–774). New York, NY: McGraw-Hill.

Crenshaw, K. W. (1991). Mapping the margins: Intersectionality, identity politics, and violence against women of color. *Stanford Law Review*, 43, 1241.

Cutri, R. M., Delgado Bernal, D., Powell, A., & Wiederman, C. R. (1998). "An honorable Sisterhood": Developing a critical ethic of care in higher education. *Transformations*, 9(2), 100–117.

Delgado Bernal, D. (1998). Using a Chicana feminist epistemology in educational research. *Harvard Educational Review*, *68*(4), 555–582.

Delgado Bernal, D., Elenes, C. A., Godinez, F. E., & Villenas, S. (Eds.). (2006). *Chicana/Latina education in everyday life: Feminista perspectives on pedagogy and epistemology.* Albany, NY: State University of New York Press.

Delgado Bernal, D., & Villalpando, O. (2002). An apartheid of knowledge in academia: The struggle over the "legitimate" knowledge of faculty of color. *Equity and Excellence in Education, 35*(2), 169–180.

Dill, B. T., McLaughlin, A. E., & Nieves, A. D. (2007). Future directions of feminist research: Intersectionality. In S. N. Hesse-Biber (Ed.), *Handbook of feminist research: Theory and praxis* (pp. 629–638). Thousand Oaks, CA: Sage.

Dillard, C. B. (2006). *On spiritual strivings: Transforming an African American woman's academic life.* Albany, NY: State University of New York Press.

Elenes, C. A. (1997). Reclaiming the borderlands: Chicana/o identity, difference, and critical pedagogy. *Educational Theory, 47*(3), 359–375.

Elenes, C. A. (2000). Chicana feminist narratives and the politics of the self. *Frontiers, 21*(3), 105–123.

Elenes, C. A. (2006). Transformando fronteras: Chicana feminist transformative pedagogies. In D. Delgado Bernal, C. A. Elenes, F. E. Godinez, & S. Villenas (Eds.), *Chicana/Latina education in everyday life: Feminist perspectives on pedagogy and epistemology* (pp. 245–260). Albany, NY: State University of New York Press.

Elenes, C. A., González, F. E., Delgado Bernal, D., & Villenas, S. (2001). Introduction: Chicana/Mexicana feminist pedagogies: Consejos, respeto, y educación in everyday life. *International Journal of Qualitative Studies in Education, 14*(5), 595–602.

hooks, b. (2000a). *Feminism is for everybody: Passionate politics.* Cambridge, MA: South End Press.

hooks, b. (2000b). *Feminist theory: From margin to center* (2nd ed.). Cambridge MA: South End Press.

hooks, b. (2010). *Teaching critical thinking: Practical wisdom.* New York, NY: Taylor & Francis.

hooks, b., & Mesa-Bains, A. (2006). *Homegrown: Engaged cultural criticism.* Cambridge, MA: South End Press.

Hull, G. T. (1984). *Give us each day: The diary of Alice Dunbar-Nelson.* New York, NY: W. W. Norton.

James, S. M. (1993). Introduction. In S. M. James & P. A. Busia (Eds.), *Theorizing black feminisms: The visionary pragmatism of black women* (pp. 1–9). New York, NY: Routledge.

Keating, A. (2000). (Ed.) *Gloria Anzaldúa interviews/entrevistas.* New York, NY: Routledge.

Keating, A. (2006). From borderlands and new mestizas to nepantlas and nepantleras: Anzalduan theories of social change. *Human Architecture: Journal of the Sociology of Self-Knowledge, 4*(Sp), 5–16.

Keating, A. (2007). *Teaching transformation: Transcultural classroom experience.* New York, NY: Palgrave.

Latina Feminist Group. (2001). *Telling to live: Latina feminist testimonios* (2nd ed.). Durham, NC: Duke University Press.

Lorde, A. (1982). *Zami, A new spelling of my name.* Trumansburg, NY: Crossing Press.

Lorde, A. (1984). *Sister outsider: Essays and speeches by Audre Lorde.* Berkeley, CA: Crossing Press.

Richardson, M. (Ed.). (1987). *Maria W. Stewart, America's first black woman political writer: Essays and speeches.* Bloomington, IN: Indiana University Press.

Saavedra, C. M. (2011). Language and literacy in the borderlands: Acting upon the world through testimonios. *Language Arts, 88*(4), 261–269.

Trinidad Galvan, R. (2001). Portraits of mujeres desjuiciadas: Womanist pedagogies of the everyday, the mundane and the ordinary. *International Journal of Qualitative Studies in Education, 14*(5), 603–621.

Walker, A. (1983). *In search of our mothers' gardens.* New York, NY: Harcourt Brace Jovanovich.

Washington, M. H. (Ed.). (1975). *Black-eyed Susans: Classic stories by and about black women.* Garden City, NY: Anchor.

The Process of *Reflexión* in Bridging *Testimonios* Across Lived Experience

Michelle M. Espino

University of Georgia

Irene I. Vega

University of California, Los, Angeles

Laura I. Rendón

University of Texas, San, Antonio

Jessica J. Ranero

Del Mar College

Marcela M. Muñiz

Stanford University

From Latinas' locations in the margins of academe and society emerges a unique set of challenges complicated by racism, sexism, and classism. One form of resistance to these multiple marginalities involves drawing upon and (re)telling one's lived experience to expose oppression and systemic violence. *Testimonio* is a conceptual and methodological tool that transforms personal narrative into this type of resistance. In this article, the authors employ *testimonio* to document, from an intergenerational perspective, critical consequences and benefits of the academic socialization process for Latina academics. In examining the exchange between and among four established and four emerging Latina scholars, the authors uncovered an innovative methodological technique for bridging *testimonios* across lived experience; this technique is referred to as *reflexión* and enhances the level of knowledge construction that *testimonio* offers in formulating a collective consciousness across generations and social identities, crafting theories about Latina scholars in academe, and demonstrating that lived experience is integral to knowledge creation.

If we are to create a critical framework to analyze systemic inequity and injustice; if we are to actualize a form of authentic justice, we must act to (re)appropriate and exercise our right to be

This manuscript is based on a symposium presented at the 2009 Association for the Study of Higher Education (ASHE) conference. The authors thank Estela Mara Bensimon, Sylvia Hurtado, Anna Ortiz, and Laura I. Rendón for granting permission to use their transcribed remarks from the ASHE symposium and for providing helpful feedback during the preparation of this article.

subjects of knowledge and of theoretical construction (Aquino, Machado, & Rodriguez, 2002). We cannot afford to leave this task in the hands of those who oppress us with their excluding theories and ideologies. As such, the *testimonios* you witnessed today become conduits to decolonize ourselves with an oppositional feminist consciousness. I commend you for your courage, your wisdom, your inner strength, your resilience and your resolve. *Hermanitas*,[1] you are the ones we were waiting for. (L. I. Rendón, personal communication, November 7, 2008)

In November 2009, we presented an intergenerational dialogue among emerging and established Latina[2] scholars at the Association for the Study of Higher Education (ASHE) annual conference (Espino et al., 2009). The symposium emerged over several years from ongoing discussions among our collective of four emerging Latina scholars who were either completing our doctorates or beginning our academic careers. Our conversations focused on bridging cultural commitments to research and the challenges we faced as Latina scholars in racist, sexist, and classist environments. We often questioned whether our concerns were unique or common issues experienced by a more seasoned generation. Our intentions were to: (1) seek answers to assuage our apprehensions, (2) heal the fragmentations caused by oppressive environments, (3) critique oppressive educational structures, and (4) formulate strategies for social change within academe. As emerging Latina scholars, we centered our lived experiences during the symposium and then invited established Latina scholars as dialogue partners to reflect on our *testimonios* and share their truths in light of what we discussed.

Although grateful for the opportunity to share our experiences in a public forum, we had not anticipated the profound emotional, intellectual, and healing connections that emerged. We, together with the audience, enacted resistance by transforming silence into language (Anzaldúa, 1990) and transgressed the boundaries of an academic, "mainstream" space. By making public those private stories of pain, triumph, uncertainty, conviction, and growth, we wove the strands of lived experience along with *sitios* (spaces) of contention (Hurtado, 1998) to "translate ourselves for each other" (Latina Feminist Group, 2001, p. 3). As we interpreted how our established *colegas* made sense of these translations, affirming and challenging the ways in which we perceived ourselves in each other, we realized the power of intersectional dialogue. Through this exchange we uncovered a process within the method of *testimonio* that mirrors the (un)conscious, "the inner faces, *las caras por dentro*" (Anzaldúa, 1990, p. xxvii) among our collective. We refer to this process as *reflexión,* one that allows us to analyze and interpret our individual *testimonios* as part of a collective experience that reflects our past, present, and future, thus moving us toward a collective consciousness.

Reflexión entails an examination of the inner self and sharing that inner self with a trusted dialogue partner. Through *reflexión* we move beyond self-reflection and self-inquiry toward a shared experience where our dialogue partners reflect our truths back to us as they share their own life journeys. This process accounts for the distortions and (mis)perceptions of ourselves based on the vestiges of oppression that continue to manifest within academe, tethering us to one another in the midst of racist, sexist, and classist environments. *Reflexión* helps us situate and explain how our lived experiences exist within a broader set of social and institutional structures. Through this process we analyze data at multiple moments in time. First, through the documentation and interpretation of the emerging scholars' *testimonios*, then through the feedback offered among our smaller collective of emerging scholars as we prepared for the established scholars' analyses and responses to the finalized *testimonios*. The final step involved analyzing the *testimonios* and responses as a larger collective. *Reflexión* created opportunities to move beyond traditional notions of goodness and trustworthiness in qualitative research and focus more on catalytic validity (Lather, 1993). The construct of catalytic validity was evident, not only in displaying "the reality-altering impact of the inquiry process; [but directing] this impact so that [we would] gain self-understanding and self-direction" and thus transform our world (Kincheloe & McLaren, 2005, p. 324). A point and counterpoint dialogue uniquely enables those participating in *reflexión* to engage in meaning making, identify the shared and differing themes found in Latina experiences, and lay the groundwork for theory building. We enacted *reflexión* to craft a collective consciousness from individual sufferings and triumphs that would lead to change within ourselves and within our environments.

For this article, we present *reflexión* as a complement to *testimonio* that focuses not only on the telling of lived experience but the (re)telling of those experiences to a trusted dialogue partner. This partner may or may not bear witness to the same forms of oppression but is still able to weave her story into a shared understanding of what it means to be a Latina in academe in the U.S. We first explain how *testimonio* bridges the perceived divide between personal experience and knowledge construction in academe. We then present excerpts from the *testimonios* shared at the symposium and demonstrate how the process of *reflexión* can be practiced to affirm and encourage healing pathways for our fractured minds, bodies, and spirits (Delgado Bernal, 2006, 2008). Finally, we offer suggestions for implementing the process of *reflexión* and assert that by analyzing the collective consciousness that emerged from this process, we can conceptualize the extent to which Latina scholars can create spaces for wholeness.

SCHOLARLY CONTRIBUTIONS OF *TESTIMONIO*

Our use of *testimonio* follows a tradition established by the Latina Feminist Group (2001), a collective of 18 women who documented their private stories to expose the diversity of *Latinidades* in the U.S. and "decenter what counts as theory and who can engage in theorizing" (p. x). The collective sought to answer Moraga's call for "theory in the flesh . . . where the physical realities of our lives . . . all fuse to create a politic born out of necessity . . . by naming our selves [*sic*] and by telling our stories in our own words" (Moraga & Anzaldúa, 2002, p. 21). The Latina Feminist Group created a social and intellectual space where personal experience, situated within historical and sociopolitical contexts, is the foundation for knowledge creation. By engaging in *testimonio*, scholars avoid essentializing a Latina experience and instead, honor the various subjectivities that correspond with sexual identities, immigration status, language, and phenotype, to name a few.

Testimonio offers a venue to expose the complexities within Latina lived experience and engages individual stories to facilitate an understanding of the larger collective (Henze, 2000), while constructing knowledge that accounts for our connections and tensions. More Latinas are successfully transitioning into higher education and becoming socially and politically empowered, theorizing differently from "the Western form of abstract logic" by sharing "the stories we create, in riddles and proverbs, in the play with language" (Christian, 1990, p. 336). For example, Delgado Bernal, Elenes, Godinez, and Villenas (2006) rejected deficit interpretations of Chicana/Latina lives as "having problems or issues requiring intervention" (p. 4) and instead uncovered Chicana/Latina resilience by identifying the cultural resources they employ to navigate various social institutions. Similarly, Burciaga and Tavares (2006) used *testimonio* to establish sisterhood pedagogy within the academy in defiance of hostile, competitive environments in which limited resources and support breed distance and contempt among graduate students. Espino, Muñoz, and Marquez Kiyama (2010) also employed *testimonio* to expose the challenges they faced in negotiating their evolving identities (motherhood, social class, and public intellectual) as they transitioned to faculty life.

We believe that *testimonio* is the most appropriate framework for our work because it is a tool that functions beyond the recording of personal stories. *Testimonio* moves us into the realm of knowledge creation that is grounded in lived experience, bearing witness to issues of oppression, confronting "traditional notions of ethnicity and nationalism, [and] questioning Eurocentric feminist frameworks" (Latina Feminist Group, 2001, p. 2). Like others before us, we argue that the goal of personal narratives should be expanded from the collection of historical events to an academic venue that privileges Latinas' ways of knowing and meaning making. Through *testimonio* we formulate our collective consciousness as a space of empowerment and resilience, while recognizing the intellectual aspects of this effort. By privileging the knowledge of those in the margins, we achieve a critical raced-gendered epistemology, a way of knowing that "speak[s] to culturally specific ways of positioning" and examines "how oppression is caught up in multiply [*sic*] raced, gendered, classed, and sexed relations" (Delgado Bernal, 2002, p. 107). We cannot separate the mind from other elements of ourselves. Every element of our "bodymindspirit" (Lara, 2002, p. 435) is indivisible and influences the knowledge and theory constructed from lived experience, despite institutionalized oppression that fragments us. In this way, we are one with knowledge, affirming our lived experiences as truths.

CREATING THREADS OF CONNECTION

In 2006, Espino and Muñiz met at the American Educational Research Association (AERA) annual conference. Vega met Ranero and Muñiz when she was applying to doctoral programs. A year later, all of us met at the American Association of Hispanics in Higher Education (AAHHE) annual conference. From conversations about our doctoral journeys, we found similar challenges in negotiating between the pressures of family and academe, developing personal relationships external to our studies, and uncovering our ethnic identities that were often subsumed under the larger Latina umbrella. Energized by our connections, we decided to share our lived experiences in a more public forum and presented our first set of narratives during the 2008 AAHHE conference. Our stories focused on negotiating academic responsibilities as a new spouse, attending to traditional values as well as emerging feminist ones, shifting identities as a married academic, and contending with (hetero)sexist interpretations of women's positions within Mexican American families.

At that point, we were not completely aware that we were engaging in an act of resistance by exposing our lived experiences in an academic space. In fact, we were privileging our ways of knowing and asserting our expertise as both the objects and subjects of knowledge creation (Latina Feminist Group, 2001). Laura Rendón, who was in the audience, recognized that we were at the early stages of understanding *testimonio* and shared that many of the tensions we documented were also of concern to her generation of Latina academics. With her encouragement, we developed the idea of engaging in an intergenerational exchange to explore the possibility that our stories were reflected in those of a more seasoned generation. As a result, in Spring 2009, the second iteration of the *testimonios* shifted to include responses from established scholars. By then, the most salient aspects of our experiences also were shifting because the intersections of our identities are fluid and place us in different positions within different moments in time (Bloom, 1998). Acknowledging the fluidity of identity further establishes the function of *testimonio* as a tool to document systemic violence over time and to demonstrate how lived experiences reflect broader structural realities (Henze, 2000).

With an understanding that our "honorable sisterhood" would enable us to "critique our experiences as ... women with different cultural, class, and immigrant backgrounds without turning our differences into sites of adversity or hostility" (Cutri, Delgado Bernal, Powell, & Ramirez Wiederman, 1998, p. 101), we developed a question to guide the crafting of our revised *testimonios* and allow the malleability of our identities to shape our writing: To what extent have our intersecting identities informed our positions as Latina scholars? We individually crafted *testimonios* that drew upon our cultural intuition[3] (Delgado Bernal, 1998) to highlight the most salient parts of our experiences as *mujeres* and sister-scholars in academe. Our stories were deeply personal, reflected aspects of the literature on Latinas in higher education, and included knowledge acquired through our professional experiences.

We then began reviewing each other's drafts and hosting teleconferences where we revealed ourselves to one another, honoring "what we [could] learn from our own and each other's mistakes ... [to be] unashamed and unapologetic about our joint collaboration" (Burciaga & Tavares, 2006, p. 138). We affirmed each other and expanded our awareness about how the multiple strands of our identities (re)shape our experiences, while recognizing our privileged and marginalized selves (Delgado Bernal, 2008). Through multiple iterations, we exposed four connecting themes in our *testimonios*: embracing the borderlands between home culture and academic culture, serving our communities, facing the challenges of being "educated out" of one's community, and the transition from doctoral study to faculty life.

Laura Rendón served as our counsel, offering suggestions and helping us secure our dialogue partners. After confirming our partners, we distributed an e-mail message that included goals for the symposium, a timeline in the event that the proposal was accepted, and questions to consider such as:

1. How have the experiences shared in the *testimonio* resonated with or differed from your own experiences?
2. What one point really stood out for you in the *testimonio*?
3. What advice would you give to emerging Latina scholars as we navigate our academic careers?
4. What are some implications for the academy's ability to attract and retain Latina scholars?

When the proposal was approved in Summer 2009, we revisited our *testimonios* and made changes that reflected a more current set of circumstances. For example, as a newly diagnosed breast cancer survivor, Michelle wanted to include the pain and struggle of dealing with cancer during her first year as a faculty member. Irene decided to focus specifically on the fragmentation and reparation of her identity during her undergraduate years. As we talked with one another, we felt encouraged to expose our *papelitos guardados*, the hidden secrets that we kept close (Latina Feminist Group, 2001).

The resulting *testimonios* are heartbreaking and honest portrayals of our interactions within systems of oppression and the resulting impact on our physical, emotional, and spiritual well-being. When we presented the final versions at the symposium, our colleague, José Cabrales, videotaped our exchange, which we then transcribed verbatim. By situating *Latinidades* in the center of scholarly discourse, we were "breaking boundaries, crossing borders, claiming fragmentation and hybridity" (Hurtado, 2003, p. 216) that would lead to theories of liberation and healing. By sharing stories about our often-fractured minds, bodies, and souls, we formulated a collective consciousness that fosters resistance and builds interdependence among Latinas in the academy, making explicit, in our case, oppression and systemic violence within higher education. Figures 1, 2, 3, and 4 highlight the most evocative sections of the *testimonios* and responses from our dialogue partners. Similar to the work of Burciaga and Tavares (2006) and Espino et al. (2010), we will first introduce the emerging Latina scholars.

Michelle M. Espino identifies as a first-generation college student and a Chicana. Her father is from Mexico and her mother was born in Texas. Michelle claims Texas as her home, although she moved to several military bases throughout her childhood. She is in her fourth year as an assistant professor at the University of Georgia. Her dialogue partner was Sylvia Hurtado, Professor in the Graduate School of Education and Information Sciences and Director of the Higher Education Research Institute at the University of California, Los Angeles.

Irene I. Vega is the daughter of a Mexican immigrant mother and a Mexican American father. Her childhood is both migratory and transnational since her family followed the agricultural crop between the Arizona-Mexico border and northern California for the first 15 years of her life. She is a doctoral student at the University of California, Los Angeles. Her dialogue partner was Laura Rendón, Professor of Educational Leadership & Policy Studies at the University of Texas, San Antonio.

Jessica J. Ranero is a student affairs administrator at Del Mar College in Corpus Christi, Texas. She is a first-generation college student and was born in Arlington, Virginia. Her parents are from Guatemala and Honduras. Her dialogue partner was Anna Ortiz, Professor of Educational Leadership and Student Development in Higher Education at California State University, Long Beach.

Marcela M. Muñiz is a newly minted Ph.D. from Stanford University. A first-generation college student, she was born in Pittsburg, California to a Mexican American mother and a Mexican father, the owners of a Mexican restaurant. She is a lifelong resident of the San Francisco Bay area and is married to a native Texan. Her dialogue partner was Estela Bensimon, Professor in Educational Policy and Administration and Director of the Center for Urban Education at the University of Southern California.

HEALING FRACTURED MINDS, BODIES, AND SPIRITS

As evidenced in the excerpts, deeply emotional, intellectual, and healing connections were fostered through the exchanges among the emerging scholars and between the emerging and established scholars, as well as the consciousness-raising that occurred between presenters and the audience. By first demonstrating "individual agency—a person's socially acknowledged right to interpret and speak for herself" through the emerging scholar's *testimonio*—and then inviting "theoretically mediated interpretations" (Henze, 2000, p. 238) of lived experience through dialogue partners, we uncovered the process of *reflexión* and formulated our collective consciousness. While bounded within the space we carved at a particular moment, our exchange illustrates the core values we share that are rooted in our *Latinidad*, as well as the complexities of our multiple identities. In the following section we offer theorizations that emerged from our exchange.

In 2003, I graduated from Arizona State University with dual degrees in Political Science and Chicana/o Studies. I had come to Tempe four years prior without a plan and graduated with a political consciousness and newfound confidence in my academic and leadership potential. But this "success" did not come without its costs.

Like a ceramic bowl that breaks and is glued back together, my wholeness was restored, but the fragmentation that I experienced left its mark.

Some would say that framing this process as deficit does not recognize all that I, my family, and community have gained through education. I realize that what I call costs can also be considered assets and that what I call fragmentation can also be understood as growth. I am conscious that my "successful" socialization into the academy has facilitated important opportunities. Instead of subtractive, this process can also be understood as additive—I gained a new dimension of self. However, being optimistic about it requires hard work—it just doesn't feel natural. The truth is that most days I feel like I've lost more than I've gained.

I feel that I had to suppress the migrant farm working border girl to allow the scholar to emerge. In restraining the border girl, I also held back from my family, my culture, my community, and my roots, and I constantly wonder if it's worth it. I wonder if the social and emotional cost that I have paid for academic success is too high.

I know that the person who left San Luis, Arizona in 1999 is within me. She and her experiences are reflected in the work that I do and in the passion that fuels me. I know she's there, but sometimes I wonder if others, especially my childhood friends and family know she's actually me.

Our lives have forked so sharply and while I know that my friends and family are proud of me, I also know they suspect me of not understanding them anymore. I fear that perhaps I've veered so much from who I was that they no longer recognize me.

What is happening here is an act of courage; it's an act of resistance; it's an act of truth-telling in a very different way but still extremely valid. Those of us who are senior on this panel—20 years ago when we were your age, this session would not have been accepted at ASHE; there would not have been an audience. We would have been told we were crazy. And so this is a very significant event in the history of ASHE and I wanted to take a moment to recognize that.

Irene, *querida hermanita*, my little sister. I cried when I read your *testimonio*. I cried because your story connected me to my story. I too am a border woman. I was born in Laredo, Texas, which literally and figuratively makes me a border woman. But, I'm also a border woman in the academy. You know, I'm neither here nor there. I'm sometimes accepted; sometimes I'm not, even at my senior status.

Irene, you talk about certain dualities, cost/assets, strengths/deficits, gains/losses, comfort/discomfort, the familiar/the unfamiliar. And the academy also deals with dualities. You have research/practice, theory/practice. But these dualities exist for a reason. To know night, we have to know day. To know man, we have to know woman. So, to know our assets, we have to have some costs; otherwise, we wouldn't recognize that these are assets. And so, what I say to you is that I think that you are moving forward because you mention how you are now viewing these things in a different way.

And in actuality, those dualities exist, the Mayans and the Aztecs told us, so that we would play in those dynamics; see how things are similar and dissimilar. We are right in this middle where there is the resolution of the duality. At some point you will grow to recognize how all of these costs and all of these things that you view as very painful, and they are painful, but how those now can be assets to give you the wholeness and the identity that you seek.

So, I thank you, Irene, and know that I am walking the path with you. *Muchas gracias.*

FIGURE 1 Fragmentation by Irene Vega; Dialogue Partner: Laura Rendón.

I carry in my heart the lessons my parents taught me along with the memories of the moments that shaped my educational aspirations. These memories and lessons sustain me during the difficult times and help me feel like I am back in the safety net of home even when I am thousands of miles away.

Despite dreams for a better life for all of us, I don't think any of us understood what types of sacrifices we would all have to make in order to get *una mejor vida*. I do not think that my parents envisioned that pursuing my education would mean having to leave home and breaking away from the *familia*. They also didn't expect that an unspoken barrier would build up between us. Furthermore, they did not anticipate that education would mean that their only daughter would not marry young and give them *nietos* to spoil.

I too did not understand that my education would place me in this strange space where I am in constant conflict between old and new; home and unknown places; tradition and innovation. I naively thought that education would give me a never-ending freedom. Although in many ways my education has given me freedoms that my parents never had the privilege of experiencing, such as economic freedom and a freedom from physical labor, it has also bound me to new and unfamiliar restrictions. These restrictions come in the form of academic standards that I blindly trip over every day in my doctoral program as I am socialized into the academy. Standards such as objectivity and the ability to work autonomously are unfamiliar because they are not based on *mis tradiciones, ni mis valores*.

Even as I struggle to hold on to the lessons and values given to me by my parents, the academy is covertly pushing me into solitude and confinement. I am left wondering if solitude was the *buena vida* my parents had envisioned for me. Somehow, I don't think so because I do not think the *buena vida* means feeling lonely and confused more often than affirmed and enlightened.

You talked about several polarities in your *testimonio*. I think the polarity between tradition and innovation is really key because we are constantly creating; we're creating research, we're writing, we're creating courses. Sometimes that is in contrast to tradition where we do what's expected, but remember there's autonomy in creation too. You have a disposition for collaboration and that's another tension—I think we work at the intersection of autonomy and collaboration.

I was also struck by the way you contrast economic freedom and freedom from physical labor to the restriction that academe offers us, requires of us. Sometimes we think that we have to buy into that restriction because we have chosen this career, this life. But know that you can reconstruct that reality just as you are reconstructing what it means to be a Latina in your family.

In fact, that's one of our greatest opportunities—we are reconstructing what it means to be Latina. This is part of that innovation that you spoke of in your *testimonio*. We are creating a new existence and new gender role patterns for ourselves in relation to our traditions.

I, too, have experienced the unspoken barriers that emerge as we educate ourselves, move up in the academy, and acquire a new language. This makes us more conscious of how we interact with the people who are so important to us and adds to our responsibilities as Latina academics. For me, it means that I have to be more intentional about connecting with my external family so that they don't think that I think I'm better than them. Because that is one of the things I really fear.

Overall, I loved reading your story, Jessica, because it made me think so much of my own. The advice I'll offer is to combat that loneliness and isolation no matter where you go. Lastly, because we come from an ethic of hard work, we often think we can take on a lot in the academy, but we must remember to balance our health. Reach out to those around you; please reach out to me in whatever way that I can help you.

FIGURE 2 *Haber Mi Gorda* by Jessica Ranero; Dialogue Partner: Anna Ortiz.

As the child of a tortilla maker and Bracero Program laborer turned entrepreneurs, I learned the value of hard work not simply by hitting the books, but by cleaning and waiting on tables in support of the family business. In my world, the term *service* has a few connotations. My culture and upbringing in a community service-oriented family have taught me that giving back in a heartfelt way is absolutely essential. However, service in academe seems less essential for tenure, often taking a backseat to research and teaching. It pains me that I would question any decision to engage in service, particularly the activities from which I draw great personal gratification, yet the pressures within the academy that will judge my success impact my decision-making process.

Throughout graduate school, I've found myself limiting my service involvement and now make decisions against a backdrop of other demands, such as my need to make academic progress, develop other aspects of my vita, and aim for greater balance between my work and family life. There is no question that I am influenced by the cues from my academic socialization, and this is something I have struggled with. As I see others passionately engaging in diversity advocacy, I sometimes wish that I could be fully in the trenches and question whether my decision to play a more limited role has been the right decision. Am I succumbing to a socialization process that limits or even denies culture and community? I'm not so naïve that I believe such a change in how we value service in tenure – a revolution, really – could easily take place at research universities, but I hope that, with supportive allies, change can indeed occur.

Until that time, I ground myself in the reality that this is not the world that I live in at my research university. Despite the tradeoffs, it is highly likely that I will continue to take those calls from the Upward Bound counselor who wants me to meet her high school students, the summer research program that needs mentors for undergraduates of color, and the students who need academic help. It may not contribute to my tenure case, but it might encourage or better equip a few more students to consider and complete a stage of higher education that they might not have considered or thought possible otherwise. It's difficult to have any regrets about that.

I suppose that my story is very different, and I probably should have titled this, if I would have written it, "How I became a Latina." I come from an Argentinian family where we were voluntary immigrants, and I'm not a first-generation college student. My story of immigration is not a story of struggle at all; it was a planned immigration. The biggest struggle was, and it's kind of ironic now when I hear some of the [other] stories, is that my father was a surgeon in Argentina and, at the age of 40, when we decided to come to the U.S., he had to start his medical profession all over again.

I think that one of the things that really surprised me was how self-directed you are and how you're thinking about things I never thought of when I was a doctoral student. When I read your *testimonio* about service I thought, "This is not about service. This is about activism." In the academy, we define service as unpaid administrative work for the university. What you're talking about is a kind of activism that enables people who are in positions of power, as tenured professors, to use the resources to enable the success of others. In order for you to be the activist that you want to be, it is very important that you not do service. Because, the way in which you will be able to do what you want to do for others, what has been done for you, you will need to reach that position that gives you the power to help others. We often think that service and teaching and research are separate. Research to me is to, as in Freire's words, to act in the world to change it. And that's the kind of research that I was able to start doing after tenure, but drawing much on the experience of being in community organizing. I encourage you to think about becoming as Ricardo Stanton-Salazar would say, "an institutional agent" that has the social network to help others become like you.

When I read your *testimonio*, the first thing I thought about was my first student at USC, Marta Soto, who died of cancer two years ago. Her parents also had a restaurant, and I thought of Marta and how much she would have enjoyed to have been here with us, so I thank you for inviting me and for helping me keep Marta's energy and sensibilities alive with me.

FIGURE 3   Heeding the Call to Service by Marcela Muñiz; Dialogue Partner: Estela Bensimon.

On February 20, 2009, during my first year as a faculty member, I was supposed to attend admissions interviews. Instead, I was in the doctor's office hearing the words, "You have cancer." Too many questions entered my mind: How would I handle the pressures and stresses of academia while dealing with cancer? How would my vulnerability affect my relationships with colleagues and students? As I began to lose my hair and my level of energy decreased, I incorporated the consequences of the chemotherapy into my schedule. I had chemo on Thursdays, knowing that I could recuperate during the weekend and then resume teaching on Tuesdays. I updated students, faculty, family, and friends through a blog. Students sent care packages and cards and raised money for breast cancer research. When others said I should not focus on my research, I argued that my work was what I should think about. I wanted to believe that there was life for me after this battle was a distant memory. While engaging in scholarly activities, I could take a break from facing the horrors of cancer and the difficult surgical decisions that would later occur. On the days I lost hope, I prayed for just one more day so that I could be remembered for doing something of value, one more day to make a difference in the lives of those around me, one more day to write about and advocate for the communities I loved. Perhaps this was a bit unorthodox, but keeping that routine and those ambitions uplifted my spirits.

What it meant to be a faculty member changed on the day of my diagnosis. Cancer reminded me that I should not fear my journey to tenure; that I am strong enough to endure the challenges with grace and gratitude. Cancer granted me an opportunity to have faith in others, to have patience in myself. Now, my scholarship has greater meaning for me. I believe in waging some battles, but only if they lead to enhancing the work that we do as faculty, the work we do in developing practitioners and policymakers, and most especially, the work we do to advocate for students and their families. As I continue to face the consequences of my diagnosis, I am confident that having and defeating cancer will make me a better researcher, colleague, and friend. I am *La Sobreviviente*.

When I read your *testimonio*, I was surprised how relevant it was to aspects of my life. The one thing that comes through is the amazing strength we have within us. We are full of insecurities, and we never realize how strong we are until it comes to a test. Yours is an amazing story of hope; enabling us to understand that we can get beyond the challenge. What I hear in your story is your strength in accepting who you are; you have a wisdom that many of us still are acquiring. To understand where we get our strength will only make us more useful to a variety of communities. As an assistant professor, you're going to doubt yourself every day. But, academia is a trapeze act, and the next bar you're going to catch; you've done it before, so you can catch it again. I never really thought about this before but, if you don't catch that bar, you have a net. It's okay to fall. You have to ask: what am I to learn from this experience? I think that is key.

During a serious illness, the first thing you have to do is plan the rest of your life, which is difficult to do because you're not gonna care about that syllabus, you're not gonna care if you deliver the perfect lecture. When I was diagnosed with a tumor on my spine, I knew I had to make a will and contact my brothers and sisters to let them know. These are the things that when you're young, you don't want to think about, but they really put things in perspective. During my illness, I started doing a lot of reading about the body and healing. Now I believe that everything happens for a reason.

So, what's the advice? Do what you love to do. You love the questions, ask the questions. You love finding the answers, go find the answers. Do what you love to do whether it means taking some time out or exploring other pieces of yourself. Thank you for your strength and for sharing what you learned because it's a valuable lesson. One of the things we learn is that the body is an amazing creation. Our bodies want to naturally heal and get back to equilibrium. The only reason the body cannot get back to equilibrium is because something is preventing it, and that could be our own thought processes; it could be a health issue. That's the one thing that I learned that was most amazing, the healing power of ourselves. Thank you for your *testimonio*.

FIGURE 4 The First Year of Survival by Michelle Espino; Dialogue Partner: Sylvia Hurtado.

Enduring the Emotional and Social Costs of Socialization to Higher Education

Our successful socialization into the academy has required the segmentation and compartmentalization of our identities. Like so many Latinas in higher education, we are positioned in the liminal spaces between multiple worlds of womanhood, family, community, and profession, striving to bridge our cultural and scholarly commitments. We fear that we are no longer recognizable to our childhood friends and families; that we have acquired a language that prevents us from communicating with the people we love; that we cannot reciprocate the opportunities that others provided us. We acknowledge that the process of socialization can be isolating for all academics; however, we assert that multiple marginalities based on Latinas' various subordinated identities compound the expected challenges. (See Delgado Bernal, 2008; Godínez, 2006; and Trueba, 2002 for discussions about intersecting identities and complexities of lived experience.)

Resisting Racialized, Gendered, and Heteronormative Expectations among Work, Family, and Community

As heterosexual women within patriarchal and homophobic environments, some of us face the pressure of managing and resisting heteronormative, gendered expectations within our families and communities. Specifically, we contend with imposed expectations about romantic partnerships and child-bearing and piece together (temporary or final) resolutions that satisfy our personal desires and work priorities. For those who identify as such, we acknowledge that our heterosexual privilege in sharing our lived experiences may not reflect salient aspects of experience for our LBTQ sisters. A recommendation for future work is to bring women with marginalized sexual identities into the process of *reflexión* and disrupt traditional academic spaces that would otherwise ignore their lived experiences.

Much of our success is attributed to members of our families and communities who invested their time and scarce resources so that we could fulfill our potential. As a result, we feel a social responsibility to contribute to the efforts of which we were once beneficiaries. Unfortunately, our commitments toward family and community are often at odds with the expectations of the academy, which refuses to acknowledge that scholars are committed to more than just their work. The fact that we are so passionate about our academic work further complicates the career-life balance. Our resistance is illustrated in the bridging of our research, teaching, and activism (Ayala, 2008).

Honoring Experiences of Pain and Healing

As members of multiple marginalized groups, we have experienced a sense of isolation and doubt stemming from our racialized, classed, and gendered experiences in academe. These socioemotional experiences and their physical consequences require that we take a more holistic perspective on our journeys—prioritizing bodymindspirit while drawing from our cultural resources to ensure our well-being (Lara, 2002). Seeking a healthy balance proves difficult as we face various academic commitments, deadlines, and the constant pressure to prove ourselves as scholars. We challenge ourselves to reflect on the nexus between our physical and mental conditions and our profession. When we are tested, we need to reframe our professional community, our friendships with one another, aspects of our own vulnerabilities, and even our work. The strength within us may not be recognized until there is a moment of difficulty, but when that strength is harnessed, we can resist against structures of oppression within higher education and the greater society.

REPLICATING THE PROCESS OF *REFLEXIÓN*

The exchange with dialogue partners who, in our case, were established scholars, deepened our understanding of the process through which a collective consciousness is formed; the process we have named *reflexión*. Through the process of *reflexión*, we moved from *testimonios*—sharing our truths—to engaging in a deeper examination of our truths and how they intersect and represent a sense of wholeness. The wisdom expressed first among our group of four emerging scholars and then among our group of eight scholars provided a sense of wholeness as we affirmed that we were not alone in our journeys and that just as our dialogue partners continued to navigate their own paths, we too would create new paths toward wholeness. The middle place where *testimonio* and *reflexión* meet is the spiritual place of identity; it is the place where two consciousnesses meet to create a collective consciousness. By sharing our personal struggles and exposing our vulnerabilities, we opened pathways between two generations of scholars who could share wisdom with one another, validate lived experiences, and (re)frame these lived experiences as legitimate, academically rigorous, and emancipatory projects.

By examining our inner selves and sharing those inner selves with trusted dialogue partners, we documented how our individual experiences diverged and converged with one another. The result was a collective consciousness through which we resist oppression in its various forms and empower ourselves and other scholars to continue doing so throughout the academic journey. Similar to the ways that Delgado Bernal's (1998) reflections after her study on Chicana school resistance and the 1968 Blowouts in Los Angeles led to uncovering the value of cultural intuition, we realized only after the symposium that the process of *reflexión* offered methodological clarity in formulating collective consciousness. Based on our experiences, we offer how the process of *reflexión* unfolded.

First, one should identify aspects or moments of her life that have been critical to the development of her intersecting identities. For us, the process started with our experiences as Latina scholars but evolved into aspects of our lives that were much more personal as we gained a greater sense of community with one another and were more willing to delve into the essence of who we each were at that given time. Second, one crafts a *testimonio* as an individual, either using a guiding question agreed upon with a dialogue partner or without such a question. A dialogue partner is identified as one who has wisdom (regardless of age or circumstance) and ways of knowing that parallels or differs from one's life experiences. In our case, we chose established Latina scholars because our intentions were to understand ourselves within the context of academe but soon realized that we, too, had wisdom to share with our established *colegas*. When the *testimonios* are exchanged through the written word, through discussion in person, or via teleconference/videoconference, guiding questions are formulated so that the dialogue partners are able to respond to similar prompts. In the responses we showcased in this article, the questions we formulated gave our dialogue partners opportunities to read our *testimonios* with particular questions in mind, but the reading of the *testimonios* in a public space also encouraged more organic reactions based on that public interchange. The process of *reflexión* is made evident when the partners engage in a dialogue. Given geographical constraints, our dialogue prior to the symposium was done in writing, but without the limitation of distance, we would have done so in person. *Reflexión* is the dialectical process that we followed in formulating a collective consciousness among ourselves and with the established scholars.

Based on our experiences, we believe that *reflexión* enables participants to engage in meaning making, to identify the shared and differing themes of their experiences, and to lay the groundwork for theory building. *Reflexión* allowed us to situate our lived experience within a broader set of social and institutional structures. By engaging in this dialectical process, we simultaneously honored the "multiplicity of positions and border-crossing identities" (Diaz Soto, Cervantes-Soon, Villarreal, & Campos, 2009, p. 771) we inhabit, while formulating theories about our experiences in academe.

Underlying both the creation of *testimonios* and the process of *reflexión* is the practice of reflexivity. Reflexivity is "the process of reflecting critically on the self as researcher, the 'human as instrument'" (Merriam, 2002, p. 26). As Latina scholars, we all reflected critically on ourselves as individuals, but we also employed reflexive practices as we engaged in *reflexión* and developed our collective consciousness. Just as the teachers in Ladson-Billings' (1995) study of culturally relevant teaching pedagogies used dialectical relationships to make meaning of their experiences, we emerging and established Latina scholars made meaning of our experiences through reflexive dialogues with one another. As Latina scholars committed to creating transformative change in the academy, we were further motivated to engage in the practice of reflexivity because it enabled us to challenge the status quo and examine our own privileges. As stated by herising (2005), we engaged in reflexivity because we knew that as Latina scholars we needed to

consider politics of location as a serious form of enquiry, to map the ways in which we are socially and historically constituted, intertwined, and intersect with(in) the world and in relationship to the subjects of our research, reflexivity requires a resistance to theoretical generalizations and monolithic truth claims. (p. 136)

CONCLUSION

As Latina academics, we claim Chicana feminist discourse to expose the cultural and social costs that we pay for success in academe. These costs are evidenced in the ways that our minds, bodies, and spirits are fractured. Through the process of *reflexión,* we combat the "alchemy of erasure" (Latina Feminist Group, 2001, p. 2); this is our effort to transcend the effect of time and the insidious effects of academic socialization. *Reflexión* is an exceptionally productive technique for doing this because of the learning and collective consciousness that can emerge from the process. In our particular experience, it allowed us to engage with colleagues in not only intergenerational exchanges that exposed how little the culture of academe has changed across generations but how we are, in some ways, more prepared to think about and expose oppression. As we encounter similar obstacles of a more seasoned generation, they simultaneously relive their pain through ours.

By using dialogue partners to share our *testimonios,* we are also better able to identify the structural and systemic roots of our individual and collective struggles through higher education.

This affirms our belief that what the academy frames as "individual subjectivity" is more collectivist in nature. "By virtue of [our individual] process of understanding [our] relationships to [our] social milieus, the groups [we] identify with become better able to represent [our] members in political struggles against oppression" (Henze, 2000, p. 230). Our personal experiences are tied to a larger community memory and a collective history that includes those who share several characteristics to include our sociocultural and sociohistorical backgrounds. As a collective of women that represents both emerging and established scholars, we created our own space of healing and empowerment in a hostile academic environment where we could begin to heal the fractures of our minds, bodies, and spirits.

As a result of theorizing the status of Latinas in the academy through the eyes of two different generations, we are both disheartened by the ongoing struggles and encouraged by the empowerment achieved through the process of *reflexión*. Feelings of isolation, confusion, physical pain, and spiritual yearning were evident across all of our lived experiences. We recognize that the fracturing experienced in the academy is a result of how higher education is structured to promote the success of those in the dominant culture. We are encouraged because despite the barriers, we Latinas have created our own spaces as we move from the margins to the center of the discourse.

We encourage other scholars to build upon the process of *reflexión* for larger empirical studies of Latinas in academe that focus on crafting lived experience as an aspect of knowledge creation. The process we highlighted in this article represents the first steps we took in our process of *reflexión*. We recognize that *reflexión* is an ongoing process; where it will lead us in the future remains to be seen, but we eagerly continue to come together in community as we forge ahead to create spaces for Latina scholars in the academy and beyond. We hope that others will move our work forward by continuing to theorize about *testimonios* and *reflexión* as mechanisms of transformative change. We end with an excerpt of Rendón's concluding remarks from the ASHE symposium (L. I. Rendón, personal communication, November 7, 2008). Her words reiterate the profound personal meaning of our exchange, while calling attention to its scholarly significance:

> [I]f research is, at its core, the simple yet complex act of uncovering truth, then *testimonios* become confessional narratives, which portray one's own truth. *Testimoniando* . . . is an act of liberatory courage. What you're saying to the academy . . . is that to be a good scholar, you must first confront your past, your pain, and your sorrow, and your evolving identity because all of this is deeply and profoundly related to your philosophical grounding and the way that you view the world. You simply cannot operate in the academy without this clarity; without pausing and taking in the enormous challenge of seeking to uncover truth, because you are a part of that truth. However, the academy has not created a space for us to engage in this profound self-reflexivity, and therefore, as Latinas, we are called to create it.

NOTES

1. Throughout the article, there are particular Spanish words and phrases that were not translated to English for the purpose of signaling to readers that we respectfully wish to convey meaning that cannot be directly translated; a collective consciousness that incorporates linguistic differences; and a connectedness to our ancestors. Those words and phrases are important references to our culture and our experiences as Latina scholars who straddle multiple worlds and languages.

2. We use the term Latina to encompass multiple ethnic identities within Latina/o populations, especially accounting for the ethnic identities of the authors. We use specific racial/ethnic identifiers when citing from the literature.

3. Cultural intuition is a complex analytical process that extends beyond theoretical sensitivity, which is "the attribute of having insight, the ability to give meaning to data, the capacity to understand and capability to separate the pertinent from that which isn't" (Solórzano & Yosso, 2002, p. 33). Cultural intuition is based on four sources: personal experiences, existing literature, professional experience, and analytical processes (Delgado Bernal, 1998).

REFERENCES

Anzaldúa, G. (Ed.). (1990). *Making face, making soul, haciendo caras: Creative and critical perspectives of feminists of color.* San Francisco, CA: Aunt Lute Books.

Aquino, M. P., Machado, D. L., & Rodriguez, J. (2002). *A reader in Latina feminist theology: Religion and justice.* Austin, TX: University of Texas Press.

Ayala, J. (2008). Voces in dialogue: What is our work in the academy? In K. P. Gonzalez & R. V. Padilla (Eds.), *Doing the public good: Latina/o scholars engage civic participation* (pp. 25–37). Sterling, VA: Stylus.

Bloom, L. R. (1998). *Under the sign of hope: Feminist methodology and narrative interpretation.* Albany, NY: State University of New York Press.

Burciaga, R., & Tavares, A. (2006). Our pedagogy of sisterhood: A testimonio. In D. Delgado Bernal, C. A. Elenes, F. E. Godínez, & S. Villenas (Eds.), *Chicana/Latina education in everyday life: Feminista perspectives on pedagogy and epistemology* (pp. 133–142). Albany, NY: State University of New York Press.

Christian, B. (1990). The race for theory. In G. Anzaldúa (Ed.), *Making face, making soul, haciendo caras: Creative and critical perspectives by feminists of color* (pp. 335–345). San Francisco, CA: Aunt Lute Books.

Cutri, R. M., Delgado Bernal, D., Powell, A., & Ramirez Wiedeman, C. (1998). An honorable sisterhood: Four diverse women identify a critical ethic of care in higher education. *Transformations, 9*(2), 101–117.

Delgado Bernal, D. (1998). Using Chicana feminist epistemology in educational research. *Harvard Educational Review, 68*(4), 555–582.

Delgado Bernal, D. (2002). Critical race theory, Latino critical theory, and critical raced-gendered epistemologies: Recognizing students of color as holders and creators of knowledge. *Qualitative Inquiry, 8*(1), 105–126.

Delgado Bernal, D. (2006). Mujeres in college: Negotiating identities and challenging educational norms. In D. Delgado Bernal, C. A. Elenes, F. E. Godínez, & S. Villenas (Eds.), *Chicana/Latina education in everyday life: Feminista perspectives on pedagogy and epistemology* (pp. 77–79). Albany, NY: State University of New York Press.

Delgado Bernal, D. (2008). La trenza de las identidades: Weaving together our personal, professional, and communal identities. In K. Gonzalez & R. Padilla (Eds.), *Doing the public good: Latina/o scholars engage in civic participation* (pp. 135–148). Sterling, VA: Stylus.

Delgado Bernal, D., Elenes, C. A., Godinez, F. E., & Villenas, S. (Eds.). (2006). *Chicana/Latina education in everyday life: Feminista perspectives on pedagogy and epistemology.* Albany, NY: State University of New York Press.

Diaz Soto, L., Cervantes-Soon, C. G., Villarreal, E., & Campos, E. E. (2009). The Xicana sacred space: A communal circle of compromiso for educational researchers. *Harvard Educational Review, 79*(4), 755–775.

Espino, M. M., Muñoz, S. M., & Marquez Kiyama, J. (2010). Transitioning from doctoral study to the academy: Theorizing trenzas of identity for Latina sister scholars. *Qualitative Inquiry, 16*(10), 804–818.

Espino, M. M., Muñiz, M. M., Ranero, J. J., Vega, I. I., Rendón, L., Bensimon, E., Hurtado, S., & Ortiz, A. (2009, November). Negotiating identities in academe: An intergenerational dialogue among Latina scholars. Symposium presented at the annual meeting of the Association for the Study of Higher Education. Vancouver, B.C.

Godínez, F. E. (2006). Haciendo que hacer: Braiding cultural knowledge into educational practices and policies. In D. Delgado-Bernal, C. A. Elenes, F. E. Godinez, & S. Villenas (Eds.), *Chicana/Latina education in everyday life: Feminista perspectives on pedagogy and epistemology* (pp. 25–38). Albany, NY: State University of New York Press.

Henze, B. R. (2000). Who says who says?: The epistemological grounds for agency in liberatory political projects. In P. M. L. Moya & M. R. Hames-García (Eds.), *Reclaiming identity: Realist theory and the predicament of postmodernism* (pp. 229–250). Berkeley, CA: University of California Press.

herising, F. (2005). Interrupting positions: Critical thresholds and queer pro/positions. In L. Brown & S. Strega (Eds.), *Research as resistance: Critical, indigenous, & anti-oppressive approaches* (pp. 127–151). Toronto, Canada: Canadian Scholars Press.

Hurtado, A. (1998). Sitios y lenguas: Chicanas theorize feminisms. *Hypatia, 13*(2), 134–161.

Hurtado, A. (2003). Theory in the flesh: Toward an endarkened epistemology. *Qualitative Studies in Education, 16*(2), 215–225.

Kincheloe, J. L., & McLaren, P. (2005). Rethinking critical theory and qualitative research. In N. K. Denzin & Y. S. Lincoln (Eds.), *The SAGE handbook of qualitative research* (3rd ed.) (pp. 303–342). Thousand Oaks: Sage.

Ladson-Billings, G. (1995). Toward a theory of culturally relevant pedagogy. *American Educational Research Journal, 32*(3), 465–491.

Lara, I. (2002). Healing sueños for academia. In G. Anzaldúa & A. Keating (Eds.), *This bridge we call home: Radical visions for transformation* (pp. 433–438). New York, NY: Routledge.

Lather, P. (1993). Fertile obsession: Validity after poststructuralism. *Sociological Quarterly, 34*(4), 673–693.

Latina Feminist Group. (2001). *Telling to live: Latina feminist testimonios*. Durham, NC: Duke University Press.

Merriam, S. B. (Ed.). (2002). *Qualitative research in practice: Examples for discussion and analysis*. San Francisco, CA: Jossey-Bass.

Moraga, C. L., & Anzaldúa, G. E. (2002). *This bridge called my back: Writings by radical women of color*. Berkeley, CA: Third Woman Press.

Solórzano, D. G., & Yosso, T. J. (2002). Critical race methodology: Counter-storytelling as an analytical framework for education research. *Qualitative Inquiry, 8*(1), 23–44.

Trueba, H. T. (2002). Multiple ethnic, racial, and cultural identities in action: From marginality to a new cultural capital in modern society. *Journal of Latinos and Education, 1*(1), 7–28.

Making Curriculum from Scratch: *Testimonio* in an Urban Classroom

Cindy Cruz

University of California, Santa Cruz

Testimonio, as a genre of the dispossessed, the migrant, and the queer, is a response to larger discourses of nation-building and has the potential to undermine the larger narratives that often erase and make invisible the expendable and often disposable labor and experiences of immigrants, the working class, African Americans, and others. This essay explores the use of *testimonio* in urban classrooms in Los Angeles and its use as a mediating tool in critical thinking and community based learning projects. I argue that there is a pedagogy to *testimonio* that is intersubjective and accessible and that, under certain circumstances, re-centers and revitalizes curriculum in this era of standardization and accountability, a hearkening to social justice movements that begin in education.

> From our different personal, political, ethnic, and academic trajectories, we arrived at the importance of *testimonio* as a crucial means of hearing witness and inscribing into history those lived realities that would otherwise succumb to the alchemy of erasure. (The Latina Feminist Group, 2001, p. 2)

Before I became an education researcher, I was a radical teacher, a street outreach worker with LGBTQ youth, an HIV educator, a community organizer, and an activist. With this kind of mission came the commitment and the responsibility to work with and from the communities of people in ways that re-centered voice and story. In my work with young people, I thought about the best and most inclusive ways to develop sustainable leadership, reflexivity, and critical thinking, tools that helped the young people with whom I worked to think praxically and to begin analyzing our own and our sisters', brothers', and others' lived experiences. As a teacher, I wanted to make sense of what was happening in my own and the students' families, communities, and within our own bodies. We were practicing what Moraga (1981) calls "a theory in the flesh" (p. 23) and armed with Freire, Anzaldúa, Marx, safe sex education, liberation theology, harm reduction, and community-based learning, we began by interrogating the lived experience of our bodies, the stories that our bodies tell us through our scars and lesions (Cruz, 2001). In our sharing of critical stories, we practiced radical storytelling in the classroom. In this essay I examine the use of *testimonio* in urban classrooms with at-risk and LGBTQ youth, where the process of radical storytelling starts with an interrogation of our bodies. I begin with my story as a teacher in Los Angeles, California, one week after the civil unrest in Spring 1992.

I LISTEN, YOU SPEAK, AND WE HONE A REPRESENTATIVE VOICE

Yudice (1985) defines *testimonio* as:

> an authentic narrative, told by a witness who is moved to narrate by the urgency of the situation (war, revolution, oppression). Emphasizing popular oral discourse, the witness portrays his or her own experience as a representative of a collective memory and identity. Truth is summoned in the cause of denouncing a present situation of exploitation and oppression or exorcising and setting aright official history. (p. 4)

Testimonio, for Yudice, becomes the narrative of the "dispossessed"—the criminal, the queer, a child, a woman who has experienced sexual violence, a community that has organized and talked back to a history of substandard educational opportunities, an African American, the indigenous, a migrant, or a narrator who is illiterate. It is a story of a subject who has experienced or witnessed great trauma, oppression, forced migration, or violence, or of a subject who has participated in a political movement for social justice. Beverley (1993) describes *testimonio* as the "dialogical confrontation" (p. 41) with the global institutions that structure and maintain the dominance of hegemonic discourse. *Testimonio*, for Beverley, is a storytelling that challenges larger political and historic discourses and undermines other official knowledge meant to silence or erase local histories of resistance. Jameson (Stephanson, 1987) notes that while testimonial narratives involve displacement of the "master subject" of modernist literature, they do so paradoxically via the insistence on the first-person voice and proper name of the testimonial narrator:

> I always insist on a third possibility beyond the old bourgeois ego and the schizophrenic subject of our organization society today: a collective subject, decentered but not schizophrenic. It emerges in certain kinds of storytelling that can be found in Third World literature, in testimonial literature, in gossip and rumors and things of this kind ... It is decentered since the stories you tell there as an individual subject don't belong to you; you don't control them in the way the master subject of modernism would. But you don't just suffer them in the schizophrenic isolation of the first world subject of today. (Jameson, cited in Stephanson, 1987, p. 45)

When stories you tell do not belong to you, *testimonio* begins to move a reader away from an epistemology of a first world narrative to an other world narrative, where the "I" of the speaker is not configured as a "hero." Instead, the speaker is configured as one of a community of people who have suffered great trauma. The "I" of autobiography, of nation-building narratives, is not the intent of the testimonialist. The purpose of testifying is to talk back to these larger and often subsuming histories, to carefully craft truth-telling that is polyphonous in its voice and political in its intent. It is asking for a "faithful witnessing"[1] (Lugones, 2003, p. 7) from an audience or a listener, a positioning that may or may not be achievable.

One of the controversies surrounding the *testimonio*, *I, Rigoberta Menchu* (1984), derives from what Sommer (1991) argues is the rejection of the reader's "imperialist substitution" of herself with the narrator of the story. Unlike fiction's process of "*ser ella*" [being the speaker], *testimonio* lends itself toward solidarity with the subject—"*estar con la hablante*" [being with the narrator] (Sommer, 1991, p. 129). Fiction and literature ask for a suspension of beliefs, while *testimonio* asks a reader to position herself as a listener and witness. When Stoll (1999) critiques Rigoberta Menchu's *testimonio* as unreliable, he is critiquing Menchu's thesis that without the indigenous guerrilla soldier there would have been no war in Guatemala. Stoll hails from a logic of neutrality that is dangerous in its revision of histories and in its erasure of the impact of colonization on subjugated bodies. Like Rosaldo's (1989) criticism of anthropology as an instrument of empire, Stoll's positioning as the academic authority to discount or even dismiss Menchu's testimony becomes very problematic. Stoll writes:

> For scholars insecure about their moral right to depict "the Other," *testimonio* and related appeals to the native voice have been a godsend. By incorporating native voice into the syllabus and deferring to it on occasion, we validate our authority by claiming to abdicate it. This is not necessarily a bad thing—anthropology and Latin American studies are hard to imagine without it. But in an era of truth commissions, when there is a public demand to establish facts, privileging one version of a history of land conflict and homicide will not do. What if, on comparing the most hallowed *testimonio* with others, we find that it is not reliable in certain important ways? Then we would have to acknowledge that there is no substitute for our capacity to judge competing versions of events, to exercise our authority as scholars. That would unravel a generation of efforts to revalidate ourselves through idealized re-imaginings of the Other. (1999, p. 277)

In Stoll's quest for objective truth, Menchu's lies, her supposed unreliability, become the lies of all Guatemalans. Accordingly, our solidarity with the Other in the academy is nothing more than our left-leaning, romanticization of the Che-ghost of revolutionary fervor. Stoll exercises his authority as the credentialed scholar to effectively distance himself from solidarity with the victims of violence and war, where only an unbiased and neutral researcher can judge these competing versions of events. Here is where Stoll's standpoint comes into play, where *testimonio*'s collective identity and story cannot compare to an anthropologist whose belief in science and rationality cloaks his own myopic truths and subjectivities. Perhaps Stoll has developed a new syllabus that eliminates those romanticized Others from his reading lists, only able to see himself and his unbiased research as both innocent and omniscient. In his rejection of "the most hallowed" *testimonio*, Stoll reclaims the nostalgic imperialism of the neutral, distant researcher as *ser ella*, unwilling, or maybe unable, to connect to *testimonio* as "*estar con la hablante*."

What Stoll overlooks is that Menchu's *testimonio* is directed at particular audiences for political purposes, and the reader's identification with the subject is not resolute. Maybe a listener can be positioned for reflection or even with a faithful witnessing in the movement toward knowing what Lugones (1987) states as a "non-imperialistic understanding between people" (p. 11). Traveling with playfulness and loving perception is about knowing other people's worlds "to understand what it is to be them and what it is to be ourselves in their eyes. Only when we have traveled to each other's worlds are we fully subjects to each other" (p. 17).

What *testimonio* does best is offer an opportunity to "travel," positioning a listener or an audience for self-reflection. Under certain open circumstances, a listener or an audience member is given the opportunity to become complicit as an observer and as a witness. Rejection of this positioning might come from a reader's or an audience's inability to feel solidarity with the subject, an inability to travel. Perhaps Stoll and other readers of *I, Rigoberta Menchu* who reject *testimonio* cannot move outside their own Eurocentrism—it is a refusal or an inability to travel. Within this methodology of travel, it is important to contextualize *testimonio* in a critical multiculturalism that is concerned with the praxis of anti-racist and anti-oppressive pedagogies. Part of this intense criticism of *I, Rigoberta Menchu* is also the criticism of Third World storytelling displacing a western hegemonic canon and away from the "I" of individualism or the "I" of autobiography. There are no Supermen in these stories, but the stories are truth-tellings and are survivor-rich.

"Radical listening,"[2] in this sense, helps guide a listener toward an in-depth understanding of what Langout (personal communication, November 15, 2011) argues is the structural critique necessary to contextualize many of these stories as local responses to globalization, how laissez faire policies in the U.S. impact the social safety net, and the effects of austerity cuts in the everyday lives of community. The testimonialist theorizes from the body, the word made flesh. This embodied evocation is made even from the streets, where *testimonio* offers LGBTQ youth a space to talk back to the larger discourses of poverty and criminalization. In one narrative I compiled from a participant in my ethnography with queer street youth, the praxis of *testimonio* is made explicit as this narrator claims a representative voice:

> I'm writing a novel, a story of all of us who live on the streets. I'm writing it for all of those kids who can't or won't write, because someone has to know what it's like being a kid and homeless. Someone has to listen to what we have to say, because something is wrong in this country—terribly wrong when so many of us are on the streets, when so many of us are abused or thrown away, or just told to get the fuck out because our parents can't afford us anymore. Something is terribly wrong when there isn't even enough beds for those of us who want them, or that we have to wait months before we can get a home, or that we have to whore our bodies just to get something to eat. I have a story to tell to whoever wants to listen to it—and I'm writing it all down. (19-year-old street youth, cited in Cruz, 2006, p. 115)

Like the testimonialists of *This Bridge Called My Back: Writings by Radical Women of Color* (Moraga & Anzaldúa, 1981), this youth subject evokes a similar collective voice and identity to craft a narrative that is inherently a political project. As a "story of all of us who live on the street" (Cruz, 2006, p. 114), this narrator demands his right to be heard, to testify, to hone a collective story deliberately, and to claim experience and authority as part of a community of youth whose struggle for very basic rights to live without fear of reprisal or arrest, to receive consistent, appropriate, and non-judgmental medical attention, and to access clean and decent shelter. Much like the testimonies of *Bridge*, whose writers offer a critique of the feminist movement that is urgent, collaborative, and radical in their testimonies of their experiences of racism in the Women's Movement and their centering of the concepts of intersectionality and interdependence, this youth writes for his very life. This is not only a narrative of one young man's experience of homelessness and survival but also a call for social justice. The role of education researcher as a compiler of stories becomes one of listener/ethnographer, and like *Bridge*, this young speaker positions himself not only in the crafting of his story but in just a very few sentences, names an experience that reverberate through each of the queer street youth *testimonios* that I have collected. In what I argue is a critique of the neo-liberal policies that cut funding for youth and their families and programs that offer transitional housing for foster youth and people living with HIV, this story becomes the vehicle through which a radical project can be engaged and enacted.

Although not all participants in the study have developed a language and a political consciousness to begin to make sense of their world, *testimonio*, in this sense, becomes one of the few means by which LGBTQ youth can connect with and assess the conditions around which they survive. *Testimonio* demands rapt listening and its inherent intersubjectivity when we have learned to do the kind of radical listening demanded by a testimonialist, turning all of us who are willing to participate as listener, storyteller, or researcher into witnesses whether we come from a place of political solidarity or even from places of conflict.

CURRICULUM IS POWER

Curriculum, how we shape it, whose communities are represented, and how histories are depicted is power. As an English teacher, I understood that the American canon of literature was demarcated in ways that subsumed the experiences of the young people in my classrooms. The canon, with its center and margins and peripheries, created a territoriality that dictated whose stories were to be validated in the classroom, in textbooks, and in the university, and whose stories would be ignored and overlooked—Ethnic and Women's Studies, LGBTQ histories, and the erasure of working people's stories, among others. Much of the work of being an effective teacher has been about finding ways to place students' experiences central in curricula and to find ways of knowing that gives meaning to students' and their family's histories of migration, work, and community building. Multiculturalism's translation into food, festivals, and the ethnic favor-of-the-month (Banks, 1995) means that its impact would require little in the standard curriculums of U.S. public schools The struggle for re-imagined multicultural and multi-ethnic curriculums and pedagogies in the public schools reflect the much larger social and political struggles in the U.S., a war of positionality in the academy, where *testimonios* such as *I, Rigoberta Menchu* are depicted as threats to the very foundations of Western knowledge (D'Souza, 1998).

Yet telling a story of forced migration or of surviving drastic fiscal changes in the community and in the families of students, offers a way to respond to the political, cultural, and economic struggles that young people bring with them into the classroom. With an increasingly fragmented civil society, demographic transformations, and wars on multiple fronts, public schools have been embattled for decades. Under mandatory testing regimes, community-based curricula are more difficult to fund and maintain. With politicians consistently blaming the public education system for the country's loss of economic and political prestige—a nation at risk all over again—it becomes the refrain heard repeatedly from conservative pundits to teachers, parents, and students. In what ways, then, do young people and their families have the opportunity to "talk back" to these larger discourses, to tell or teach a counterstory? When do we create space in the public schools for students to critique these larger narratives of labor, masculinity, and compulsory heterosexuality?

> Sometimes I think there's more for me out there, you know? I see my friends hooking up with girls, making families, having babies, working. I don't want that shit. I mean, it's what's in place for someone like me, a man, to work and take care of his family. My family doesn't expect anything else. I don't think anything else exists for any of my family, my brothers and sisters. What I see out there is that Latinos like me are meant to work for someone else. We work hard, and we have our families and our children work hard too. Maybe that's good. But I don't want to work until my body can't work no more like my mom and my dad. I want something more, you know what I mean? What if I don't want what my dad wants me to do? What if I want a body that I'm not supposed to want?
> (17-year-old, Latino youth)

In this *testimonio*, the speaker questions his inheritance of a racialized, working-class masculinity and wonders what his father would say if he knew that his son desired a male lover? The speaker rejects the social and cultural norms of his family, questions the positioning of Latino immigrants as exploitable and ultimately expendable laborers, and in his "want[ing] something more," speaks of desire. The truth-telling in this testimony is of how a young person assesses the options that have been already put in place for him as a young Latino and how his decision to pursue his desires may move him in unexpected directions. The speaker demands a different life for himself and of life-loving practices. Pérez (1999) states, "If the subaltern could speak, would not desire be the subject of that discourse?" (p. 157). The story of this young, gay Latino becomes more than a life-story but also a narrative that moves past survivance[3] and into a space of hope and yearning. If a teacher or a researcher listens carefully, she will hear stories of love and desire, notions that both trouble and extend not only knowledge production in education research but further nuance our understandings of the lived experiences of LGBTQ youth.

CREATING A CURRICULUM FROM SCRATCH

The Aztec informants of Bernardino de Sahagun, who recited *náhuatl* poetry that had been conserved by oral tradition and who thus gave him the story of the terrible experiences of the Conquest—weren't these informants actually testimonialists? (Bueno, 1978, p. 13)

I began teaching in Los Angeles one week after the civil unrest of the Rodney King trial exploded on the city streets. I remember riding past shattered storefront windows and still-smoldering businesses to the schools I was partnered with, and I saw people armed with brooms and shovels working together to rebuild their neighborhoods near Crenshaw and 52nd, Santa Monica and Sycamore, Vermont and 82nd, and Avalon and 79th—all places where I met and worked with young people and their teachers in community schools. In these parts of the city that were deeply affected by civic neglect and now fire, I was convinced that we needed to tell our stories of the violence and the burnings, to make spaces where young people could reflect and interrogate what they had witnessed. This was not to be business as usual in the classroom, where the histories and narratives of young people and their families were marginalized. *Testimonio* became central in teaching and reflecting on the everyday experiences of post-Rodney King Los Angeles.

In her work as an adult educator and poet in Nicaragua, Randall (1984) writes, "It is no accident, because recognition of, knowledge of, and understanding of one's personal and collective identity is essential to people's revolution" (p. 10), where *testimonio* was seen as an integral part of a Sandinista literacy program. Like Randall's project where teaching reading and writing was taught along with compiling the oral histories of the Nicaraguan people, storytelling in this project is configured as part of a community-based curriculum. Video poems and short truth-telling narratives serve as vehicles for documenting the present and also as a tool for the recovery of a collective identity wrought out of histories of migration and struggle.

In the experiential education program I taught for in Los Angeles schools, approximately 32 high school students participated in the community-based learning program from two continuation schools.[4] I also met and worked with students from other continuation schools that were working with the community-based learning program in other capacities. Students interned in paid local community-based organizations in their neighborhoods, such as the Red Cross, local libraries and archives, legal aid services, health clinics, and immigration service centers, for approximately 8 to 12 hours a week. Working closely with teachers, curriculum coordinators would research and develop learning activities and help students create curricula based on the experiences and observations of students at their community sites. A record of daily events and curriculum goals and objectives was collected in teaching journals to help assess whether an activity or learning environment or pedagogy worked effectively with students. The teaching journals also captured the daily activities and the stories I heard from students and teachers and my observations of the school community. Unstructured interviews of students and teachers continued weekly throughout the program's tenure to assess the efficacy of the schools with which I worked.

My role at the schools was primarily as teacher-researcher and, as part of the teaching team, I was to assist in moving community-based learning forward in an effort to help foster a critical, interdisciplinary curriculum within continuation schools. I met often with students and their teachers while debriefing the week's events from their field sites, where issues of migration, language, and translation; access to basic resources; and police brutality were common. Thinking about the demographic and economic changes in our communities was foundational for the curriculum. In 1992, Los Angeles already reflected a massive reduction of core services for inner city residents, and tensions ran high between communities. There was a sense of urgency in teaching during this time; building a community of critical thinkers in these schools began with sharing their life stories.

I often begin curricula with sharing life-stories, through which students begin to learn about each other. But this was the first day after a week of chaos and violence, and I remember distinctly the nervous energy both students and teachers brought with them into the classroom. Students formed a circle and we began to talk about our fears, our bodies, and what we saw in these last few days. I asked them to tell me a story about a scar:

> This scar on my arm, I love this scar. My mom accidently burned me with an iron and now that she's gone, it's the thing that reminds me of her everyday.
> [Pulling up shirt to show a quarter-sized indentation on his back] This scar is where they cut me when I was walking home from school last year. And I try all the time to forget about it, but it's still there. I remember who did this. It's a reminder written on my skin!
> This scar I made myself when I was too scared to tell my dad I was pregnant.

One student told us that she was washing clothes for her mother in a laundromat on the first night (April 29, 1992) of the uprisings. She said she saw men pushing open the doors and smashing the machines for the quarters inside. She scratched herself on the edge of a corner backing away from it all. That was her scar. She said she was so scared that she could not move from where she was. "My mouth opened but nothing came out," the student told us.

Felman (1999) writes that testimony is composed of "bits and pieces of a memory that has been overwhelmed by occurrences that have not settled into understanding" (p. 5), and that this snapshot of memory is simply a discursive practice, a "speech act." Surely these memories overwhelm both emotionally and psychologically. Yet I would not have these stories stay in the realm of language, as a "speech act," no matter what the impact. Is it enough to tell you my story in an era of ever-widening disparities between rich and poor? Because it seems to me that in 1992 L.A., we were always already mired in an economic downturn. These neighborhoods of Los Angeles never recovered. In 1992 Angelenos burned what had been smoldering decades earlier. Now these communities bear witness to the aftermath of rage and destruction in these continuation school classrooms where short pieces of truth-tellings are offered by students to anyone who cares to listen to them.

Scarry (1987) suggests that under extreme circumstances, language becomes unintelligible or inadequate to describe certain kinds of traumatic experiences. In this instance, the student in the laundromat describes how, in the immediacy of witnessing the chaos of the first nights, she was unable to respond. *Testimonios*, in this case, are not only the fragments of information that students offer, but also are fragments of memory of an experience that cannot be assimilated. Language fails some students, and words cannot describe what so many students have witnessed. I am no counselor, yet we all required this space of healing and trust in these classrooms, where on that first day teaching after the five days of civil unrest, we all laughed and cried so hard that it was difficult to distinguish among any of our emotions. To tell our stories in our own words and to name ourselves in those classrooms was about reconnecting and affirming our refusal of an uncomplicated response to civil unrest.

TESTIMONIO AS SOCIAL JUSTICE PRACTICE

Bishop (1998), in his work with Maori communities, makes explicit a teaching and research agenda committed to social justice, suggesting that pedagogy and methodology must be:

> Positioned in such a way as to no longer need to seek to give voice to others, to empower others, to emancipate others, to refer to others as subjugated voices, but rather to listen and participate in a process that facilitates the development in people as a sense of themselves as agentic and of having an authoritarian voice [that] challenges colonial and neo-colonial discourses that inscribe "otherness." (pp. 207–208)

In the schools in which I worked, developing *testimonio* as a social justice practice meant centering youth stories and experiences in the classroom. These stories of the body became the cultural artifacts that allowed students to interrogate their experiences, to mediate how these personal narratives needed to be theorized as political maneuvers. Combining perspectives of Freire (1970) and Vygotsky (1978) allowed me to help scaffold students into other levels of consciousness. The queer body became a mediating tool. "We all have them—scars—and they all have stories beneath the skin." I would ask of them: "Tell me a story about a scar." and one by one, students would begin to tell stories about their lives, suturing together narratives of their families, their bodies, and their desires. Students and teachers learned to listen to each other's bodies and learned to share the stories of a community surviving in this post-Rodney King Los Angeles. Teaching near the intersections of Manchester and Vermont, or Santa Monica and Highland Boulevards, students told stories of violence and abuse, migration, loneliness, and sometimes resistance. As part of pushing back against school policies that created often brutal environments for queer and questioning youth, students wrote and narrated the stories they always wanted to read. They wrote and created stories that "talked back."

> I've known I've been gay since I was 5 years old. I had crushes on my friends, and I was aware that I had feelings for other boys. But it was a little easier in my family for me because my uncle is gay, even though my father was very upset that he had a "queer" son. My mom is okay with it. She said she knew it was coming, but my dad has a harder time with it. I don't know what my sexuality has to do with his manhood, but I've learned to walk a wide circle around him. I'm at [local LGBT educational center] because my school either refused or ignored all the abuse and harassment I was getting every day at my old high school. Every day I was called "faggot" or "punk" in the hallways, in the classrooms, even teachers didn't stop it when students called me names right in front of them. When I complained, teachers would say things like, "Well, if he didn't flaunt it all over the place,"

or "He just wants attention." And these were black teachers! So I'm here to finish my senior year without all the shit. 'Course that don't mean there ain't shit here too, you know? (17-year-old student)

The work of *testimonio* demands that listeners acknowledge these experiences. This scenario tells the truth—the truth of a student critical of the rampant homophobia and impunity in the public schools— and his story of the inaction of teachers and administrators to create a safe learning environment for LGBTQ students explains what led him to drop out of his comprehensive high school and into a drop-out recovery program. Beverley (1993) and Ferman (2001) suggest that *testimonio* tells much larger "truths" as "the question of whether our self-description ought to be constructed around a relation to a particular collection of human beings" (Rorty, 1991, p. 24). Truth, in these ways, is multiple—or *toda la realidad de un pueblo*—the truth of a whole people rather than the singular "reality of a whole people" (Menchu, cited in Beverley 1993, p. 89). These youth narratives, mediated by a compromised social body[5], privilege the voices and histories of poverty and displacement, tell much different truths, stories that often talk back to nation-building ideologies. What does it mean when a student says that he "walk[s] a wide circle around [his] father"?

For this gay, black student's narrative, the story becomes a stand-in for hundreds of LGBTQ youth who have been pushed out of schools because of harassment and violence unchecked. Sharing these truths among students becomes a valuable mediating tool (or "codification," (Freire, 1970, p. 106) as youth begin to examine closely their own communities, homes, and schools. *Testimonio* becomes central in the efforts to build curriculum that helps students think critically about their experiences in and outside of the schoolyard. To bear witness as part of a community of young people thinking together is about transgressing a stance of isolation, to speak for other at-risk and LGBTQ students (the two are not mutually exclusive) and to other students, is to move beyond oneself. A pedagogy of social justice depends on this movement beyond the student and knowledge or reflexive understanding of the experience cannot be separate from the *testimonio*. A listener is not what Laub (1999) asserts as "a blank screen on which the event comes to be inscribed for the first time" (p. 57). Listeners bring their own histories and experiences to this "hearing." But maybe *testimonio* is asking a listener to travel:

> We are fully dependent on each other for the possibility of being understood and without this understanding we are not intelligible, we do not make sense, we are not solid, visible, integrated, we are lacking. So travelling to each other's worlds would enable us to *be* through *loving* each other. (Lugones, 1987, p. 8)

A speaker, especially a witness to a social upheaval, violence, poverty, or impunity, requests a tremendous libidinal response, one of *loving*. It is something that we teachers and researchers have yet to talk about, to involve the body present and the recognition that to be a faithful witness to a story of trauma or oppression, there is a responsibility we owe to the speaker. The openness required to listen with love necessitates that our bodies be present, not exhausted, not distracted, but wholly focused and vulnerable in a way that allows travel. Lugones (1987) states that for many, "our travelling is done unwillfully to hostile White/Anglo worlds, and makes it difficult for us to appreciate the value of this part of how we live our lives and its connection to loving" (p. 3). It is not only a profound empathy with the testimonialist but a skill necessary to move forward social justice work.

CONCLUSION

The stories that came out of these Los Angeles classrooms serve to emphasize the urgency of the work with at-risk and LGBTQ youth. What did it mean to teach these stories of the body, to make this brown and queer body the center of radical politics? Students located their stories in the classrooms, students wrote their own books, re-invented themselves in video work and poetry, talked about their bodies and what becomes inscribed upon them and how, and together students and teachers looked at our communities and tried to understand the trauma and anger and sometimes even the hope that comes out in these streets. We also learned how hard it was to be present and to listen; without these skills of radical listening and decolonizing pedagogies it becomes that much more difficult to lay a foundation for a social justice curriculum. I am reminded again of Lugones' wisdom when she writes about learning to "world"-travel with an attitude of playfulness and loving perception: "I could practice" (Lugones, 1987, p. 13). Schools should be the place where "practice" happens everyday.

Now teaching at the university, I bring these tools I used in the streets and communities—the decolonizing pedagogies, radical literacies, new readings of the body, *testimonios*—into courses and into educational research, using the *testimonio* practices that are familiar to me and to other activist researchers. In this way, *testimonio* is configured not only as the oral histories of members of the community but also as a means of honing new subjectivities for emerging social and political youth movements. *Testimonio* is political narrative, oral history, traumatic memory, pedagogical, radical methodology, and is part of the cognitive requirements for new radical literacies and subjectivities with youth.

For academics who are seeking new methodologies of solidarity with the communities they are working with, *testimonio* sets in motion a process that recognizes the manner in which "truth" is constructed in education and social science research. *Testimonio*, as a storytelling genre for the dispossessed and the displaced, offers a way of collecting and compiling narrative that makes complicit both the roles of a researcher and the subject. It is an acknowledgement of the constructiveness of personal narrative and life history and of how science, as defined by Stoll (1999) as "hypothesis, evidence, and generalization," (p. 247) implicitly positions itself in studies of the "subaltern" as a colonial project. It is the recognition that the production of knowledge in anthropology and education is an ideological project and despite the objections of Stoll, the choice of *testimonio* as a methodology forces reinvention and radical repositioning of power for both researcher and subject. In essence, *testimonio* begins the process of unpacking truths and "truth-tellings" from its Western epistemological speculations. LGBTQ street youth who offer *testimonios* construct if not the real as such, then certainly as Jara and Vidal (1986) suggest, "a trace of the real, of that history which, as such, is inexpressible" (p. 3). Often these fragmented narratives are all we have of youth experiences, inexpressible, a little bit of their time compiled, but a short testimony of the daily conditions of their lives. We must ask ourselves as researchers, is it enough just to tell you my story? If research or "truth-telling" is intersubjective (and thus pedagogical), maybe this renders positivism obsolete—and from here we recoup these new truths.

NOTES

1. Lugones (2003) defines "faithful witnessing" as "providing ways of witnessing faithfully and of convey-ing meaning against the oppressive grain. To witness faithfully is difficult, given the manyness of worlds of

sense related through power so that oppressive and fragmenting meanings saturate many worlds of sense in hard to detect ways. A collaborator witnesses on the side of power, while a faithful witness witnesses against the grain of power, on the side of resistance" (p. 7).

2. Langout explains radical listening this way: "Angela Davis defines "radical" as "grasping things at the root." Radical listening, therefore, is listening for root ideas that are connected to a structural analysis. This means listening for what is being said and what is left unsaid. It means co-creating a space where what has been rendered invisible can be seen, spoken, and heard. To practice radial listening is to take seriously what is being said and to be in dialogue with the speaker in ways that facilitate a structural, radical analysis" (Personal communication, November 15, 2011).

3. Survivance is a term used by Native scholar Gerald Vizenor (2008) to describe the Native American active sense of presence over historical absence, deracination, and oblivion, an acknowledgement of endurance and creative persistence of life-loving practices under colonialism.

4. Continuations schools are often small schools designed by school districts to help recover credits for students who have left or dropped out of a comprehensive high school.

5. By "compromised social body" I intend to describe the unhealthiness or toxicity of the environment and those who live/work in it, but in particular the body made ill or frail because of environmental and poverty-based issues.

REFERENCES

Banks, J. (1995). Multicultural education and curriculum transformation. *The Journal of Negro Education*, *64*(4), 390–400.

Beverley, J. (1993) *Against literature*. Minneapolis, MN: University of Minnesota Press.

Bishop, R. (1998). Freeing ourselves from neo-colonial domination in research: A Maori approach to creating knowledge. *International Journal of Qualitative Studies in Education*, *11*(2), 199–219.

Bueno, S. (1978). Testimonio en campana. *Revolucion y Cultura*, *71*, 9–17.

Cruz, C. (2001). Toward an epistemology of a brown body. *International Journal of Qualitative Studies in Education*, *14*(5), 657–669.

Cruz, C. (2006). *Testimonial narratives of queer street youth: Toward an epistemology of a brown body*. (Doctoral Dissertation). Retrieved from ProQuest Dissertations and Theses. (Accession Order No. AAT 3251434).

D'Souza, D. (1998). *Illiberal education: The politics of race and sex on campus*. New York, NY: Free Press.

Felman, S. & Laub, D. (1999). *Testimony: Crises of witnessing in literature, psychoanalysis and history*. New York, NY: Routledge.

Ferman, C. (2001). Textual truth, historical truth, and media truth: Everybody speaks about the Menchus. In A. Arias (Ed.), *The Rigoberta Menchu controversy* (pp. 156–170). Minneapolis, MN: University of Minnesota Press.

Freire, P. (1970). *Pedagogy of the oppressed*. New York, NY: Continuum.

Jara, R., & Vidal, H. (1986). *Testimonio y literatura*. Minneapolis, MN: Institute for the Study of Ideologies and Literature.

The Latina Feminist Group. (2001). *Telling to live: Latina feminist testimonios*. Durham, NC: Duke University Press.

Laub, D. (1999). Bearing witness, or the vicissitudes of listening. In S. Felman & D. Laub, *Testimony: Crises of witnessing in literature, psychoanalysis and history* (pp. 57–74). New York, NY: Routledge.

Lugones, M. (1987). Playfulness, "world"-travelling, and loving perception. *Hypatia*, *2*(2), 3–19.

Lugones, M. (2003). *Pilgrimages/Peregrinajes: Theorizing coalition against multiple oppressions*. Lanham, MD: Rowan & Littlefield.

Menchu, R. (1984). *I, Rigoberta Menchu: An Indian woman in Guatemala*. (E. Burgos-Debray, Ed., A. Wright, Trans.). London, UK: Verso.

Moraga, C. (1981). Entering the lives of others: Theory in the flesh. In C. Moraga & G. Anzaldúa (Eds.), *This bridge called my back: Writings by radical women of color* (p. 23–25). Boston, MA: Kitchen Press.

Moraga, C., & Anzaldúa, G. (Eds.). (1981). *This bridge called my back: Writings by radical women of color*. Boston, MA: Kitchen Press.

Pérez, E. (1999). *The decolonial imaginary: Writing Chicanas into history*. Bloomington, IN: Indiana University Press.

Randall, M. (1984). *Testimonios: A guide to oral history*. Toronto: Participatory Research Group.

Rorty, R. (1991). *Objectivity, relativism, and truth: Philosophical Papers, 1*. New York, NY: Cambridge University Press

Rosaldo, R. (1989). *Culture and truth: The remaking of social analysis*. Boston, MA: Beacon Press.

Scarry, E. (1987). *The body in pain: The making and unmaking of the world*. New York, NY: Oxford University Press.

Sommer, D. (1991). No secrets: Rigoberta's guarded truth. *Women's Studies, 20*(1), 51–72.

Stephanson, A. (1987). Regarding postmodernism: A conversation with Fredric Jameson. *Social Text, 17*, 29–54.

Stoll, D. (1999). *Rigoberta Menchu and the story of all Guatemalans*. Boulder, CO: Westview.

Vizenor, G. R. (2008). *Survivance: Narratives of Native presence*. Lincoln, NE: University of Nebraska Press.

Vygotsky, L. (1978). *Mind in society: The development of higher psychological processes*. Cambridge, MA: Harvard University Press.

Yudice, G. (1985). *Central American testimonio*. Unpublished manuscript.

Getting There *Cuando No Hay Camino* (When There Is No Path): Paths to Discovery *Testimonios* by Chicanas in STEM

Norma E. Cantú

University of Texas at San Antonio

This essay outlines how the book, *Paths to Discovery: Autobiographies from Chicanas with Careers in Science, Mathematics, and Engineering* (Cantú, 2008) came about. I then use *testimonio* theory to analyze the narratives in this book as the data of a qualitative study, and I describe the general themes that the analysis highlights.[1] I scrutinize the factors that affected the authors' success in school and career, including the roles of parents, teachers, extended family, and community; I also describe the impact of the intersection of gender, race, and class on their academic journeys. This article looks at Chicanas[2] in science, technology, engineering, and mathematics (STEM) fields and concludes with policy recommendations for increasing the number of Chicanas and Latinas in STEM.

May we do work that matters. *Vale la pena*, it's worth the pain. (Anzaldúa, 2005, p. 102)

As a Chicana in south Texas, I loved science, but there was no infrastructure to nurture or present the option of pursuing it as a field of study. My junior high counselor dissuaded me from aiming too high. When I said I wanted to be a physicist, he smiled and said I might consider being a teacher of science, and since I was good in English I should consider teaching English. Such perceptions, coupled with teachers who mostly "baby sat" and assigned memorization and rote learning, doomed me. Also, I did not have access to much mathematics beyond high school trigonometry, and as an undergraduate I was not required to take math beyond college algebra. I avoided the biology class where we were required to dissect a frog, so my limited exposure to science consisted of a physics class in high school and a chemistry class as a college freshman. Both were disappointing and turned me off, mostly due to poor teaching: My college chemistry professor was always late to class and reeked of alcohol. He was so inebriated some times that we could not understand what he was saying as he lectured. To add to the problem, our class was held in an old army barracks converted into a chemistry lab. While my high school physics teacher, Mrs. Baird, was a female, I did not feel any kind of connection to her; she favored the males in the class.

Perhaps it is my own frustration that has impelled me to work on the topic of Chicanas and STEM, as I see similar conditions, including poorly prepared teachers and lack of resources, in today's classrooms. I think of the young Chicana student brimming with curiosity, with a desire to know how the world works, wanting to be a scientist, a Chicana sitting in classrooms without competent teachers or with poor facilities or without an encouraging word from anyone. In the future she could be traveling to Mars, engaged in medical discoveries or even be the one to push science to the next scientific revolution. But she may never get to do any of these things if no one nurtures her scientific spirit or gives her the solid preparation it will take to succeed in college.

The backdrop to this analysis is the crisis presented by the very small number of Chicanas and Latinas who major in mathematics or science disciplines and the even smaller percentage who enter doctoral programs in STEM. Seeking to give *Paths to Discovery* a context, I asked Puerto Rican education researcher Deborah Santiago to compile data on Latinas in STEM. I knew of her excellent work as Vice President for Policy and Research at *Excelencia* in Education, the organization that focuses on Latino student success in higher education. In her brief piece, she cites National Center for Education Statistics figures: Latinas earned 60% of all bachelor's degrees awarded to Latinas/os in 2005 but only 37% of the bachelor's degrees awarded to Latinas are in STEM (Santiago, 2008, p. 226). Additionally, she notes, "Latinas earned more than half of the bachelor's degrees awarded to Hispanics in biological and biomedical sciences (63%), and almost half (46%) in mathematics. While pointing out that there has been progress in the last 30 years, she notes that Latinas "lagged behind males in degrees earned in all STEM fields except biology and biomedical sciences" (p. 226). She especially notes that only 22% of Latina/os enrolled in engineering programs are female.

A look at more recent data reveals that the situation is not much better. The data gathered by the National Science Foundation (NSF), show the low number of Latinas/os in STEM areas, overall, and in certain fields, such as computer science or mathematics, in particular. Table 1 shows that almost half of the doctoral degrees awarded to Hispanics in 2007 were in science and engineering (48.5%); about one-quarter (25.4%) of those were in psychology, and only .3% were in mathematics and statistics, and .2% were in computer science. The statistics reveal that there is still much to be done to raise the numbers in particular fields of science and engineering.

However, the numbers do not tell the whole story. The student participants and the speakers at the *Adelante* Project, part of the *Mujeres Activas en Letras y Cambio Social* (the Organization of Women Active in Letters and Social Change) (MALCS), conference in San Antonio in 2003, did not see themselves as statistics breaking barriers, but that is what they are as Chicanas in STEM fields. The Chicana students heard stories from Chicana scientists and mathematicians; I subsequently gathered these stories in a book, *Paths to Discovery,* a collection that indeed shows that numbers do not tell the whole story. The narratives by the Chicana mathematicians, scientists, and engineers as well as Chicana[3] students in STEM fields certainly do defy the expectations of some of their counselors and teachers, as revealed in their *testimonios*, and continue to break barriers today, as they continue working in STEM areas and achieve their goals of earning doctorate degrees and pursuing careers in science.

So, while I celebrate the accomplishments of the women who gave their written *testimonios* for *Paths to Discovery*, I note the tremendous impact they have had on their fields and bemoan the lost advances that others, who did not succeed, might have made. Among the young scholars who attended that MALCS gathering in 2003, several did not reach their goals due to financial or other concerns. Invariably in our discussions, the authors noted and observed the negative impact of the racist and oppressive conditions on the success of the majority of their classmates; such was specifically noted in narratives focused in the Southwest, such as Nogales, Arizona or in California. The authors in *Paths to Discovery* acknowledge the help that certain teachers,

TABLE 1
Doctorates Awarded to U.S. Citizens and Permanent Residents, by Sex, Field and Race/Ethnicity: 2007
(Percent Distribution)

Sex and Field	Hispanic
Female (number)	1,242
All fields	100.0
S&E	48.5
Science	44.8
Agricultural sciences	0.4
Biological sciences	9.3
Computer sciences	0.2
Earth, atmospheric, and ocean sciences	1.0
Mathematics and statistics	0.3
Physical sciences	2.7
Psychology	25.4
Social sciences	5.6
Engineering	3.6
Non-S&E	51.5
Education	24.1
Health	12.2
Humanities	7.0
Other non-S&E	8.2

Source: Women, Minorities and Persons with Disabilities (National Science Foundation, 2012).

neighbors, family members, or even strangers provided and marveled at the ways that certain colleagues or mentors had come into their lives and been "angels" helping them to achieve their goals. Such was the case, for example, of Niebla (2008) whose high school mathematics teacher assisted her with higher mathematics that was not taught in the school. Unfortunately, these "angels" do not eliminate barriers for every Latina who is drawn to the STEM fields. While the overarching reach of the *testimonios* described here lies in their potential to motivate and inspire students to continue their studies in STEM, the work cannot stop there. We must delve deeper into the systemic and structural elements that need to be in place for all Chicanas and Latinas to navigate the educational system in STEM areas successfully. In the following section, I trace the development of the *testimonio* theory I use, grounding it in an earlier book project, *Telling to Live: Latina Feminist Testimonios* (The Latina Feminist Group[4], 2001). In discussing the idea or concept of *testimonio* in this earlier book, my goal is that we can see these life stories or *autohistorias*, as Anzaldúa (1987) calls her own genre of life-writing, as fitting vehicles for narrating the struggles and triumphs of the Chicanas in these STEM fields.

FINDING *PATHS TO DISCOVERY*

In the 1990s, I participated in a project to theorize our conditions as Latinas in academia. The Latina Feminist Group utilized the practice of *testimonio*, or life story, as the preferred and most appropriate tool to document what our paths had entailed. Thus, we set about gathering first-person accounts of the pitfalls and the serendipitous routes each of us had taken to arrive at our individual places in academia. Some of us were professors—from different disciplines in the humanities and social sciences—a few were administrators, and a couple were still graduate students; altogether 18 Latinas—Puerto Ricans, Costa Ricans, Dominicans, Cubans, and Chicanas—met over a period of six years in different locations from New York City to Colorado to California. We worked as a collective, attempting to gather perspectives from various *Latinidades*[5]and disciplines. The result of our work is the book, *Telling to Live: Latina Feminist* Testimonios (The Latina Feminist Group, 2001). However, something was lacking from our project: the stories of our sisters in science, mathematics, and engineering.

While I was very familiar with the marginalized status of Chicanas in academia, especially in Humanities fields, as a professor of English I had little knowledge of the crises that Chicanas who work in the STEM fields face; my continuing interest in documenting stories led me to the intriguing and necessary work of helping to give their stories a voice. In 2003, soil chemist Elvia Niebla and I applied for a small NSF grant to bring together senior scientists and mathematicians at the annual meeting of the Latina academic organization, MALCS, that we were hosting at the University of Texas at San Antonio (UTSA). We titled the effort the "*Adelante* Project" and held concurrent sessions during the MALCS conference.[6] Our goal was to have the eight scientists and mathematicians speak to 27 graduate and undergraduate Chicana students majoring in science, mathematics, and engineering who were attending the MALCS symposium, so that those students could interact with successful Chicana scientists, mathematicians, and engineers well into their careers and be motivated to stay on their chosen STEM path.

The invited students heard the personal stories and current work interests of the Chicana scientists and mathematicians.[7] Our goal was met as we saw the intense and engaged reaction of the students. The evaluation forms submitted by meeting attendees confirmed that for many of the students, it was tremendously affirming to see and hear other Chicanas who had achieved what they aspired to achieve: careers in mathematics, science, and engineering. The invited speakers, administrators, professors, and doctoral students cared deeply and wanted to be involved in a project that would encourage other Chicanas to seek a career path in the STEM fields. Upon hearing the inspiring stories that these faculty members and administrators told, I remembered our Latina Feminist Group and our pledge to duplicate the process with other Latinas who had traversed a similar path but whose stories remained untold.

Thus our book, titled *Paths to Discovery: Autobiographies from Chicanas with Careers in Science, Mathematics, and Engineering*[8] (Cantú, 2008) was conceived. I guided the eight Chicana presenters from that *Adelante* Project part of the MALCS conference plus several other Chicanas with STEM careers through the process of writing their own *testimonios*. This article presents the process by which these autobiographies, or *testimonios*, were created and came to publication; my own analysis and findings from the essays; and finally a set of policy recommendations for helping to alleviate the low numbers of Chicanas in STEM fields and for helping every young Chicana who dreams of being a scientist to achieve her dream.

FORGING *PATHS TO DISCOVERY*

In this section, I discuss the gathering of the *testimonios* and thereby trace the path from idea to publication, for it illuminates the path that I hope other groups, especially other women of color, will follow in recapturing the stories of women of color in STEM or in other areas where our stories have been erased.

The *testimonio*s for *Paths to Discovery* were put together by means of writing workshops held at meetings of the Society for the Advancement of Chicanos and Native Americans in Science (SACNAS) and funded in part by the *Adelante* Project grant. Participants included the eight Chicana scientists and mathematicians who presented at the MALCS conference in addition to a Chicana engineer and two other Chicana scientists who had been invited but had not been able to participate in that conference.

At the writing workshops, participants were asked key questions around which to construct their narratives, questions about significant events along their paths, persons who had influenced them, and obstacles they had overcome. These questions allowed the authors to explore how they had navigated the rough, often inhospitable, waters of academia, to acknowledge the positive influences along the way, and to recognize the significance of their achievements.

This process also included spending time talking as a group, telling our stories *platicando*, talking and chatting, in much the same way we had done with the Latina Feminist Group, although without the luxury of extended periods of time to experience each other's company. Many of the writers found relating the most challenging aspects of their stories to be difficult. My previous experience gathering stories has shown that reliving painful experiences and revisiting difficult times, while therapeutic, can drive the writer to subterfuge and to writing that is not in touch with their core feelings. Our intent was to foster a supportive environment in which the participants felt trusting enough of themselves and of one another to be able to share as truthfully as possible in their essays.

While most of the Chicana participants in the *Adelante* Project knew one another, there were some who were meeting for the first time. For those who knew each other, stories and backgrounds were not new or revelatory; for those new to the group, trust had to be established. Perhaps their excitement at being with other Latinas in STEM assisted in the creation of an environment in which they all felt at ease. Inherent in qualitative research methods is the factor of serendipity (Fine & Deegan, 1996). For this enterprise, trust and serendipity played a large role in the success of the *testimonio* strategy. Given that none of the participants had written autobiographies or had much experience in writing reflective personal essays, my collaborator, Elvia Niebla, and I felt it necessary that they read *Telling to Live* and come to an awareness of what *testimonio* entails. The participants were given copies of the book to prepare for writing their *testimonio*s. Reading of other Latinas and the process of *testimoniando*, I believe, added to establishing the necessary trust among the participants. In like fashion, chance brought together these generous Latinas who were willing to engage in a writing experience so outside of their academic and professional expertise. They exhibited reticence and some concerns, but serendipitously the group arrived at a self-monitoring standard that allowed for a high level of trust. The tears and the laughter they shared, as well as the commonality of experience, soon soothed any rough edges or misgivings of some members of the group about displays of emotion; in general the group cohered and supported each other. Observing these interactions and the essay writing process was an integral part of the study; analysis of these observations incorporates ethnographic methodology and is discussed further below.

To complete the project, I gathered the essays, gave the authors editing feedback, and received their final drafts. I then added an introductory essay by social psychologist Aída Hurtado, who wrote an overview of the book, noting specific concepts that are critical for an analysis of the narratives. I submitted the book manuscript to the American Association for the Advancement for Science (AAAS) to be published with the title, *Flor y Ciencia (Flower and Science): Chicanas in Mathematics, Science and Engineering* (Cantú, 2006). After the initial print run, a revised and enlarged manuscript was published in 2008 by UCLA's Chicano Studies Research Center as *Paths to Discovery: Autobiographies from Chicanas with Careers in Mathematics, Science and Engineering* (Cantú, 2008).

WALKING THE *PATHS TO DISCOVERY*

Paths to Discovery is a path-breaking publication in that it informs us about what nurtures and sustains Chicanas/Latinas who follow a STEM path. Several key questions come to mind as I reflect on how the collection of autobiographical stories lay out a trajectory and critical factors along the way for Chicanas/Latinas in STEM: How can *Paths to Discovery* be used to increase the number of Chicanas/Latinas in STEM? Who will listen/read these stories—in other words, who is our audience? And how will *Paths to Discovery* help shape the environment for future Chicana students and faculty in STEM. The first question is somewhat answered by the other two; as Chicana/Latina students and faculty read the first person narratives, they will identify and gain confidence and trust that they, too, will succeed. But the answer is a bit trickier in that the book must reach all its intended audiences. Yes, students are a critical source but so are the faculty members who teach them. I want the book to become a fund of knowledge for educators to draw from as they work with Chicana/Latina students. In addition, the lone Chicana assistant professor at a small liberal arts college, or even at a large research institution, who is feeling alien in that inhospitable environment that is the academy, can find comfort in knowing that she is not the first, that there are others like her, and that she can tap them and other networks that can sustain her in her chosen field. SACNAS and MALCS, for example, are academic organizations in which she might find like-minded women and thereby feel part of a larger network of Chicanas in STEM. So, while the first audience is the student and the faculty member who is herself a Chicana—or a Latina, for the issues seem to be the same for non-Chicanas/Latinas in STEM—a second audience is the mainstream STEM faculty member, the scientist, the engineer, or the mathematician who may be oblivious to the predicament faced by Chicanas/Latinas in STEM classrooms and STEM careers. Those who make decisions about these Chicanas' careers and academic standing must understand the context of their lives. *Paths to Discovery* teaches us all—the students, the faculty, and the policymakers—what an invaluable resource Chicanas/Latinas are and what values, cultural and otherwise, inform their success stories. The lens through which we view the stories (i.e., the way we read the narratives) also informs the reader about the academic and scholarly framework that reflects cultural and historical ways of telling stories. While the numbers reveal the statistical data and tell a compelling story, the narratives offer solutions and tell the complete story of Chicanas in STEM. The storytelling itself, then, the *testimoniando*, becomes a way to gather information.

TESTIMONIOS THEORY AS ANALYTIC LENS

I anchor my analysis of the *testimonios* gathered in *Paths to Discovery* on a theory developed for analyzing the narratives of certain subjects, mostly in Latin America. *Testimonio* theory represents, as the editors of *Telling to Live* (Latina Feminist Group, 2001) state, "a crucial means of bearing witness and inscribing into history those lived realities that would otherwise succumb to the alchemy of erasure" (p. 2). My use of *testimonio* reframes the ways that Beverley (2004) and other scholars have deployed *testimonio* as a methodology for investigating and analyzing oral histories or interviews of specific populations in a number of disciplines. For example, in education, Pérez-Huber (2009) cites specific methodological strategies for employing *testimonio* in Latino critical race research. Beverley indicates that the Latin American *testimonio* tradition includes an abject subject whose voice is mediated by an interlocutor. *Paths to Discovery* deviates from this oral tradition and is more in line with the Latina Feminist Group's use of the term and the theory by gathering written *testimonios*. It could be argued that while most of the contributors to *Paths to Discovery* come from abject subject positions, they no longer belong in that position as university professors and scientists. Further, the *Paths to Discovery* authors combine oral and written narratives, injecting their positionality and often revealing how the academy othered their experiences and negated their "funds of knowledge,"[9] (Moll, Amanti, Neff, & González, 2001)—the assets that a student brings to the classroom.

In her analysis, Hurtado (2008) observes that the "Master Narratives" of success have excluded non-traditional stories and have entirely ignored the variant paths that Latinas have used to achieve success. The contributors in *Paths to Discovery* seek to inscribe into the history of science their "lived realities," so as to resist that "alchemy of erasure" (Latina Feminist Group, 2001, p. 167) that their absence and the absence of their stories would constitute. As I cull through the *testimonios* in *Paths to Discovery*, the subject position of the authors becomes apparent, regardless of their class position, and invariably underscores gender and ethnic positionality in STEM. More importantly, I also glean how certain common elements and topics surface; thus, we can ascertain that *testimonio* methodology fits the content and is most useful as we mine the narratives for information that leads to successful strategies and policies for increasing the number of Latinas in STEM. Using *testimonio* as a methodology allows for discussion of how such a strategy reveals a more in-depth appreciation than a traditional close reading would reveal. The common threads that emerge from an analysis of the collected *testimonios* offer insights into the ways these Chicanas in STEM fields managed to survive often against apparently insurmountable odds. The use of *testimonio* theory opens the discussion of the texts in useful ways to help us discern the key elements that Chicanas in STEM fields must contend with, both in academic settings and in their formation as scientists, mathematicians, and engineers.

FINDINGS AND ANALYSIS OF *TESTIMONIOS* FROM *PATHS TO DISCOVERY*

I base my analysis of the *testimonios* written by these Chicanas with careers in STEM on what could be called ethnographic methods of observation as well as on what I conclude from a reading of the essays through that theoretical lens. Combign through the narratives for common themes, I find certain repeated topics. I have used these themes to highlight findings from the project: family and community; teachers and mentors; bilingualism and a love of reading; and constant negotiation of differences from typical STEM students in order to overcome stigmas and achieve success. I share Hurtado's (2008) observation that the participants often remained unconcerned about their accomplishments and understated how significant their work really is, given the odds they overcame. I was initially surprised by their humility and self-effacement, given the stories they told of survival in academia. However, after getting to know these strong, successful women better, I realize that it is, perhaps, that very humility and resilience in the face of obstacles that may account for their success. Family, professors, and colleagues expected nothing less.

The Role of Parents, Family, and Community

Many of the authors link their strong family support systems and their subsequent success in math and science, what educators sometimes call "intellectual scaffolding" (Hurtado, 2008, p. xix). Biologist Mary Elena Zavala (2008) writes that her grandparents and parents "told [her] to observe the plants and animals and maybe they would reveal the answers" (p. 34) to her many questions about the natural world. She further states that her parents encouraged the biologist-to-be by giving her a chemistry set and allowing her experiments, even after she started a small fire in the kitchen. Maria Elena's family took her interests seriously, and their nurturing and support, in very palpable ways, strengthened her resolve to become a scientist. In similar fashion, soil chemist Elvia Niebla (2008) credits her mother with instilling a sense of wonder and curiosity by feeding her incipient inclination for chemistry. For example, she tells the story of how when she wanted a pink dog, her mother helped her dye her white dog pink with food coloring and *voila*! She had a pink dog! Mathematics educators Cleopatria Martínez (2008) and Elsa Ruiz (2008) tell of growing up in working-class households that also valued education, which helped them develop a sense of adventure and *ganas*—that ineffable quality that motivates and gives children the desire to learn. Cleopatria lovingly tells of her mother's supportive advice and, in the section titled "Truths my mother taught me" (Martínez, 2008, p. 70), she tells of how she and her siblings basked in the unique feeling of luxury when her mother purchased a brand new blanket for them. Elsa Ruiz narrates warm memories of learning mathematics from her father and how a supportive mother and siblings reinforced her desire to learn, a desire that teachers did not always recognize or whet.

In some cases not just family but the community at large offered the scaffolding that allowed the authors in *Paths to Discovery* to succeed. Lupita Montoya (2008) and Elizabeth Rodríguez-Johnson (2008) expressed that their communities held education in high regard and that those high expectations along with their support countered the negative messages found in school and offered solace and hope. The sensing of a collective investment in their future through a supportive community is one I know well, too, for often the whole community celebrated good grades. I recall the owner of the neighborhood corner store who gave us nickels for As on our report cards. These examples attest to the value that parents, home, and community support provided these successful Chicanas.

The Role of Teachers and Mentors

In like fashion, the authors recount how key teachers and professors offered not only encouragement but viable and tangible support. Professor Emerita from UCLA, biologist Elma González (2008) speaks of how one of her professors lent her money "to pay rent" and another lent her "some sweaters and a blanket" during the winter quarter at the University of California, Santa

Cruz, because her fellowship stipend had been "delayed while Rutgers confirmed her degree" (p. 21)—and coming from South Texas, she did not own the necessary clothes for the chilly northern California weather. Lydia Villa-Kamaroff's (2008) junior high school teacher, Laura Beheler, remained a mentor and introduced Lydia to a friend who gave the high school senior a check for three hundred dollars, "enough to pay tuition, deposit and at least start the school year " (p. 208). Such stories resonate with my own experience as I, too, experienced the generosity of teachers and others as I made my way through college and graduate school. But it was not always financial help that teachers and supporters provided.

When academic preparation may have been lacking, mentors and teachers provided support that often supplemented and enhanced the poor preparation that under-funded or limited schools offered. Niebla writes about a dedicated high school mathematics teacher, Mr. Summers, who taught her calculus after hours, and about how a community college start prepared her for the rigors of a chemistry major and subsequent graduate work in the area. Montoya remembers Lynn Hindemann, a professor who advised that she be easier on herself when Montoya was going through a particularly rough time made more difficult by the death of her grandmother. She also credits Noe Lozano at Stanford and Rick Ainsworth at California State University, Northridge, with mentoring and assisting her in deciding whether to major in science or to make engineering her career choice. Marinez (2008) and Montoya (2008) also point to the roles that teachers had in their development and success as a biologist and engineer, respectively. Marinez's Catholic school professor in her undergraduate science program guided and inspired the budding scientist, providing support and a strong belief in the young student's abilities to succeed in graduate school. Time and again, these authors tell of sympathetic professors or caring teachers who gave of their time and energy to protect, sustain, and offer a different kind of scaffolding, providing support beyond what financial aid or student loans could provide.

English Proficiency and the Written Word

I found that a love of reading seemed to pervade all of the authors' lives. Their *testimonios* are rife with stories of finding comfort in the public library as children and of being fascinated by the written word. Elma González (2008) beautifully narrates a story of how she found a treasure trove of books abandoned in a shed, which was her family's home while they worked as migrant workers in Nebraska. For over 30 years, scholars have noted the correlation between English reading proficiency and success in mathematics courses (Zepp, 1981). Lydia Villa-Komaroff's (2008) stories of being a reader as a child in New Mexico illustrates the desire for and the link between reading and overall academic success, especially in mathematics and science. By age nine Lydia already knew she wanted to be a scientist, no doubt a desire born of having a supportive family and her reading of science fiction. I contend that being readers, and not just in their own disciplines, better prepared these women to handle the rigors of science and mathematics classes.

Through their love of reading, the authors, who mostly spoke Spanish as a first language, developed English language proficiency. They spoke of what could be called a "linguistic terrorism" (Anzaldúa, 1987, p. 80)—imposed by a monolingual English educational system. Their success in navigating such a system is linked to their proficiency in English obtained through their love of reading.

The participants insisted that Spanish was an asset, categorically stressing that the hostile and anti-Spanish environment in school impacted them negatively. Similarly, they were adamant about the lack of access to proper preparation; they called for stronger and better opportunities to be academically prepared for college and graduate school in the sciences. For example Elvia Niebla, Elsa Ruiz, and others insist that without the proper mathematics preparation, success in more advanced courses is jeopardized. Several of the participants posit that without the right academic preparation, they would not have been prepared for, or even been admitted to, graduate programs, much less have survived to graduation.

Stories from Maria Elena Zavala and Elizabeth Rodríguez-Johnson highlight how their home education countered any racist or negative views of Spanish and of their Spanish-speaking home environments but they also illustrate the negative and dismissive attitude towards Spanish they encountered in school. Maria Elena's (Zavala, 2008) home knowledge of Spanish allowed her to succeed in a college-preparatory course she needed. She recounts how a high school counselor retorted to her request to switch from typing to Spanish, "Your kind of people need some kind of skill." When she explained that she was "going to be a scientist and that Spanish was a better college-prep course, he laughed dismissively" (p. 41) telling her that if she could convince the Spanish teacher, Mr. Dávila, to accept her, he would allow it. Where she got the courage to resist and persist is part of the narrative that is untold in her *testimonio*, but we can deduce that it came from the supportive family and community where she was raised. Her sister and her family prepared her so she could take the test that would allow Mr. Dávila to let her enroll in the class. Even though she minimally met the requirement, Mr. Dávila let her in; she earned an "A" in the class. Elizabeth Rodríguez-Johnson (2008) also tells of travails because of views of Spanish in school. She tells how in elementary school she was physically punished for speaking Spanish at recess. However, her uncertainty with English nudged her to mathematics as a subject of study, "Solving math problems does not require a mastery of the English language." She continues, "Therefore, at a very early age I devoted more time and energy to mastering mathematics rather than English" (p. 82).

NEGOTIATION OF STIGMA: CLASS, RACE, AND GENDER

In all of the authors' stories we find the need to negotiate difference. Whether it is the dilemma faced by the authors such as Diana Marinez (2008) and Martha Zuñiga (2008), who as daughters of Mexican parents from South Texas navigated an unfamiliar academic culture, or the dilemmas of coming from poor families and poor school districts, as did Cleopatria Martínez, Elsa Ruiz, and Lupita Montoya. Mathematics professor Cleopatria Martínez (2008) tells a poignant story of being so poor that her aspiration was to reach the poverty line.

The authors relate that negotiating academic culture was a challenge, but the "alien" world of STEM, where most professors and professionals are white, male, and middle-class, posed an even greater challenge for these brown, working-class Chicanas. What is extraordinary is that they succeeded despite these challenges. There are well-known, long-standing stigmas imposed on girls and women drawn to STEM fields; for Chicanas, as indeed for most women of color, the barriers are multiplied, a network of interlocking biases. Navigating the differences that come with marginalized social conditions, however, was only part of these women's stories.

With support from their families, communities, teachers, and mentors, these women overcame class bias and racist and sexist conditions—for example, the poor, under-funded and limited curricula, the assumption that Chicanas could not aspire to much more than finishing high school—in public schools and in undergraduate and post baccalaureate programs. Still, they faced further obstacles in graduate school cultures that denied their right to be there. The next step was getting into those graduate programs and deciding that, indeed, they wanted to and could do the research in their chosen STEM fields. Martínez (2008) expresses that not until she was in her doctoral program did she take a bilingual mathematics class with a Latino professor and finally "found out what comfort in the classroom [felt] like" (p. 75).

Elma González (2008) recounts encounters with the racist and sexist climate rampant in graduate schools in the late 1960s when she was applying for doctoral programs. At one school where she interviewed, the professor asked what she wanted. When she answered, "'A Ph.D.' he urged [her] to consider 'who you are' and [that] for a woman who was probably going to get married a doctorate was not a practical ambition" (pp. 18–19). There are unfortunately many other stories like these that have gone untold. But these women managed to "not listen" (p. 72), as Martínez (2008) advises; they did go on to complete their graduate work.

Their struggles did not end with graduation from graduate school. Even armed with doctoral degrees, the negotiating continued as they became assistant professors and traveled onward in the academic world. While none of the authors expressed feelings of inadequacy outright, some did write of facing what Clance and Imes (1978) coined the "imposter syndrome" or "imposter phenomenon" (p. 241). (Zavala asks when considering her location within her field, "What does a Chicana botanist look like?" [Zavala, 2008, p. 43]). Reflecting on her graduate school experiences at the University of Texas, Austin, Martha Zuñiga (2008) writes, "Often I wondered if I had the creativity and insight to create my own projects" (p. 123). Diana Marinez (2008) recounts her battle to challenge the sexism she found as a post-doctoral fellow at Michigan State University and claims, "I had not experienced such overt sexism, and while I had always been an advocate for women, this incident solidified my commitment and converted me into a more proactive advocate" (p. 193). She goes on to tell of her continued struggle as a faculty member and administrator to challenge the status quo.

Many of these path makers were the only females of color in their science or mathematics classes; and while today more women of color are entering these disciplines (see below), the fact remains that there are still many young Chicanas/Latinas who are alienated and feel shunned by the STEM fields.

Many of the conditions faced by these authors during their schooling still exist today; in particular, the lack of access to a rigorous preparatory curriculum (many high schools still do not offer the courses required to succeed in college), and the sexism and racism faced by many young assistant professors in departments that do not recognize their abilities. The stigma of not being "good enough"—due to academic preparation (resulting from ethnic, racial, or class subject position) or due to belonging to a group believed not to belong in STEM—still poses challenges for women who choose, against all odds, to pursue careers in the STEM fields.

I conclude from reviewing the *testimonios* that these authors have passion for their field of study; they desire to give back to the Chicana community, and they are involved with programs and organizations that support increasing the number of Chicanas/Latinas in STEM (e.g., SACNAS or the *Adelante* Project). Eight of the nine are or have been intimately involved with SACNAS in various ways, from being president and board members of the organization to working with a biography project that seeks to provide role models and mentors to young Chicanas and Latinas in the sciences. Lupita Montoya has also been very active in the Society for Hispanic Professional Engineers. Evidence of these women's commitment to increasing the number of Chicanas/Latinas in science is that they traveled to San Antonio that hot summer of 2003 to present their research and their life stories to students and that they agreed to engage in writing their *testimonios*, creating roadmaps and marking pitfalls and routes of success to guide those coming next.

DISCUSSION

This final section draws from the key lessons gleaned from the authors' *testimonios* and lays out several steps that can address the problems of (1) numbers and (2) environment for Chicanas in STEM fields. The goal of increasing the number of Chicana and Latina students in the disciplines of science, mathematics, engineering, and technology is best addressed through strategies that may appear simple but are quite complex. Beverley (2004) says, "Something is asked of us by *testimonio*" (p. 1). Further, he claims, "We are in effect interpellated *from* the subaltern" (p. 2). Thus, the person, the *testimoniante*, speaks to a reader, to us, with a purpose. While Beverley is referring to a particular kind of specifically political *testimonio*, I believe we can also say the same of the *testimonios* in *Telling to Live* (Latina Feminist Group, 2001). They are asking something of us, the readers; they are *testimoniando* about a political condition as are the *testimonios* in *Paths to Discovery* (Cantú, 2008). As I offer the suggested policies for changing the condition of Latinas, especially Chicanas, in STEM, I highlight that we have heard from those in the trenches, those whose *testimonios* attest to the conditions and the solutions.

As the *testimonios* reveal, the educational path from preschool through undergraduate school must include an emphasis on preparation and on building a solid foundation that will allow students to envision choosing these areas of study and to succeed in STEM once they embark on that trajectory. Using the funds of knowledge that students already bring with them and building upon their cultural assets is part of this effort. Additionally, academic preparation is a key factor, for without it, students are doomed to fail. Taking mathematics courses from middle school on and being exposed to the sciences in exciting and challenging courses will no doubt yield an increase in the number of Chicanas/Latinas who major in these areas in college and pursue STEM as a career. In a previous section I referred to how various authors alluded to deficient curricula that did not prepare them for college. For example, Niebla's (2008) high school did not offer calculus classes and Zavala (2008) discovered in science journals that "scientists were still writing about their discoveries" (p. 44). The lack of culturally relevant courses, the poor preparation in mediocre or poor high schools, a weak undergraduate curricula that does not prepare Chicana/Latina students for college, or weak college preparation that does not prepare them for graduate school are at the core of policy changes that need to occur. Implicit in such a cursory summary of these needed changes is the call for systemic change as well as an underscoring of the complexity of the solutions to the problem at hand. A cycle that perpetuates the low numbers of Chicanas in STEM appears to be a Catch-22, for if we do not have the college professors preparing the competent teachers, then we do not have the students entering college or graduate school prepared for the rigors of these fields. Courses that are culturally relevant, that build on what students bring from their root culture, and that link them to the excitement of discovery—perhaps through internships in laboratories or with research professors—would impel well-prepared students to choose STEM career paths. Additionally, having well-trained high school—and even elementary and middle school—mathematics and science teachers who not only inspire but foment a love of science and mathematics will translate into greater numbers of Chicanas/Latinas in these fields. Specifically, teacher education programs in STEM that target the culturally relevant needs of Chicana students provide a move toward increasing the number of such students in the STEM fields; these students then will nurture their students' love of science. Furthermore, sensitive and caring college professors who build on what the students entering graduate school bring with them and who provide a scaffolding to help them succeed in graduate programs are needed. As I discussed in the section above, teachers and professors were a determining factor in the success of the authors in *Paths to Discovery*.

A corollary to a firm and solid foundation of curricular design and restructuring is the preparation of teachers and counselors. As the findings above also show, the teachers and counselors who care and go beyond their duties are a determining factor in the attraction to and the success in the STEM fields for Chicanas/Latinas. Well-trained, caring teachers at all levels, from kindergarten to graduate school, adequate resources and infrastructure, and good counseling services will increase the number of Chicanas/Latinas entering the STEM fields. The support of teachers and the critical role they played in the success of the authors comes to light when we consider the findings: Mr. Dávila, the Spanish teacher allows María Elena Zavala to enroll in the college prep course; Elvia Niebla's algebra teacher, Mr. Summers, stays after school to teach her calculus; Sister Mary Daniel Healy at Incarnate Word College takes Diana Marinez under her wing and prepares her for graduate studies; and Lydia Villa-Kamaroff's teacher, Laura Beheler, introduces her to a friend who financially assists Lydia as she moves away to college. All of these teachers demonstrated what Rendón (2008) calls *sentipensante* pedagogy, a caring and holistic approach to teaching. That is what I call for—caring teachers and professors. Another critical issue is access, for if Chicanas and Latinas do not have access to programs because of limited funding or because of geographical isolation, they will continue to have minimal participation in STEM fields.

Second, we must improve the environment so that the experience for Chicanas entering STEM fields is a positive one. The surroundings that shape and allow for their growth are necessarily dependent on a number of policies: more faculty of color, more role models, state-of-the-art classrooms and laboratories and, most critically, a safe space so that there is absolutely no harassment of or discrimination against Chicanas/Latinas in academia at any level, from undergraduate student to full professor. In the findings delineated above, I laid out the challenges that Chicanas in STEM encountered in academia. Elma Gonzalez's predicament as an assistant professor at UCLA, Maria Elena Zavala's experiences at Cal State Northridge, and Lupita Montoya's location within engineering programs illustrate the need for a working environment that is welcoming and conducive to fulfilling one's potential. Such an environment would provide the stimulus to stay in college or in academia. A study of the ecology of STEM for women of color, and for Latinas in particular, may reveal the difficult climate that the *testimonios* attest to, a climate that must change if we are to see the numbers rise.

A final policy recommendation would be to fund research on issues of gender access, specifically on the barriers faced by Chicanas and Latinas who wish to major in STEM areas. We need to better understand what hidden shibboleths are in place that keep Chicanas and Latinas from pursuing work in STEM areas at all levels, from high school to undergraduate to graduate school, and ultimately from pursuing academic careers in these fields. For example, at each level—high school, college, graduate work, post-doctoral fellowship and, finally, in faculty positions—the academic or scholarly culture could deter advancement for Chicanas and Latinas. Just like segregated neighborhoods resisted integration, the STEM fields continue to isolate and alienate those who are "other," that is, those Chicanas and Latinas who do not fit the mold, who do not conform to the mainstream academic or cultural milieu. Although this is not the place to introduce the issue of immigrant students and faculty who secure the postdoctoral fellowships or academic positions, it is an issue that disguises the quandary for Chicanas in STEM. When recently immigrated scientists from South America secure these positions, the end result may not be entirely what is hoped for; they may not have the same cultural or historical disempowerment as those Chicanas who have survived the educational hurdles within the United States educational system. As a result, they may not be as sensitive to the needs of Chicanas.

CONCLUSION

I recognize that instituting policies that play a role in increasing the number of Chicanas/Latinas majoring in and succeeding in the STEM fields will not be easy, but we are already heading in the right direction. My concern is that merely gathering to share our stories and our ideas stops short of actions that can produce innovative and dynamic actions resulting in an increase of women of color in these fields. I am heartened by the recent focus on this critical issue, and I know that various gatherings and actions have already begun to make a difference. In 2010, the Academy of Teacher Excellence at University of Texas at San Antonio held a Summit on Latino Student Success in STEM fields; CEOSE held a mini-symposium on women of color in STEM in 2009, and there are others contributing solutions to this critical situation. Young scholars in graduate school, and the young *Chicanitas* in high school or even elementary schools who dream of being scientists or who love mathematics will be the beneficiary of the work and will follow their own paths to discovery, paths forged by those who have come before, one that I hope is a less treacherous and challenging one.

As I conclude, I recall Chicana philosopher Gloria Anzaldúa's (2005) words: "May we do work that matters. *Vale la pena*, it's worth the pain" (p. 102). I used this quote in my epigraph because I want to keep these words at the forefront as we work to increase the number of Chicanas and Latinas in STEM. We must believe that we can do it, that we can increase the number of Chicanas and Latinas, indeed of all women of color, in the STEM fields. By focusing on the *testimonios* of these successful Chicana scientists, mathematicians, and engineers and illuminating the key characteristics that these authors exhibit, I offer their stories as lessons about what works for Chicanas in these fields.

NOTES

1. *Testimonio* as theory (Latina Feminist Group, 2001) is useful when looking at life stories of abject or marginalized subjects, for it allows them a voice and agency that the conditions described may not allow.
2. I use the term "Chicana" or "Chicano" for the Mexican origin population because it is the preferred term of our book contributors who are all of Mexican origin. I use the term "Latina" or "Latino" to refer to the larger group of Latinas/os that includes Puerto Ricans and those of Central and South American origin.
3. Because demographically the *Latinidades* is the largest group of all, and because I am Chicana, I have chosen to focus my academic work on Chicanas. The MALCS annual meetings, while not limited to

Chicanas, is attended predominantly by Chicana students and professors. I do not know of any study that has tracked the stories of Latinas in STEM, but my own personal observation is that often immigrants from Latin America and Puerto Ricans are more likely than Chicanas to be in graduate school or in jobs in the STEM fields, albeit this number is also miniscule.

4. The Latina Feminist Group (2001) is a collective of Latina scholars who came together to create a theory of *testimonio*-based epistemologies.

5. *Latinidades* refers to the various origins for Latinas and Latinos in the United States; in other words, it is an umbrella term for the peoples and cultures from, for example, Mexico, Puerto Rico, Central America, Columbia, Cuba.

6. At least one other MALCS annual meeting also secured NSF funding for a similar effort: the MALCS meeting held in 2008 at the University of California in Santa Cruz.

7. For the final publication, we added an engineer and two other working scientists who had been unable to attend the conference.

8. The title was changed several times as we attempted to find one that would reflect the book's content. The editor discouraged us from using the term, "*testimonio*" as she feared that it might be misunderstood as being more akin to the religious concept of bearing witness to a spiritual event. While I resisted, I queried the participants and they agreed to using "autobiographies," instead of *testimonios*.

9. Funds of knowledge (Moll et al., 2001) refers "to the historically accumulated and culturally developed bodies of knowledge and skills essential for household or individual functioning and well-being" (p. 133). In a later work (González, Moll, & Amanti 2005), they developed these ideas further, especially in reference to classroom practices.

REFERENCES

Anzaldúa, G. (1987). *Borderlands/La frontera: The new mestiza.* San Francisco, CA: Aunt Lute Books.

Anzaldúa, G. (2005). Let us be the healing of the wound: The coyolxauhqui imperative—La sombra y el sueño. In C. Joysmith & C. Lomas (Eds.), *One wound for another/Una herida por otra: Testimonios de Latin@s in the U.S. through cyberspace (11 de septiembre de 2001–11 de marzo de 2002)* (pp. 92–103). Mexico City: Universidad Nacional Autónoma de México.

Beverley, J. (2004). *Testimonio: On the politics of truth.* Minneapolis, MN: University of Minnesota Press.

Cantú, N. E. (2006). *Flor y ciencia: Chicanas in mathematics, science, and engineering.* Washington, DC: American Association for the Advancement of Science.

Cantú, N. E. (Ed.). (2008). *Paths to discovery: Autobiographies from Chicanas with careers in mathematics, science and engineering.* Los Angeles, CA: UCLA Chicano Studies Research Center Press.

Clance, P. R., & Imes, S. A. (1978). The imposter phenomenon among high achieving women: Dynamics and therapeutic intervention. *Psychotherapy: Theory, Research & Practice, 15*(3), 241–247.

Fine, G. A., & Deegan, J. G. (1996). Three principles of serendip: Insight, chance, and discovery in qualitative research. *International Journal of Qualitative Studies in Education, 9*(4), 434–447.

González, E. (2008). What I did on my summer vacation. In N. E. Cantú (Ed.), *Paths to discovery: Autobiographies from Chicanas with careers in science, mathematics, and engineering* (pp. 3–25). Los Angeles, CA: UCLA Chicano Studies Research Center Press.

González, N., Moll, L., & Amanti, C. (2005). *Funds of knowledge: Theorizing practices in households, communities, and classrooms.* Mahwah, NJ: Erlbaum.

Hurtado, A. (2008). Introduction: Un cuadro—A framing. In N. E. Cantú (Ed.), *Paths to discovery: Autobiographies from Chicanas with careers in science, mathematics, and engineering* (pp. xv–xxvi). Los Angeles, CA: UCLA Chicano Studies Research Center Press.

Latina Feminist Group. (2001). *Telling to live: Latina feminist testimonios.* Durham, NC: Duke University Press.

Marinez, D. (2008). A's in academics, C's in conduct. In N. E. Cantú (Ed.), *Paths to discovery: Autobiographies from Chicanas with careers in science, mathematics, and engineering* (pp. 177–196). Los Angeles, CA: UCLA Chicano Studies Research Center Press.

Martínez, C. (2008). Life lessons. In N. E. Cantú (Ed.), *Paths to discovery: Autobiographies from Chicanas with careers in science, mathematics, and engineering* (pp. 61–76). Los Angeles, CA: UCLA Chicano Studies Research Center Press.

Moll, L. C., Amanti, C., Neff, D., & González, N. (2001). Funds of knowledge for teaching: Using a qualitative approach to connect homes and classrooms. *Theory into Practice, 31*(2), 132–141.

Montoya, L. (2008). Claro que sí se puede! In N. E. Cantú (Ed.), *Paths to discovery: Autobiographies from Chicanas with careers in science, mathematics, and engineering* (pp. 95–112). Los Angeles, CA: UCLA Chicano Studies Research Center Press.

National Science Foundation. (2012). *Women, minorities, and persons with disabilities in science and engineering.* Retrieved from http://www.nsf.gov/statistics/wmpd/minwomen.cfm#degrees

Niebla, E. E. (2008). The education of a Chicana scientist. In N. E. Cantú (Ed.), *Paths to discovery: Autobiographies from Chicanas with careers in science, mathematics, and engineering.* Los Angeles, CA: UCLA Chicano Studies Research Center Press.

Pérez Huber, L. (2009). Disrupting apartheid of knowledge: Testimonio as methodology in Latina/o critical race research in education. *International Journal of Qualitative Studies in Education, 22*(6), 639–654.

Rendón, L. I. (2008) *Sentipensante (Sensing/Thinking) pedagogy: Educating for wholeness, social justice and liberation.* Sterling, VA: Stylus.

Rodriguez-Johnson, E. (2008). Our history, my life. In N. E. Cantú (Ed.), *Paths to discovery: Autobiographies from Chicanas with careers in science, mathematics, and engineering* (pp. 79–93). Los Angeles, CA: UCLA Chicano Studies Research Center Press.

Ruiz, E. C. (2008). Aprendiendo a vivir. In N. E. Cantú (Ed.), *Paths to discovery: Autobiographies from Chicanas with careers in science, mathematics, and engineering.* (pp. 157–175). Los Angeles, CA: UCLA Chicano Studies Research Center Press.

Santiago, D. (2008). Appendix: Latinas in science, technology, engineering, and mathematics. In N. E. Cantú (Ed.), *Paths to discovery: Autobiographies from Chicanas with careers in science, mathematics, and engineering* (pp. 225–227). Los Angeles, CA: UCLA Chicano Studies Research Center Press.

Villa-Komaroff, L. (2008). On the inside, looking in. In N. E. Cantú (Ed.), *Paths to discovery: Autobiographies from Chicanas with careers in science, mathematics, and engineering* (pp. 199–223). Los Angeles, CA: UCLA Chicano Studies Research Center Press.

Zavala, M. E. (2008). *Haciendo caras*: The making of a scientist. In N. E. Cantú (Ed.), *Paths to discovery: Autobiographies from Chicanas with careers in science, mathematics, and engineering* (pp. 27–58). Los Angeles, CA: UCLA Chicano Studies Research Center Press.

Zepp, R. A. (1981). Relationships between mathematics achievement and various English language proficiencies. *Education Studies in Mathematics, 12*(1), 59–70.

Zuñiga, M. (2008). *Mi viaje en esta vida*: The life of a Laredo girl. In N. E. Cantú (Ed.), *Paths to discovery: Autobiographies from Chicanas with careers in science, mathematics, and engineering.* (pp. 115–131). Los Angeles, CA: UCLA Chicano Studies Research Center Press.

Testimonio as Praxis for a Reimagined Journalism Model and Pedagogy

Sonya M. Alemán

University of Utah

The differences between journalism and *testimonio* are stark: One is premised on verifiable truths (Mindich, 1998), while the other treats truth as fractional, relative, subjective, and communal (Arias, 2001; Binford, 2001; Delgado Bernal, 2006a; Latina Feminist Group, 2001). Nonetheless, Chicana/o journalism students developing a raced-and-gendered conscious journalism practice have merged the two by utilizing a Chicana feminist inspired *testimonio* to fashion a journalistic practice that resonates with the racialized experience of communities of color. By examining how student journalists describe their practice, their interviewing and editing techniques, and their published content publish, this essay documents the four ways that *testimonio* informs these newsgathering efforts. They include: (1) personal vignettes, (2) rhetorical devices that foster transparency, (3) *confianza* (trust) and reciprocity with interviewees, and (4) collaboration with sources. Consequently, *testimonio* bolsters efforts to pursue traditionally neglected stories, incorporates reciprocity into newsgathering, and empowers student journalists as agents in the representation and transformation of their communities. It also raises concerns about academic privilege—the advantage college-going Chicanas/Latinas have to edit, frame, collect, and represent stories from their communities. Lastly, it establishes Chicana feminism as a foil for the academic biases in regards to truth and facts and reorients journalists as subjective storytellers rather than impartial beings.

The function of journalistic writing and *testimonio* narratives appear to be quite disparate: One is premised on the notion of verifiable truths (Mindich, 1998), while the other treats truth as fractional, relative, subjective, and communal (Arias, 2001; Binford, 2001; Delgado Bernal, 2006a; Latina Feminist Group, 2001). Mexican journalist Elena Poniatowska (1971) wove these two approaches together, which she described as a collection of *testimonios* from eyewitnesses and survivors of the tragic government-ordered slaughter of college student protestors and their supporters during a rally demanding that the Mexican President Díaz Ordaz's administration reinstate university and student autonomy. Criticism of this convergence is predicated on the same Western-based cultural logics of truth that Stoll directed toward Rigoberta Menchu's *testimonio*—that some of the claims and retelling of injustices suffered at the hands of the military lacked evidentiary support (Arias, 2001; Binford, 2001; Brooks, 2005; Irizarry, 2005). Poniatowska ultimately issued an updated version of her book on its 30th anniversary, correcting many misquotes and misinformation sources said were peppered throughout (Lopez, 1998).

Despite the seemingly contrasting paradigms of journalism and *testimonio*, Chicana/o journalism students developing a raced-and-gendered-conscious journalism practice have reconciled the two approaches by incorporating the epistemology and methodology of a Chicana feminist-inspired *testimonio* as a viable platform from which to fashion journalistic techniques, values, and processes that better correspond to the multiple oppressions racially marginalized communities experience that mainstream news media outlets disregard or discredit (Mize & Leedham, 2000; National Association of Hispanic Journalists, 2006; Poindexter, Smith, & Heider, 2003; Rivas-Rodriguez, 1998). This essay chronicles the way this type of *testimonio* informs the newswriting and newsgathering efforts of alternative student journalists by analyzing three elements: the ways the activist-practitioners make sense of their practice, the interviewing and editing techniques employed by these alternative correspondents, and the content published by these politicized reporters.

As advisor for the student staff engaging in this practice, I drew from autoethnographic methods, written reflections, focus group interviews, student-generated media content, and field notes from staff meetings to generate data that would reveal the nuances and complexities of this nonconventional journalism model. I analyzed this material using thematic or content analysis to reveal four ways that *testimonio* manifests in the content and production of their publication: (1) the use of personal vignettes, (2) the transparency of the reporter, (3) the trusting and reciprocal relationships with interviewees, and (4) the collaboration with sources to write and edit content. I argue that the resultant work showcases the ways that *testimonio* bolsters efforts to pursue traditionally neglected stories, incorporates reciprocity as an element of newsgathering, and positions student journalists as agents in the representation and transformation of their communities. It also problematizes an academic privilege—the advantage college-going students or scholars of color have to edit, frame, collect, and represent stories from their communities—an issue minimally discussed among Chicana scholars engaging in scholarly research using a lens of *testimonio* (Téllez, 2005; Villenas, 1996a, 1996b). Lastly, it solidifies existing Chicana feminist scholarship that challenges academic biases toward truth and facts and reorients all journalists as human storytellers rather than as automatons operating in an invented vacuity.

First, I ground this project with a brief overview of my association with these student journalists and a history of their racialized and gendered practice. Next, I summarize the scholarship on *testimonio* produced by Chicana and Latina scholars as the theoretical keystone buttressing this project. Then, I share some of the ways students drew on the notion of *testimonio* in conceptualizing their distinctive journalism practice and the resulting attributes. A mélange of material, including student written reflections, formal focus group conversations, in-class discussions, and published articles, serve as the sources of data for this section. I then document the tensions that students identified in coalescing these two idiosyncratic approaches. Finally, I suggest the contributions that this project offers Chicana scholars, as well as mainstream journalists and journalism educators.

VENCEREMOS[1]

During the 2007–2008 academic year, a group of 12 Mountain Valley University Chicana/o students, led by the paper's first Chicana editor, revived *Venceremos*, an alternative campus newspaper dedicated to serving and representing the Chicana/o communities on campus and in the larger Chicana/o and Latina/o community by advocating for social change and equality in its content and news production. Initially published in the Fall of 1993 at a predominantly white, Research-I institution, this tabloid-sized newspaper debuted by defining the endeavor as a "progressive Chicana/o journalism." This practice was intended to allow the producers of *Venceremos* to achieve the following:

- Openly stand against social injustices, such as racism, sexism, and class oppression;
- Report the important events, issues, and struggles of Latina/os at Mountain Valley University, at local high schools, in the community, and from around the region;
- Publish articles on Chicana/o history and political thought;
- Bridge the gap between working-class Latina/o communities and Mountain Valley University and, thus, make the university more accessible to youth;
- Encourage the recruitment and retention of Latina/o students, faculty, and staff at the Mountain Valley University;
- Strengthen the ties among students of different cultural and national backgrounds;
- Expose and oppose the negative depictions of Chicanas/os that often appear in the media of the dominant culture; and
- Support all struggles that are aimed at combating racial, gender, and class inequality at Mountain Valley University (Marcial, 1993).

Since that ambitious launch, 32 issues of *Venceremos* have been published with varying frequency and consistency, with the most recent iteration occurring after a five-year-hiatus. After the first nine issues, *Venceremos* published intermittingly. It struggled to remain sustainable, as it has lacked designated campus office space, desktop publishing or design software, computer equipment, funding, training, or salaries for its staff. A consistent challenge has been securing a steady pipeline of student staff. When there was enough student interest, the university provided operational funding to cover printing costs and sometimes, the mainstream campus daily newspaper shared computer and distribution resources. Various faculty also took the time to serve as advisor during these periods. Together, these factors have contributed to its inconsistent publication history.

After its revival in 2007, I learned of the publication and its rich history on the campus and community; my interest was piqued immediately. As a U.S.-born Chicana, my fascination with mass media representations of my community has driven my academic pursuits in the field of Communication. I explored ways of teaming up with *Venceremos* in ways that could fuse my racialized identity, my passion for equal and accurate representation in media discourse, and my academic expertise. Eventually, I collaborated with the student producers of *Venceremos* to institutionalize the publication at Mountain Valley University, as well as to evolve and articulate the elements of this distinctive Chicana/o journalism practice. This occurred through an upper level communication course that I designed to support the publication of the newspaper in the Fall of 2008. A year-long independent study course for three *Venceremos* student staff members, including the editor-in-chief (L. Marzuli, personal communication, Winter 2008) enabled the dormant publication to re-debut in January 2008. Inspired by this configuration, I successfully proposed creating and teaching a journalism course to support the publication of *Venceremos* to various stakeholders—including *Venceremos* staff and the Department of Communication.[2] I also informed the *Venceremos* staff that I intended to use the *Venceremos* classroom as my dissertation research site, as it melded my interests in media, race, and journalism pedagogy. The course was offered for the first time during the Fall 2008 semester, has been offered for six semesters since then, and has enrolled 32 students, 90% of whom have been Latinas/os (all but three, who identified as African Muslim, Tongan, and white) and represent various countries of origin. Most—but not all—have self-identified as Chicana/o, but all embrace the designation bestowed by the newspaper's founders to name their journalism practice. Half a dozen have revealed their undocumented status.

After the inception of the course, the student staff published twelve successive issues, with a fourteenth and fifteenth planned for fall 2012. *Venceremos* increased the frequency of publication in Fall 2011 to two issues a semester rather than just one and is exploring the plausibility of a hybrid online/print format. *Venceremos* launched a corresponding website in Fall 2009.

INFORMING A CHICANA/O JOURNALISM MODEL THROUGH *TESTIMONIO*

The course has utilized literature from race-conscious and gender-conscious theoretical frameworks—namely critical race theory and Chicana feminism—to buoy the students' efforts. Because of their personal crusades toward social justice, several students have been exposed to concepts from these frameworks through other coursework, individual research, or through their activist work, but very few enroll in the course having studied either theory in depth. Critical race theory and its complementary counter-storytelling methodology have been useful heuristics for plotting out a Chicana/o journalism product. Students have identified six benchmarks of Chicana/o journalism that correspond to key tenets of critical race theory. These include content that: (1) centers on Chicana/o-centric topics and/or themes, (2) challenges majoritarian ideology and dominant discourses, (3) encourages activism on the part of the reader, (4) is written in accessible language, (5) validates experiential and cultural knowledge from marginalized communities, and (6) is grounded in a Chicana/o sensibility (Alemán, 2011).

One of the forms of counterstories utilized by critical race theorists recounts someone else's story, but it stops short of delineating guidelines for that exchange. How do you cultivate relationships that draw out someone's counterstory? How do you conduct these exchanges? How much do you share? How much do you take? How do you identify whose counterstory to tell? To seek answers to these questions, *testimonio,* as practiced through a Chicana feminist epistemology, authenticates the lived and embodied experiences of Chicanas as a source of sagacity about how structural marginalization impinges on their opportunities and quality of life. It emerged as an apt tool to inform the newswriting and newsgathering techniques Chicana/o journalists could use to collect the stories of members of racially disenfranchised communities. Moreover, staff members enrolled in the first semester used the term "*testimonio*" in their discourse and sense-making about their unique journalism practice, solidifying the use of Chicana feminism as a foundation for this distinctive journalism practice. Here is how they operationalized their approach, using the six attributes of critical race theory and a specific reference to *testimonio: Venceremos* articles are "written by individuals who have experienced and/or understand the effects of racism, discrimination, or other forms of marginalization and can bring this insight to report and write about issues, themes, or topics relevant to Chicana/o or similarly oppressed and colonized communities (Aleman, 2011, p. 343)." Chicana/o journalists collect and honor "the *testimonios* of members of marginalized communities and recount those tales in humanizing and accessible" language(s) to "expose and challenge stereotypes about those communities and/or white supremacist and liberal ideologies (p. 343)." These pieces advocate "activism or action to address the issues presented in the article" (p. 343).

This conceptualization attends to both the finished product and to the process of Chicana/o journalism. Collecting and honoring "the *testimonio* of members of those communities" (Aleman, 2011, p. 343) specifically alludes to the modes of practice, and this essay maps out how a Chicana feminist-inspired *testimonio* informs the mechanisms, strategies, tactics, and ways of relating to, connecting with, and documenting the stories community members in an honorable and respectful exchange. Based on the conceptualization students generated, *testimonio* is integral to Chicana/o journalism practice. Elements five and six, referenced above, specifically correspond to a Chicana feminist epistemological lens that (1) the lived experiences of oppression cultivate an expertise and knowledge in how these systems operate and that (2) people more attuned to the experience of marginalization are uniquely suited to hear, understand, collect, and honor this knowledge in the form of their stories, or *testimonios* (Delgado Bernal, 1998). As such, their conceptualization of a Chicana feminist-inspired *testimonio* is one that understands *testimonios* as a methodological, pedagogical, and epistemological tool.

The following section encapsulates out how Chicana feminist scholars have expounded the notion of *testimonio*.

REVIEW OF *TESTIMONIO* IN CHICANA FEMINISM

Chicana feminist scholars have marshaled the process, aesthetics, and purpose of *testimonio* to legitimate the life experiences of Chicanas and Latinas (Delgado Bernal, Godinez, Villenas, & Elenes, 2006; Latina Feminist Group, 2001), theorize the imprint of multiple oppressions on their minds, bodies, and spirits (Anzaldúa, 1987; Nayar, 2006), detect the faculty needed to surmount marginalization (Delgado Bernal, 2006b; Galván, 2006; Villenas, 2006), and forge a gender- and race-based knowledge production previously disregarded by the academy (Pérez Huber, 2009b). *Testimonio* has been anchored in Latin America for decades, where it emerged as an anthropological project between a subaltern and interlocutor that gave voice to an experience of gross injustice and those with the tenacity to surmount it to bring about a respite to the suffering (Binford, 2001; Pérez Huber, 2009b; Irizarry, 2005). The *testimoniante* (person giving the *testimonio*) is often positioned in a liminal space, while the interlocutor is situated in a different and often, greater sphere of power, but he or she strives to channel the raw, unedited *testimonio* into a written product (Nayar, 2006). The tale is frequently narrated in the first person, but the singular experience alludes to a broader collective experience (Irizarry, 2005; Nayar, 2006). This rhetorical strategy functions to raise awareness to the plight endured by this individual and the members of her or his community in order to engender progressive change in the living conditions, policies, or treatment of those peoples. It is meant to reach those with life experiences far removed from the *testimoniante* in order to evoke empathy, sympathy, and advocacy (Binford, 2001; Cruz, 2006; Nayar, 2006). These purposeful literary devices make *testimonio* pragmatic, performative, and overtly political. Consequently, *testimonio* can be differentiated from the genre of life history or autobiography, because the narrator skillfully crafts a tale that is both his or her own and communal while deliberately drawing attention to the experience of disenfranchisement (Delgado Bernal, Godinez, Villenas, & Elenes, 2006).

As referenced earlier, *testimonio* writing of this sort has been besieged with critiques regarding its authenticity. These censures rely primarily on Western cultural values (Arias, 2001; Binford, 2001; Brooks, 2005; Irizarry, 2005). The logics of representation make any kind of retelling naturally fraught with complexities (Binford, 2001; Brooks, 2005; Gutiérrez, 2008; Pérez Huber, 2009a), but Chicana scholars who have taken up *testimonio* as a method, pedagogy, research, or activist tool have lessened the power differential between interlocutor and witness by either fusing them together—as when they recount their own story (Burciaga & Tavares, 2006; Espino, Muñoz, & Marquez Kiyama, 2010; Flores & Garcia, 2009; Latina Feminist Group, 2001; Pérez Huber, 2009b)—or by bringing their own experiences of disenfranchisement to bear on the sense-making and analysis of *testimonios* by other Latinas (Cruz, 2006). *Testimonio* also somewhat eases the social distance between *testimoniante* and intended audience. While most writing has occurred in academic environments, sometimes it has been shared with Chicana communities in popular and public formats outside of the ivory tower. Lastly, both of these approaches soothe abrasions caused by marginalization, a balm that heals both seen and unseen wounds (Pérez Huber, 2009b).

When Chicana feminist scholars employ *testimonio* to document, reframe, transmit, or illuminate their own multiple subjectivities and the oppressive burdens they entail, the need for a second party to translate their personal stories is eliminated. The ability to author one's own tale serves as a source of empowerment and healing. This approach promotes a sense of agency because the *testimoniante* is simultaneously the subject and object of inquiry, fostering a self-reflexivity of identity formation and an acknowledgement of the capacity to thrive despite unjust social and institutional barriers (Delgado Bernal et al., 2006).

When Chicana scholars collect *testimonios* from other Latinas, this *testimonio* process often occurs by reciprocating stories of marginalization and empathizing during the interview or pedagogical process (Pérez Huber, 2009a, 2009b), by collaborating with the *testimoniantes* during the analytical phase (Pérez Huber, 2009a, 2009b), or by drawing on their cultural intuition (Burciaga & Tavares, 2006; Delgado Bernal, 1998; Latina Feminist Group, 2001) to theorize the *testimonios* collected. One additional outcome of this research framework is to forge solidarity among women with various *Latinidades*, whose varied countries of origin, language abilities, phenotypes, religious or spiritual views, geographic ties, citizenship status, and cultural traditions are often indistinguishable by dominant society but that are indicative of the rich tapestry enveloped by the label, "Latina."

Because Chicanas are an under-researched community in the academy, *testimonio* as a methodological tool focuses needed attention onto a group overlooked both by researchers and, unfortunately, by Chicana women themselves, whose academic training may have dissuaded such inquiry. *Testimonio*-based research challenges the Eurocentric timbre of research protocol and invigorates race and gender scholarship with its erudite insight into the material and social reality of multiply-layered oppression (Pérez Huber, 2009b). The work validates the experiential knowledge of those who subsist with the discursive and material residue of racism, racialization, race, sexism, patriarchy, and/or genderization,in their instititional, individual, and ideological forms. As an incarnate node of these various oppressions, Chicana scholars often develop an insight into the phenomenon of disenfranchisement in ways that might differ from scholars whose various forms of privilege can buffer such intimate knowledge (Delgado, 1989). Moreover, in both instances (personal *testimonios* and collecting *testimonios* of other Chicanas), the resulting *testimonio* often is fastened to a form of praxis or activism that, like its precursor in anthropology and literary disciplines, endeavors to right social wrongs in the lives of their community.

The facets of *testimonio* that have found purchase with Chicana scholars have similar appeal to *Venceremos'* Chicana/o student journalists evolving their unique practice. The section below fleshes out how these students conceptualized congruencies between their endeavor and *testimonio*.

HOW CHICANA/O STUDENT JOURNALISTS TALK ABOUT *TESTIMONIO*

Venceremos staff members ascribed three attributes of *testimonio* onto their Chicana/o journalism practice. Culled from formal and informal reflections and sense-making about their distinctive approach, as well as the published product, these attributes include: (1) focusing on topics that reflect the experiences and struggles of Chicana/o and Latina/o communities to endure, and persevere through, all forms of oppression; (2) prioritizing members of their communities as the principal sources of information for the issues reported; and (3) retelling these accounts in ways that name, challenge, and begin to dismantle the systemic injustice suffered by these communities. I delineate each quality below.

Themes

The themes and subject matter that the *Venceremos* staff recognize as pertaining to the experiences and actualities of Chicana/o and Latina/o communities include—but are not limited to—the following types of accounts:

- overt and covert acts of racism
- struggles with identity
- bilingualism/biculturalism
- access to education or other institutions
- community activism or civic engagement
- labor and class issues
- anti-immigration attacks, rhetoric, and legislation
- reclaiming Chicana/o history
- artistic or cultural achievements of Latinos/as

These various themes reveal individual, systemic, discursive, and material patterns of colonization, discrimination, and oppression. They also celebrate tactics of resistance, navigational strategies, and accounts of perseverance. For instance, Chicana/o journalism articles, wrote Gino,[3]

> focus on themes of identity, discrimination, culture, and history, with an emphasis on validating the Mexican (Latin) American experience or Chicana/o culture in the United States . . . important themes of Chicana/o journalism include the experience of immigration, and the situation of living between two languages.

Angel said the types of tales found in *Venceremos* include "the narratives of migrant workers," or the "anecdotes of local shop owners trying to stay open for business despite ordinances passed to ensure their downfall." *Venceremos* is an opportunity to "validate the stories of your elders, speak of the struggles of your sisters and brothers," continued Angel. As Chicana/o journalists, he continued, our job is "to represent the stories that are of importance to the Chicana/o community. Capture the stories of the people who do the work, live in the communities, and are marginalized." Hortencia echoed this sentiment when she wrote, "You, as a Chicano writer, need to find the immigrant's story, their views, and their ideas from the perspective of an immigrant dealing with the immigration issues."

Staff members also advised incoming staff members to look to their own lives for inspiration. "Since racism and oppression are part of everyday lived experience, these stories are not hard to find if you only keep your eyes and ears open," Citlaly surmised. Analisa argued that what makes true Chicana/o journalism "is demonstrating the struggles of the Chicana/o and Latina/o people, instead of ignoring them as if they did not exist." *Venceremos* student staff recognize the value of the untold narratives of their community and use their publication as a vehicle to authenticate them. Given that news coverage of Latina/o or Chicana/o communities has repeatedly been relegated to crime, festivals (Heider, 2000), and immigration (National Association of Hispanic Journalists, 2006), *Venceremos* contributors aimed instead to convey the breadth of experiences that are distinctive to racialized, ethnicized, minoritized, or colonized communities.

Experts

Seeking sources directly from racial and ethnic communities was an imperative way Chicana/o journalists wanted to counteract the absence of these groups in mainstream news media (Heider, 2000; National Association of Hispanic Journalists, 2006; Poindexter, Smith, & Heider, 2003). This resolution further functions to legitimize the communal, cultural, collective, and historical knowledge inherent in communities that are often framed by reporters, pundits, and academicians as inferior, pathological, or deficient. Several staff members implored contributors not to rely solely on campus administrators, students, faculty, or government officials for information. Staff felt obligated to cultivate sources who were clearly experts in their own lives by communicating with them in their own language, earning their trust, and treating their stories with care and respect. "As news writers, we are conscious of who we interview," explained Rolando. "Mainstream media often interviews people deemed experts as decreed by a diploma or through social status, often overlooking the voices of communities of color who are at the center of the issues they are reporting on," he added. What I gleaned from their exhortations is that the person telling the story is as important as the story itself. The heuristic guiding them here qualifies "expertise" remarkably different from traditional news values.

For an assignment that asked students to explain the components of Chicana/o journalism to future staff members, Hortencia clarified that

> when you begin to write your story and to look at people you can potentially interview, find the people who will give you the story that mainstream and even most alternative presses won't cover. Don't go to the white legislator or white business owner, go to the Latina/o community, the Latina/o business owner or official because they are the ones who have traditionally been oppressed and can tell you who is really being affected and can personally tell you how.

Angel similarly directed student staff to "find the story first hand from the people." The community focus of the newspaper necessitates that Chicana/o student journalists step beyond campus to "hear from everyone, not just students or those in academia," Mireya stressed. "Our people/community are/is the expert," that Chicana/o journalists should turn to, wrote Joaquin. "We place value on the experiences of those in our stories," the voices "of the workers and oppressed," he added. Citlaly encouraged staff members to "get details about what is happening from their own point of view and how it is affecting their lives and the lives of people in their communities." As Chicana/o journalists, Elena explained,

> We want to be the source of media that draws information from the community. We validate their input. Our readers can easily connect to the articles because they see how news affects their lives by reading their own voices, the *testimonio* of the community in our paper.

She also recognized that Chicana/o student journalists "reach out to sources whose voices are often silenced or disregarded." For Sarita, Chicana/o counter-news stories create a canvas "for the underprivileged minority to tell their stories from their perspective and in their language, enabling the untold stories of our people, our *gente* [people], to come to light." Finally, Rolando claims that a fundamental premise of this journalism practice is "that our communities possess a knowledge brought upon their individual experiences in our society, our newspaper seeks to emphasize this knowledge." By relying on sources that are chronically underrepresented in mainstream news content, Chicana/o journalists create the opportunity for these marginalized individuals to speak for themselves, rather than being spoken for (Pillow, 2003).

Dismantling Systems of Oppression

Validating communal experiences of marginalization and racism operates concurrently with exposing and dismantling the systemic inequities that undergird that disenfranchisement, another quality analogous to the *testimonio* practice of Chicana feminists. For a Chicana/o journalist, this entails deconstructing majoritarian ideas regarding the supremacy of whiteness and heteronormativity, the inferiority of communities of color, the primacy of individualism and meritocracy, the appeal of colorblindness, and the detrimental ways communities of color uphold these systems, such as through a colonized mentality or internalized racism. For Rolando, the tone of *Venceremos* "places value in the voices and experiences of Chicana/o and other subjugated communities as means to subvert deficit thinking and build solidarity between disenfranchised groups." Analisa contends that Chicana/o journalism provides liberation, "letting the *gente* speak what they have kept silent." Sarita understands the newspaper as a vehicle to foster solidarity among readers and an embodiment of "the greatest sources of resistance" students of color have on campus. Yvette conceptualized their publication as a weapon of resistance in the struggle for racial reform, and wrote that she hopes "our community can hear" their voices in the pages of the newspaper.

As is evident through the discourse of the student staff, a Chicana/o journalism model clearly exudes a *testimonio*-informed praxis. Similar to Chicana feminist scholars who have reclaimed *testimonio* to theorize and improve their own lives and that of their brown sisters, *Venceremos* staff deliberately validate and amplify the voice of the marginalized, feel they have a proclivity to tell those stories wholly (unlike those not positioned in those communities), and want to tell those stories of oppression and multiple identities to transform and empower their Latina/o communities. For example, *Venceremos* reported on campus government elections where a slate of candidates of color had their posters and other campaign materials defaced with racial slurs and were victimized by hate speech. The staff not only covered the incidents to allow the harassed individuals to legitimize their experience, but they also organized an anti-racist rally to raise awareness among the campus community about these circumstances. Another issue ran a feature titled, "Carne Asada is not a Crime," that profiled taco stand vendors targeted by discriminatory city ordinances that sought to limit their presence on city streets. The staff listed the locations of several taco stands and encouraged readers to visit and support these owners. They also published the name and contact information of the councilman responsible for the new rules so that readers could demand a stop to such ordinances.

With a Chicana feminist-inspired *testimonio* serving as a pivotal keystone of their sense-making and the ideals shaping their approach, several modes of practice were wrought from this foundation. In the next section, I detail how activist student journalists fashioned a newsgathering and writing process informed by *testimonio*.

A *TESTIMONIO*-INSPIRED CHICANA/O JOURNALISM PRACTICE

Testimonio manifests in four different ways in the production of *Venceremos*. These are (1) the use of personal vignettes, (2) rhetorical strategies to make the reporter transparent, (3) trusting and reciprocal relationships with interviewees, and (4) collaboration with sources to write and edit content.

The most common technique occurs when students opt to disclose personal vignettes from their lives for publication. One of their first in-class written assignments asks them to reflect on how they became politicized students or to document their journey toward critical awareness. For another prompt, students recount their journey into higher education. These assignments are often not published in their entirety, but this exercise helps the staff find a way to locate personal aspects of their lives to incorporate into their final contributions. For example, Citlaly documented her connection to a space on campus about to undergo renovation. Mireya shared a piece defending her identity as Chicana even though she was light-skinned and did not speak Spanish. Nabila wrote about the stereotypes she encountered daily as an African Muslim student, garbed in a *hajib*. Joaquin described his experience living in Puerto Rico and how that helped him see the common experience of colonialism between Chicanas/os and Puertorriqueñas/os. Fatima wrote about the challenges she copes with as a single mom and college student. She authored a second piece around her concept of Latina motherhood and how it is irreconcilable with the dehumanizing concept of "anchor baby," a derogatory term invented by anti-immigrant activists to refer to the citizen children of undocumented mothers. The assignment about higher education inspired a two-page spread outlining steps to successfully enroll in college one semester.

Several contributors also submitted pieces about their experiences. Diana wrote about her trip to Nicaragua that combined her interest in Nicaraguan art and connecting with family she had never met before. She also wrote about her efforts to reclaim the Spanish language through various courses and by immersing herself in a study abroad program. Leo offered a peek into his life as a Latino punk band member, revealing the context of this particular genre. A recent issue published three *testimonios* of DREAMers, undocumented students who actively mobilized to help pass the DREAM Act. Two other undocumented community members also submitted pieces for publication that reveal the tenuous existence of their lives in the midst of such restrictive legislation. Finally, an article by five high schoo-aged research interns told of their experience lobbying during a legislative session. In all, about 15% of the content published since the inception of the course has originated from a *testimonio*.

A second manifestation of *testimonio* in the news writing practice for *Venceremos* are the rhetorical techniques students use to place themselves in their stories. Often, this is done using the first person. For example, when Rita outlined the steps high school students should consider to prepare themselves for college, she wrote,

> I almost did not make it into college myself. I allowed my fears and insecurities about my abilities as a student to control me. I also became discouraged because I had no idea how to get into school, and did not have help from teachers or advisors.

Mireya's coverage about woeful graduation rates of Latina/o students included this passage: "On the last day of my freshman year of high school, I had a teacher tell me she was glad that I had been in her class. She told me she thought I was going to be trouble, but was pleasantly surprised that I was not." A frequent contributor wrote about the misinformation about the indigenous population of Mexico and wrote that he learned of their worth because

> Every day I work with young Mexicans who are fighting to make their country a better place. I have met civil engineers from wealthy families who came here to make a difference. I have met nuns and priests dedicated to fighting for human rights.

In an article about the importance of student of color groups, one contributor included her motivation for belonging to a Hispanic student business group: "I am often one of the only minority students in my courses. Hispanic Business Student Association has become a place where I can feel comfortable sharing personal experience about campus life." A story discussing the failure of college diversity courses to incorporate critiques of white privilege and power included the author's observation: "I have observed that my white peers are often not 'well-intentioned' in their remarks, but rather insensitive or cruel."

Other times, the students placed themselves in the story more subtly. For instance, a student participant of a campus-community partnership at an elementary school wrote about the transformation in that school but included comments about her role in the collaboration. Diana reported on the enactment of a performance art piece at the state capitol and informed her readers that she took a class from the artist to be a part of that exhibition. A story about undocumented workers in the fast food industry was prompted because one student "was compelled" to bring his voice to light amid such negative legislation and rhetoric. Co-authors Leticia and Emily wrote about how they visited several Home Depots to interview day laborers looking for work to support their families because they wanted to convey their integrity. Bella recounted how she became aware of the concept of social justice and programs that enabled her to advocate for her community. Angel reflected on leadership training he received that had a Hawaiian-based epistemology. Selena profiled a 19-year-old, undocumented resident facing deportation, and she revealed her personal friendship with him since high school. These techniques are used to let the reader know what motivated the author to pursue a particular story, and it acknowledges that the writer reports through the lens of his or her experience, personality, and history.

A third rhetorical device students rely on to situate themselves in their coverage is their frequent use of the pronouns "we" or "our." Most frequently this occurs in references to "our community." In a story about the various forms of activism against anti-immigration legislation, Rolando wrote, "Year after year, we see these types of bills emerge whose sole purpose is to make the life of immigrants more complicated." In a piece about the Brown Berets, Hugo wrote, "Self-determination is the idea that we have the right to live our lives and run our communities in the way our culture teaches us to." Angel wrote about the media framing of a brown-on-brown tragic crime, claiming that "false identities" of brown males "disguise the problems in our communities and pit community members against their neighbors while labeling our young adults." In an article encouraging Latinas/os to reclaim the ancient and modern artifacts of a pending exhibit of Mexican art, Simon wrote,

> What we must do is educate ourselves and reclaim the traditions that our ancestors left for us through their works that have been recovered and tell the stories that we know from our parents that fit into whichever particular piece we're admiring in the exhibit.

Again, this rhetorical move makes the reporter visible in the story and connects him or her as a member of the community, rather than as a dislocated, untethered voice. In a student-produced manual stipulating the guiding principles of Chicana/o journalism, the students explained:

> Every staff member should have the space for allowing self-positionality and sensibility within and among the issues they write about. Unlike the standard of objectivity prevalent in mainstream news writing, *guerrilleras/os*[4] unapologetically name their positionality, multiple identities, their group membership, and their motivation for writing about that matter. Thus, *guerrilleras/os* have the freedom to use "I," "we," or "our" in the articles and are able to place or include themselves in their stories.

In addition to personal stories and rhetorical maneuvers, a third technique informed by the concept of *testimonio* involves cultivating reporting techniques that honor the generosity, sincerity, and confidence of those whose stories are gathered, whether it be for a single quote in an article or an individual's life story featured in the article. *Venceremos* contributors understand the need to foster a relationship with sources that reflect a level of respect and that is reciprocal. Again, this stands in contrast to the way that mainstream journalists are socialized to act as neutral channels that simply ask questions rather than engage in dialogue or relationship building. One of the ways that the course draws attention to the skill set needed to cultivate this rapport is by reading *testimonios* of Latina/o students aloud in class. We discuss the significantly personal accounts and the intimacy required to share those kinds of details, which allows the student staff to envision conducting interviews that elicit those poignant stories. One student summarized this to mean that it was imperative for staff members not to take pity or sympathize. Another said to "give them something in return. Perhaps share a story about yourself that is relevant or/and shows some hardship in your life." Establishing trust was another key factor. Revealing a similar struggle, students said, establishes trust. Lastly, a common sentiment reiterated among student journalists was that connecting with a common experience allows the person interviewed to recognize a form of oppression he or she had not yet identified in their life. Desire wrote, "Sometimes people themselves don't realize what they are going through, so getting them to tell you about stories that they may not think are important" happens after you have told them something that happened to you.

Most interviewing occurs outside of the purview of the classroom, and so students self-report how they conducted the interview. Angel talked about visiting the home of a young Latino who was killed by a Tongan male—spending hours getting to know his family, eating with them, and sharing his experiences with gang violence and the means to get out of it. Selena shared how she and the individual she interviewed cried several times during the interview as they shared stories with each other. Analisa visited with owners of Latino-owned businesses in their places of work for several weeks to get a sense of their daily struggles to stay afloat. She did the same when she featured a local *panadería* (bakery). Simon interviewed taco stand owners who were facing tightened city ordinances and had to spend several weekends hanging around their street corners until they were confident enough to talk to him about their situation.

Over 40 undocumented individuals have been interviewed for *Venceremos* over the past four years, and these interviews always require extra diligence and, often, the ability to speak in Spanish. The use of these sources also means making explicit the opportunity to keep the sources' identity hidden and unexposed. Citlaly cautioned *Venceremos* staff to

> be conscious that there are risks involved for them in telling their story, especially since we often are bringing up issues that people in power would rather we ignored (like the rest of the media does). So if this is a concern, reassure your interviewees that we will protect their identities because we understand what risks they are taking.

For the most part, students report that nearly all of the undocumented sources they have approached with the opportunity to share their story with someone who can understand their plight are grateful and willing to do so. Students further describe these interactions as transformative and meaningful for them.

A final component of a Chicana feminist *testimonio*-informed journalism practice necessitates co-constructing the resulting story with sources. Even though *Venceremos* staff members across the semester articulate the importance of this reciprocity, only about a third of the students shared a final draft with their interviewees prior to publication. Two main reasons may account for this. For one, most students write in English, even when they speak Spanish fluently. Because many sources are Spanish-only speakers, they are unable to ask them to review an article written in English prior to publication. Usually, articles are translated into Spanish mere days before the pages are designed, minimizing time for additional feedback and edits. Secondly, students over-rely on e-mail to share their finished product, and a minimal number of sources have convenient access to an e-mail account. Those who do get feedback from their sources report general high satisfaction, needing very few edits to their resulting pieces.

However, a different aspect of collaboration occurs in the editing process designed by the *Venceremos* staff. All first drafts are read by every staff member, who provides feedback to the contributor in a group editing session. Those in editor positions communicate the feedback, but all staff provide comments, suggestion, and praise. This collective editing is meant to avert a hier-archical structure in determining content and newsworthiness and to foster a shared responsibility for what ultimately gets published. It also allows contributors to feel supported and appreciated for their efforts to collect, organize, and share the stories they pen. This process is in contrast to the top-down structure in most newsrooms where supervising editors and copy editors make sole determinations of edits to copy.

In summary, focus on issues that impact Chicana/o Latina/o communities, value of experiential knowledge, and engagement with systemic oppression and social change solidify the presence of Chicana feminist *testimonio* within the Chicana/o journalism model of *Venceremos* and within the pedagogy used in the *Venceremos* classroom. This engenders a media practice that encourages writers to author their own *testimonios*, allows them to locate themselves in the stories they tell, advocates for a reciprocal and trust-building interview process, and strives for a collaborative editing process. Despite the multiple points of alignment between *testimonio* and a Chicana/o journalism model, the fusion is not perfect. The following section delineate the tensions the student staff faced as a result of merging two disparate literary genres: journalism and *testimonio*.

Tensions Converging *Testimonio* and Journalism

The alternative journalism model espoused by *Venceremos'* mission purposely countered mainstream news norms, primarily the attempt to report objectively. Similar to the critiques of a decidedly Eurocentric bias in academic research, this attribute of the mainstream news has been interpreted to likewise uphold white privilege and ideology (Dolan, 2006; Heider, 2000; van Dijk, 2000, 2005). Consequently, the concern of the verifiability of "a true accounting" of an event did not preoccupy *Venceremos* staff members. Rather, they wanted to report how Latinas/os and members of other racially and ethnically marginalized groups made sense of their experiences of oppression, to document how they understood this phenomenon as it revealed itself in their social spheres, in their psyche, and on their bodies. As such, three interrelated tensions did surface. All pertain to issues of representation. First, students often struggled with the privilege they felt being in college and being responsible for editing collected *testimonios*. Second, several writers grappled with the decisions and discernments of the translation process because many interviews were conducted in Spanish, and they were writing primarily in English. Last, some students struggled with placing themselves in their stories, despite their commitment to foster greater transparency in their journalism model.

Because space limitations require students to curtail their contributions to an average of about 500 words, a finite number of anecdotes, quotes, or details from a *testimonio* could be included. Student staff frequently exceeded maximum word count on their first drafts because they could not decide what to exclude. Prioritizing only certain moments felt disingenuous to students who had invested time in building a relationship with various sources. In addition, they resisted editing responses into paraphrasing or condensed quotes. They wanted to incorporate the words of their *testimoniantes* intact. Because *Venceremos* only has funding to produce a certain size document each semester, it is impractical to run articles that exceed the designated space allotment, forcing students to determine what to exclude. Again, for some, this entailed more of a collaborative negotiation, but for the most part, these are choices students have to make once they have moved onto the production stage of the publication and are placing their story on the page. Reflecting on this dilemma, students often perceived the academic privilege that allowed them to filter voices and stories to finalize the content of the newspaper. Even though journalists of color recognized they were ostracized on a predominantly white campus, they were sometimes troubled with the power their position as a college student journalist afforded them when they were representing someone else's story, even someone else from their community. Granted, many sources interviewed were other college students of color, thus, diminishing the disquiet somewhat; however, *testimonios* from individuals not part of the campus community caused the greatest apprehension for those writers and ironically, the empowerment *Venceremos* provides them was problematized as a form of power over someone else's story.

A second tension includes the subjective art of translating direct quotes. Students frequently debated word choices, as well as whether *testimoniantes* should ever be quoted in a language they do not speak. As a result, there is no consistency across the past seven issues as to how certain words are translated—especially academic jargon that names and articulates experiences of oppression—or how often Spanish and English are mixed in the same article. The *Venceremos* staff, over the past seven semesters, has included a variety of *Latinidades*—including multi-generational U.S.-born Chicanas/os from Texas, California, New Mexico, New York, and Utah, as well as members of the 1.5 generation from Peru, Argentina, Mexico, Costa Rica, and Guatemala. As a result, various dialects of Spanish have been parried about in the classroom space. Words carry certain connotations in some Latin American countries that they do not in others, and so students wrestle with finding "universal" Spanish terminology. Moreover, students grapple unendingly with the complexities of subtext, denotation, and overtones inherent in the translation process (Marshall & Rossman, 2006). In the end, editors decided to allow each contributor to resolve how to convert quotes from one language to another, entreating the staff to ensure that all readers could read a story and its accompanying direct quotes in the language of their choosing. As the advisor and instructor for this publication, I help students articulate the particular challenges in the translation process and make the advantages and disadvantages of each option explicit, but the staff ultimately determines how to treat each article, and each word choice, on a case-by-case basis. I have tried to help them recognize patterns in their decision-making to formulate general guidelines that may aid future staff in their own decision-making process.

A final difficulty the student journalists of *Venceremos* face is situating themselves in their articles. Often *Venceremos* staff members were disinclined to acknowledge their presence in the story or had difficulty sharing a personal *testimonio* in a publication that would print between 6,000 to 8,000 copies. As mentioned, students often wrote themselves into their articles by using the first person. When students turned in drafts that did not reference their investment in the story in any way, I would encourage them to find a way to incorporate their connection to the story using "I" statements. For a handful, this caused apprehension and they did not do so. While theorizing abstractly about the necessity of having spaces for the voices of their community, telling their own story—albeit in a line or two—proved too taxing. The primary stumbling block perhaps may be that their academic training has socialized them to deliberately keep themselves out of their writing, and it feels awkward to write against that. For some, the formula for news writing has been etched into their consciousness and in an effort to write professionally, they cling to this blueprint. Lastly, the fact that their name and its accompanying story will be reprinted thousands of times is perhaps, dissuading enough. For those few *Venceremos* reporters, the private and the public grate against each other, and they wrestle with finding a common ground.

IMPLICATIONS AND CONCLUDING THOUGHTS

In this essay, I map out the benchmarks Chicana/o student journalists utilize that hinge upon a Chicana-inspired *testimonio*. By aligning epistemological approaches, Chicana feminist *testimonio* aptly scaffolds this alternative news model. This is evident in the student discourse about the stories of racism, sexism, heteronormativity, classism, and other forms of oppression, they collect, the individuals they collect stories from, and the objective those tales meet. Recognizing this derivational point for this unconventional practice exposes an unnamed epistemology that undergirds current journalism practices—an invisible Eurocentric, white supremacist ideology that privileges certain voices, stories, and frames and excludes, minimizes, or negates others. Several journalism scholars have pointed out this bias (Dolan, 2006; Dyer, 2000; Hieder, 2000;

van Dijk, 1993, 2000), but I hope to begin to plot re-imagined practices with different orienting points. I also extend a Chicana-feminist *testimonio* beyond its present academic sphere, back into the general public domain (albeit a small local market reach).

Based on the work of the *Venceremos'* activist journalists, I chart the use of *testimonio* for media consumption. Four waypoints materialize when converting this philosophy into a practical application. The first occurs when student reporters of color write their own *testimonios* for the newspaper. A second expression is the rhetorical devices student journalists engage to identify the role they play in their coverage of an issue or event, a concession that their lived experiences color[5] the way they understand the world. A reporting process that cultivates a shared trust and reciprocal exchange of stories is a third articulation. A final module compels student journalists to collaborate with their *testimoniantes* in crafting the article, which typically means asking them to provide feedback on a draft of a story.

The act of writing one's *testimonio* has some recent precedence in the journalism world, as the proliferation of blogs can be read as publicizing the observations and daily minutia of a single individual. Journalism educators are presently trying to adapt existing curricula to incorporate academic training for potential bloggers, validating this personally-situated approach as current and potentially profitable for the industry. However, not all content produced for blogs qualifies as a *testimonio*, which specifically denotes a subaltern experience of injustice shared with the intention of social transformation. This observation simply reminds journalism researchers of the established value in the industry of a particularized approach.

For *testimoniantes*, the calculated and often blurred use of "I," "we," or "our" engenders the reader to understand the tale communally, as a representative—if not wholly composite—story of injustice. For student journalists of color, the use of these rhetorical strategies helps the reader identify them as part of the larger marginalized community—not to see them as outsiders or as objective. This is also done more privately in the reporting techniques developed by the *Venceremos* staff that seek to establish trust and to develop relationships. Inviting this sense of community is part of *Venceremos'* modus operandi, and it starkly contrasts with traditional news routines that dictate that reporters assume an unattached persona and write through an omnipresent and disembodied voice in news reports. As the news industry adjusts to different news consumption patterns, perhaps cultivating news gathering methods that help readers relate to reporters as actual people will generate loyalty among readers.

Co-constructed news articles like the ones published in *Venceremos* are also antithetical to the profit-driven and fast-paced contemporary news cycle. Copy editors and supervising editors are the final arbiters in this top-down structure. While *Venceremos* staff writers are still refining this aspect of their practice, the principle of co-constructed news articles offers a re-envisioned hierarchy that privileges a bottom-up perspective.

Blending the genres of journalism and *testimonio* generated some friction regarding issues of representation. The first tension arises when student journalists are forced to exclude some portions of another's *testimonio*. Paradoxically, their position as college students of color with access to *Venceremos* becomes an uncomfortable privilege when they are forced to edit another's story who is not connected to the campus. Student of color journalists feel culturally attuned to collect, empathize, and understand the *testimonios* they collect, and there is reticence to purge parts of it. These still-hidden narratives are what cause the most anxiety for the *Venceremos* staff. Chicana scholars have begun to pursue the theoretical implications of the authorial privilege in editing down someone else's story, which must occur in preparing manuscripts based on collected *testimonios* (Téllez, 2005; Villenas, 1996a, 1996b).

When the agenda is the production of knowledge as defined by the academy, what criteria is invoked when filtering a *testimonio*? The issue is not as problematic when Chicana feminist scholars pen their own *testimonio*; they have full autonomy over what they share and do not share, and this self-editing is more authentic. The tension confronted by the *Venceremos* staff provides Chicana feminists an additional opportunity to tease out which *testimonios* remain hidden because it reveals a fissure in the narrowed gap between subaltern and interlocutor that Chicana feminist *testimonios* try to minimize.

Translating Spanish to English is a second cause for consternation because of the inexorable subjectivity inherent in transferring from one language to another and the various dialects of Spanish the students themselves know. There are no standards or guidelines in Chicana feminist scholarship either. Much *testimonio* scholarship mixes concepts and theoretical terms in Spanish, but many *testimonios* are either written in English or translated from Spanish without describing the credentials of the translator. Mainstream newspapers also provide quotes that were originally stated in another language without referencing the translation process. Given the subjective nature of converting from one language to another, both Chicana feminists and news practitioners should make explicit how these words are selected and why. The goal to these discussions should not be to standardize Spanish in the literature. The multifaceted, dysfunctional, and resilient relationships between Spanish and those of Latina/o heritage are reflected in the many dynamic iterations of the Spanish language. Consequently, translated works by Chicana feminists might begin to indicate the subjectivity and rationale behind certain word choices because they will reflect certain positions, historical contexts, and geographical roots that may or may not correspond to those of the *testimoniantes*. Transparency, rather than uniformity, would impel this move.

The apprehension that students experienced in revealing aspects about themselves has implications for journalism educators. I would like to see journalism pedagogy and curriculum re-socialize potential media practitioners to be publically accountable for the ways they are invested in newsworthy events, issues, and stories. Reporters should once more reconnect with the role of public servant as part of their professional identity and willingly become agents in the representation and transformation of their communities.

I argue that Chicana/o journalism students adopting a raced- and gendered-journalism practice, rooted in Chicana feminism and *testimonio,* offer Chicana/o communities in and out of the academy legitimate, judicious, and pertinent journalistic norms and customs that are more compatible to representing the multiple oppressions that racially marginalized communities experience. By shifting the power more evenly between news consumer to news producer, the *Venceremos'* Chicana/o journalism model strives ultimately to transform the access, opportunities, and life experiences of its community.

NOTES

1. The name of the newspaper, which means "We shall overcome," has not been changed.
2. The Department of Communication readily considered my proposal and offered the infrastructure to get the course on the books. Monies from the university publication council remain steady in order to cover printing costs. However, the staff only has access to the computer equipment and meeting space where class is held for three hours a week, and only under my supervision, a barrier several faculty in the department felt was necessary to erect because of several unfounded concerns about students using the space outside of regular class hours and on the weekends. It continues to be a challenge to have a space where students can gather and do this work.
3. Names of students have been changed

4. *Guerrilleras/os* are "warriers of the pen." The students identify themselves in this way in their bylines.
5. The term "color" refers to both the impact and influence student journalists' lived experiences has on their worldview and it implies that the very experience they are drawing from is demarcated by race, which is often signified by skin color.

REFERENCES

Alemán, S. (2011). Chicana/o student journalists map out a Chicana/o journalism practice. *Journalism Practice*, *5*(3), 332–349.
Anzaldúa, G. (1987). *Borderlands/la frontera: The new mestiza* (2nd ed.). San Francisco, CA: Aunt Lute Books.
Arias, A. (2001). Authoring ethnicized subjects: Rigoberta Menchú and the performative production of the subaltern self. *PMLA*, *116*(1), 75–88.
Binford, L. (2001). Empowered speech: Social fields, *testimonio*, and the Stoll-Menchú debate. *Identities*, *8*(1), 105–133.
Brooks, L. M. (2005). *Testimonio's* poetics of performance. *Comparative Literature Studies*, *42*(2), 181–222.
Burciaga, R., & Tavares, A. (2006). Our pedagogy of sisterhood: A testimonio. In D. Delgado Bernal, C. A. Elenes, F. E. Godinez, & S. Villenas (Eds.), *Chicana/Latina education in everyday life: Feminista perspectives on pedagogy and epistemology* (pp. 133–142). Albany, NY: State University of New York Press.
Cruz, C. (2006). *Testimonial narratives of queer street youth: Towards an epistemology of a brown body*. Unpublished dissertation,. University of California, Los Angeles.
Delgado, R. (1989). Storytelling for oppositionists and others: A plea for narrative. In R. Delgado & J. Stefancic (Eds.), *Critical race theory: The cutting edge* (2nd ed., pp. 60–70). Philadelphia, PA: Temple University Press.
Delgado Bernal, D. (1998). Using a Chicana feminist epistemology in educational research. *Harvard Educational Review*, *68*(4), 555–582.
Delgado Bernal, D. (2006a). Learning and living pedagogies of the home: The mestiza consciousness of Chicana students. In D. E. Delgado Bernal, A. C. Elenes, F. E. Godinez, & S. Villenas (Eds.), *Chicana/Latina education in everyday life: Feminista perspectives on pedagogy and epistemology* (pp. 113–132). Albany, NY: State University of New York Press.
Delgado Bernal, D. (2006b). *Mujeres* in college: Negotiating identities and challenging educational norms. In D. E. Delgado Bernal, A. C. Elenes, F. E. Godinez, & S. Villenas (Eds.), *Chicana/Latina education in everyday life: Feminista perspectives on pedagogy and epistemology* (pp. 77–80). Albany, NY: State University of New York Press.
Delgado Bernal, D., Godinez, F. E., Villenas, S., & Elenes, C. A. (Eds.). (2006). *Chicana/Latina education in everyday life: Feminista perspectives on pedagogy and epistemologies*. Albany, NY: State University of New York Press.
Dolan, K. (2006). *Whiteness & news: An ethical inquiry into the construction of "realities."* 56th Annual Conference of the International Communication Association (pp. 1–25). Dresden, Germany.
Dyer, R. (2000). The matter of whiteness. In L. Black & J. Solomas (Eds.), *From theories of race and racism: A reader* (pp. 539–548). New York, NY: Routledge.
Espino, M. M., Muñoz, S. M., & Marquez Kiyama, J. (2010). Transitioning from doctoral study to the academy: Theorizing trenzas of identity for Latina sister scholars. *Qualitative Inquiry*, *16*(10), 804–818.
Flores, J., & Garcia, S. (2009). Latina testimonios: A reflexive, critical analysis of a "Latina space" at a predominantly white campus. *Race, Ethnicity and Education*, *12*(2), 150–172.
Galván, R. T. (2006). Campesina epistemologies and pedagogies of the spirit: Examining women's sobrevivencia. In D. E. Delgado Bernal, A. C. Elenes, F. E. Godinez, & S. Villenas (Eds.), *Chicana/Latina education in everyday life: Feminista perspectives on pedagogy and epistemology* (pp. 161–180). Albany, NY: State University of New York Press.
Gutiérrez, K. D. (2008). Developing a sociocritical literacy in the Third Space. *Reading Research Quarterly*, *43*(2), 148–164.
Heider, D. (2000). White news: Why local news programs don't cover people of color. Mahwah, NJ: Erlbaum.
Irizarry, Y. (2005). The ethics of writing the Caribbean: Latina narrative as testimonio. *Literature Interpretation Theory*, *16*(3), 263–284.
Latina Feminist Group. (2001). *Telling to live: Latina feminist testimonios*. Durham, NC: Duke University Press.

Lopez, K. S. (1998). Internal colonialism in the testimonial process: Elena Poniatowska's Hasta no verte Jesús mío. *Symposium, 52*(1), 21–39.

Marcial, G. (1993, Fall). Venceremos is here! *Venceremos, 1*(1), 2.

Marshall, C., & Rossman, G. B. (2006). *Designing qualitative research* (4th ed.). Thousand Oaks, CA: Sage.

Mindich, D. T. Z. (1998). *Just the facts: How "objectivity" came to define American journalism.* New York, NY: New York University Press.

Mize, R. L., & Leedham, C. (2000). Manufacturing bias: An analysis of newspaper coverage of Latino immigration issues. *Latino Studies Journal, 11*(2), 88–107.

National Association of Hispanic Journalists Network. (2006). *Brownout Report 2006: The portrayal of Latinos and Latino issues on network television news, 2005.* Washington, DC: Author.

Nayar, P. K. (2006). Bama's Karukku: Dalit autobiography as testimonio. *The Journal of Commonwealth Literature, 41*(2), 83–100.

Pérez Huber, L. (2009a). Challenging racist nativist framing: Acknowledging the community cultural wealth of undocumented Chicana college students to reframe the immigration debate. *Harvard Educational Review, 79*(4), 704–729.

Pérez Huber, L. (2009b). Disrupting apartheid of knowledge: *Testimonio* as methodology in Latina/o critical race research in education. *International Journal of Qualitative Studies in Education, 22*(6), 639–654.

Pillow, W. (2003). Race-based methodologies: Multicultural methods or epistemological shifts? In G. R. Lopez & L. Parker (Eds.), *Interrogating racism in qualitative research methodology* (pp. 181–202). New York, NY: Lang.

Poindexter, P. M., Smith, L., & Heider, D. (2003). Race and ethnicity in local television news: Framing, story assignments, and source selection. *Journal of Broadcasting and Electronic Media, 47*(4), 524–536.

Poniatowska, E. (1971). *La noche de Tlatelolco: Testimonies de historia oral.* México: Ediciones Era.

Rivas Rodríguez, M. (1998). *Brown eyes on the web.* Unpublished dissertation. University of North Carolina, Chapel Hill.

Téllez, M. (2005). Doing research at the borderlands: Notes from a Chicana feminist ethnographer. *Chicana/Latina Studies, 4*(2), 46–70.

van Dijk, T. A. (1993). *Elite discourse and racism.* Newbury Park, CA: Sage.

van Dijk, T. A. (2000). New(s) racism: A discourse analytical approach. In S. Cottle (Ed.), *Ethnic minorities and the media* (pp. 33–49). Philadelphia, PA: Open University Press.

van Dijk, T. A. (2005). *Reproducing racism: The role of the press.* Paper Congress on Immigration, Almería Universitat Pompeu Fabra, Barcelona.

Villenas, S. (1996a). The colonizer/colonized Chicana ethnographer: Identity, marginalization, and co-optation in the field. *Harvard Educational Review, 66*(4), 711–732.

Villenas, S. (1996b). *Una buena educación: Women performing life histories of moral education in new Latino communities.* Unpublished dissertation. University of North Carolina, Chapel Hill.

Villenas, S. (2006). Mature Latina adults and mothers: Pedagogies of the wholeness and resilience. In D. E. Delgado Bernal, A. C. Elenes, F. E. Godinez, & S. Villenas (Eds.), *Chicana/Latina education in everyday life: Feminista perspectives on pedagogy and epistemology* (pp. 143–146). Albany, NY: State University of New York Press.

Digital *Testimonio* as a Signature Pedagogy for Latin@ Studies

Rina Benmayor

California State University Monterey Bay

This article proposes the curricular integration of digital *testimonio* as a "signature" pedagogy in Latin@ Studies. The *testimonio* tradition of urgent narratives and the creative multimedia languages of digital storytelling—text, voice, image, and sound—invite historically marginalized subjects, especially younger generations, to author and inscribe their own social and cultural truths. Taking inspiration from Latina writings, undergraduate students script, record, produce, publish, and theorize their own *testimonios*, building new knowledge from personal and collective experience. In this process, they construct historical and theoretical understandings of identity and belonging, reproducing and reinforcing the testimonial nexus between individual and collective story. For cyberspace generations, the digital multimedia format facilitates coming to voice. The claim for "signature" pedagogy is based on my 10-year experience with the digital storytelling genre, facilitating the creation of approximately 300 digital *testimonios* and their accompanying reflections.

I begin with an origins story. In 1993, I designed and taught an undergraduate class at Hunter College (CUNY), titled "Latina Life Stories" (LLS). It was inspired by the autobiographical writings of U.S. Latinas that, at long last, began populating bookstore shelves during the previous decade. I constructed the course around these readings and the vivid and poignant classroom discussions they invariably provoked. I asked students to write their own narratives and, as a class finale, to share portions of these in a collective reading. The class was a hit and continues to be a favorite, especially among Latina/o students because the course and the readings validate their lived experiences and place their own lives at the center, often for the very first time.

Around the same time, I also had the great fortune to become part of the Latina Feminist Group, a group of 18 teachers and writers from across the country, including Latinas of varying national, historical, cultural, and regional origins, who set out to explore our individual and intersecting personal and professional experiences through storytelling. The result of this 10-year collaboration was the anthology *Telling to Live: Latina Feminist* Testimonios (Latina Feminist Group, 2001), a volume that I now use as the backbone of LLS. We understood our stories to be *testimonios* because they were the result of an oral process of telling, recording, and bearing witness to each other's life stories. These recordings later became the written pieces in the book. In keeping with the Latin American *testimonio* tradition, we enacted over a period of five years a process of speaking out, breaking silences, and making new sense out of our commonalities and differences of experience. As with *testimonio*, our individual stories also expressed collective experiences of marginalization, resistance, and strength.

In the late 1990s, I had my own millennial turn. I was now teaching at California State University Monterey Bay, a new university that encouraged the use of new technologies. A colleague emailed me an example of some digital stories produced in workshops pioneered by the Center for Digital Storytelling in Berkeley, California. The digital multimedia world was launching new technologies and applications every day. I had never seen a digital story—a two- to four-minute movie in which the narrator tells a story in her or his own voice with the addition of images and sound. Upon seeing three sample stories, my response was instantaneous. I had already begun to experiment with web pages where students posted their written *testimonios*, but the digital multimedia story offered a whole new level of creativity and power as a testimonial form in a digital age. Since 2000, each student in Latina Life Stories, regardless of gender or ethnic origin, has created her or his own digital *testimonio* (Latina Life Stories, n.d).

To give a snapshot of the process I follow, which will be detailed further in this essay, we begin storytelling with discussions of the readings, in-class free-writes that I call "memory-writes," viewing stories of previous students, and story-circle sharing. Subsequently, students begin defining their story, writing a draft script, and after several revisions, performing the script in a recording booth. They then work in a digital lab to prepare images, edit and prepare their voice tracks, and select an optional music track. The various media pieces are then compiled in iMovie to produce a three- to four-minute digital movie. The production phase is accompanied by in-class screenings, during which we collectively theorize each story, situating it within larger social, historical, and cultural contexts. Finally, students write a theorizing paper in which they analyze and reflect upon the meanings their story contains. The class culminates with a public screening of the stories for the campus, friends, and family.

I have written extensively on the digital storytelling process in Scholarship of Teaching and Learning venues (Benmayor, 2009), and have argued for it as a signature pedagogy for the broader "new humanities," taking new fields like Cultural Studies and Ethnic Studies into account (Benmayor, 2008). Technological literacy aside, digital storytelling offers students and teachers a compelling way to discuss and understand social identities, positionalities, and inequalities. Over the 16 years in which I have taught LLS, with and without the digital multimedia component, I have consistently observed that the personal identity story opens the mind to understanding difference in ways that are deep, compassionate, and indelible. In this respect, the digital storytelling process may constitute an important curricular contribution to critical multicultural education and teacher training at the elementary and secondary levels as well. Although I do not specifically address K-12 contexts, my process as outlined in this essay may provide useful ideas and strategies for adaptation at other levels, as digital tools are no longer foreign to even the youngest students.

In this essay, my focus is more specific, drawing a distinction between digital storytelling and digital *testimonio*, and proposing digital *testimonio* as a signature pedagogy for the field of Latin@ Studies. Digital *testimonio*, in contrast to the wider category of "digital story," gives urgent and powerful voice to individual and collective Latin@ experiences and allows for broader, more democratic authorship, dissemination, and reception. But first, let me provide some definitions of terms.

DEFINITIONS

Signature Pedagogy

Traditionally applied to the professions of law, education, and medicine, signature pedagogies are acts that convey the personality, methods of performance, and values of a field. Lee Shulman (2005) former President of the Carnegie Foundation for the Advancement of Teaching, argues:

> A signature pedagogy has three dimensions. First, it has a *surface structure*, which consists of concrete, operational acts of teaching and learning, of showing and demonstrating, of questioning and answering, of interacting and withholding, of approaching and withdrawing. Any signature pedagogy also has a *deep structure*, a set of assumptions about how best to impart a certain body of knowledge and know-how. And it has an *implicit structure*, a moral dimension that comprises a set of beliefs about professional attitudes, values, and dispositions. (pp. 54–55)

Within the humanities, Calder (2006) defines signature pedagogies for the discipline of history as: "ways of being taught that require them [students] to do, think, and value what practitioners in the field are doing, thinking, and valuing" (p. 1361). In the case of interdisciplinary fields like Ethnic Studies, Women's Studies, and some Cultural Studies, signature pedagogies are grounded in liberatory values and methods. I argue for digital *testimonio* as a signature pedagogy for Latin@ Studies because it engages students first hand in reproducing the processes of (1) situated knowledge production, (2) embodied theorizing, and (3) collective practice that are foundational to the field. These processes constitute core epistemologies for Latin@ Studies, ones that we hope all of our students learn to perform in their lives as well as in their professional futures.

Testimonio

Constructing knowledge from personal experience is in the DNA of Latina writing and scholarship and is one of the key contributions that Latinas have made to the larger field of Latin@ Studies. Situating knowledge production at the intersection of race/class/gender and sexuality, pathbreaking Chicana writers demonstrated the power of knowledge that is "experienced in the flesh" and is "revealed in the flesh of their [women of color] writing," [and ultimately theorizing from the flesh] (Moraga, 1983, p. 34). Twenty-five years after its publication, Anzaldúa's (1986) *Borderlands: La Frontera* persists as a core text and continues to inspire and energize new generations of Latin@ readers. For the many Latina writers and scholars that have followed, theorizing and constructing new understandings meant breaking silences, speaking out, talking back, "writing back," and ultimately "writing for"—a voice that is both oppositional and propositional (Benmayor, 2009). Moreover, theorizing implies understanding oneself and one's experience in the context of one's own and other cultural communities. The works that we now consider foundational were the result of years of community activism and coalitional work and express not simply the truth of one individual, as compelling as it may be, but mark a collective experience, which is the critical link to *testimonio*. Sommer (1988) pointed out many years ago, apropos of Latin American women's *testimonios*, that the first person "I" of their *testimonios* stands for shared experience, for the communal "we."

Testimonio, thus, expresses the central values of situated knowledge production, embodied theorizing, and community engagement, and thus can be considered a signature pedagogy. It offers a space where students can produce their own stories to live by, the stories of their own generation, of their communities. But, what happens when *testimonios* go digital? Does the medium matter? I think it does.

Digital Storytelling and Digital *Testimonio*

Digital storytelling is a loose term used to define a variety of digital media products, some of which have little to do with storytelling in the more traditional sense. For example, even the Wikipedia (2011) entry for "Digital Storytelling" signals both specific and broad usages of this new term. The first definition is specific:

> "Digital storytelling" is a new term, arising from a grassroots movement that uses new digital tools to help ordinary people tell their own "true stories" in a compelling and emotionally engaging form. These stories are usually short (less than 8 minutes) and can be interactive. (para. 2)

The second definition is broader:

> The term "digital storytelling" can also cover a variety of new forms of digital narratives (web-based stories, interactive stories, hypertexts, and narrative computer games). It is also sometimes used to refer to any type of film-making, and is now often used for advertising and promotional work for both commercial and non-profit enterprises. (para. 3)

The stories that my students produce fall into the first definition. To complicate matters, a digital story and digital *testimonio* are not necessarily the same things. While all digital *testimonios* are generically digital stories, not all digital stories, nor all the ones my students create, should be called *testimonios*. Some stay more within the realm of personal (even though the personal is always political) and do not intentionally address collective histories of struggle. I sometimes use the broader term (digital story) to represent the full range of story genres that students produce. When I use digital *testimonio,* however, I am being specific, keeping in mind the particulars of the genre. To *testimoniar* (testify) involves an urgent voice of resistance to social injustices, an urgency to speak out, a collective interlocutor, and a collaborative process of production and interpretation. Whereas digital storytelling might be used to emphasize the medium, using digital technologies to tell stories, digital *testimonios* place the emphasis on the story and its social purpose, in a medium that is digital. Thus, in my usage I try to retain the original political and liberatory impulse of the *testimonio* genre.

My claim is that digital *testimonio* is a type of digital story that expresses core epistemologies of Latin@ Studies and involves a collaborative process of production and creation. Different from traditional autobiography or conventional digital storytelling, where the author works individually and independently to produce the narrative, digital *testimonios* involve various dimensions of collectivity. Just as the *testimonio* requires an interlocutor to generate the story and a community audience to share or understand the experience, digital *testimonios* emerge from a storytelling setting. This may be a one-on-one conversation between narrator and facilitator, a larger story circle, or a classroom of students where shared experiences interpellate the personal and spark the particular story. The texts we read are also products of collective struggles and actions. In the next section I refer to three additional collective contexts for the work the students produce: the digital media lab where collaboration and sharing are intense; the process of theorizing, placing them within larger social, historical, and cultural frameworks of meaning; and the festival where students present their finished work to a community audience. In these ways, the digital *testimonio* process quite intentionally reproduces the circle of situated knowledge production. Digital *testimonios* reenact, in form as well as content, the core dimensions of a Latin@ signature pedagogy, moving collectively from experience to narrative, to the construction of new knowledge, and to its dissemination through authorship. At each stage, the individual voice signifies a collective referent.

Before entering the classroom and the stories, let me provide a brief note about the data. I have conducted a loose form of participant observation in my own classroom over 16 years. The primary data consist of approximately 300 *testimonios* collected during this time period. The secondary data are the theorizing essays that students write at the conclusion of the course.

REENACTING THE *TESTIMONIO* PROCESS IN THE CLASSROOM

Testimonio is a dialogic process, much like an oral history, involving two interlocutors. It is the shared result of the interaction and agendas of two or more interlocutors. Expanded to the context of an ethnically diverse classroom of 25 students, however, the dialogic process takes the shape of open class discussions in which one or more students begin to tell their particular stories to the group. The assigned readings stimulate a process of *concientización*, of becoming aware of and situating one's own struggles in a larger social context. Students read Gloria Anzaldúa, Cherríe Moraga, Judith Ortiz Cofer, Aurora Levins Morales, Rosario Morales, Norma Cantú, Sandra Cisneros, Achy Obejas, and other noted Latina writers. The readings stimulate students to share their own experiences, as they begin to recognize common and uncommon situations and feelings. The classroom provides a forum for these realities to emerge. Students might say, "I can really relate to that story because the same thing [or something similar] happened to me," and the discussion switches to personal storytelling and disclosure. Other times, I might ask students to share their own stories on a particular theme, as Liliana Cabrera-Murillo remembers during a taped reflection on her experience in the class for a national project on digital storytelling conducted by scholars at Georgetown University:

> It was like a discussion session. So many times that we'd be sitting . . . We tried to make it a circle but it always end up being a square! But it was fine. We were looking at each other, and kind of saying . . . 'Cause she [the instructor] would ask us just these point blank questions, "What is your story? What is your history? What did you feel when you went to go visit your grandparents?" And even though sometimes it's like we can blow it over really easily and just kind of give everybody the, "Oh, it's great. I feel warm and fuzzy when I see my grandparents." But for that class it was like, "No. I visit my grandparents, and they live across the street from the border." And before this class, before having all these different women and their stories, I wasn't able to open up. Because it was like, "Oh, you just want to hear about my grandma's cookies or her food or something," but this was like, "Yes, I see the 10-foot tall fence with the barbed wire on top every time I visit her. Yes, I drive through a dirt driveway to get to my grandma's house. Yes, there are people who hang out and hide out in the back yard." But I never really thought about it, I never really shared it. (Digital Storytelling Multimedia Archive, 2006; cited in Benmayor, 2008, p. 199)

As Cabrera-Murillo indicates, our dialogic process can become intense when students decide to take the risk and speak their truth. As they do so, they begin to construct an incipient safe space of disclosure. I say "incipient" because safety is a relative feeling and each individual chooses what she or he wishes to share. Although the class is typically comprised of a rich mix of students—Latinas, some brave *vatos* ("dudes" in Chicano slang), other students of color, and students of European heritages (women and men), straight and gay, and sometimes of different generations—everyone is able to find points of connection with or divergence from their own experiences. Latin@s, of course, have a special relationship to the material. The readings authorize them, perhaps for the very first time, to bring their lives into the classroom and to begin to think about them as more than just "my personal story." They begin to understand that their experience is not theirs alone. Regardless of level of privilege or disadvantage, gender, age, or ethnicity, once the space of disclosure has been opened, every student positions herself or himself as a mindful, compassionate ally to one other. This is the real magic of this course.

I structure the digital *testimonio* creation process in six stages. A recent "U-Story" (university story) (Turchin, 2010) produced about the Latina Life Stories class gives a video glimpse into several parts of the process. The first stage consists of reading, viewing digital stories of previous semesters, and discussion. (Readings and discussions continue throughout two-thirds of the class.) We open each session with a five-minute "memory write," a free writing in a personal journal around one of the class themes, to jog the memory. Memory write prompts include topics such as, "identity," "family and community," "migration," "gender roles," "transgressing," and "an empowerment story." Students are invited to share their memory writes aloud in class if they choose. I do not collect their journals and never see what they have written, as I consider these private writings. Some of these are shared, and they initiate the thematic discussion, and a few may eventually make it onto the screen. At an appropriate moment in each class session, we also view students' stories from previous years that have particular relevance to the theme. These screenings also may stimulate a memory, a conflict, or aesthetic ideas for the story that each student will create.

While we are seeding ideas for scripts in the initial stage, theoretical and textual analysis and discussion play a central role in the whole process. I might give a short presentation on critical ideas and theories, or discussions can be prompted by a student summary of the assigned text and a question to spark discussion. I also pose questions, sometimes very simple and direct ones that link the text to personal experience, like, "Has this ever happened to you?" The best pedagogical strategies invariably dissolve into spontaneous personal disclosure. Sometimes difficult discussions around racial and sexual violence ensue. Students seem to listen to each other differently than the way they do in other classes, assuming responsibility as caring facilitators and mediators rather than as opponents, as happens so often in other classes. At the beginning of the course I speak openly about ways to listen and to hear stories from the heart, about the importance of not judging each other and fostering an open atmosphere of mindfulness and understanding. I also take care to present critical ideas and potential hot-button issues in a non-confrontational tone. The personal intensity of autobiographical writing also helps establish this tone of mindful engagement.

During the second stage, we continue discussing readings and view stories, but now drafts of the new stories begin to emerge, first orally ("this is what I'm thinking about for my digital *testimonio*"), then in written drafts shared in class, and finally in the form of a $1\frac{1}{2}$ page, double-spaced script. We workshop the scripts, give oral and written feedback to find the dramatic arc of the story and, in preparation for recording, insure that the syntax of the story follows oral speech patterns. I offer aesthetic and dramatic suggestions to the various drafts of the story script. Most often this involves suggestions for cutting, synthesizing, clarifying, and intensifying the dramatic twist. On occasion, I might gently challenge a statement made in a story, but I attempt to do so in an invitational manner. I try to honor the students' choices by supporting the stories they have chosen to tell, whatever they may be. In this regard, my process departs again from traditional *testimonio* in that control of the writing, selection, editing, and publishing is placed in the hands of the author, rather than in that of the oral history interviewer who gathers the testimony and then usually prepares its publication.

The third stage is recording. To facilitate the performance of the story, the prose script is displayed in poetic format (see the example from Garza below). Cutting the lines along the natural breath pauses helps turn the "reading" into a "telling." Recording takes place in a very hot and claustrophobic sound recording booth, with the narrator, a microphone, the dramatic performance coach (me), and a computer. This process is very emotional, not only because of the physical discomfort of the cramped space, but also because of the impact of voicing on the narrator. No matter how many times students practice, the performance into the microphone becomes the "real" telling, the moment of disclosure, the moment of real remembrance, and the moment when they "hear" their own story out loud. Students say that this is the most difficult moment in the production process. Ana Elías Morales (2008) writes: "The first indication that this story was very personal was in my first attempts to record it in the sound booth; I cried. I . . . felt as though my mom were speaking through me" (p. 6). Javier Tamayo (2007), who today is an actor in a barrio theater group, writes:

> Speaking my story out loud and recording it did change me. . . . I felt as if it was not just a poem but demanded social justice. This inspired me to try and write more poetry and recite them [sic] . . . I did feel intimidated because I had never recorded my voice in that type of format. (p. 4)

Emotionally challenging as it is, the recording is perhaps the most important dimension of the *testimonio*. No longer an edited transcript to be read, the *testimonio* is now in the voice of the subject, speaking directly to the viewers, and asking us to listen. More than the images, the voice is what gives these digital *testimonios* their power.

The fourth stage is production. Production takes place in a digital lab attached to the course. Here students learn everything they need to construct their story digitally—scanning and photoshopping still images, using Internet source material fairly, editing the audio recordings, embedding music, integrating video, and final timing and mixing. Although one often hears the claim that technology is alienating, the work in the digital storytelling lab effects the opposite. In response to the technology learning curve, students form natural teams, help each other, and appreciate (in the full sense of this word) each other's stories. As the technological vulnerability increases, the group support intensifies. The more savvy students help the others and share creative tricks. Their presence in the lab is important. There are students who have the skills and want to work alone at home. Yet, they miss out on a very critical process of collaboration, become disconnected from the group, turning authoring into an individualized rather than a collective process.

The fifth stage is in-class screening and interpretation of each story, anticipating the final theorizing paper each student will write. This is the first time students see each other's stories in their entirety. Seeing one's story on the big screen is a scary moment but, by this point, collaborative engagement throughout the semester has produced a strong level of solidarity and safety. The tissue box circulates. Each story is met with tears, laughter, awe, and enthusiastic applause. Students offer empowering comments to each other and vulnerability is transformed into pride. Suddenly, the classmates they have been sitting next to, hearing from, and working with for 16 weeks acquire full historical dimension, they become full people with real lives, as their stories invite the viewer into their pasts and their feelings. The story and the individual merge and produce deeper insight into that person's social reality, heightening the bond that has been created throughout the semester and creating an unusual degree of cross-cultural understanding and mutual respect among all members of the class.

All students receive an automatic "A" for completing a story, worth 60% of the class grade. I do this for various reasons. First, I do not feel it is appropriate to judge the grade value of an intensely personal story. I would not know what criteria to use. This way, students are making stories that are meaningful to them and not for a grade. The final theorizing paper, however, is a graded assignment. It is an analytical and interpretive piece in which students are asked to draw connections between their story and its historical and cultural contexts, and to reference the class readings and concepts. Here I feel it appropriate to assess and grade their attention to and care in analysis. In the end, students come to value their experience in the class more than the formal grade because they are given the space to tell their own truths. Although students do get a grade for the class, the vast majority of students engage and perform at a very high and outstanding level.

The sixth stage is public presentation. The class finale is a public digital *testimonio* festival for friends, family, faculty, and staff, which has now become an annual event on campus. Whereas the in-class screening intensifies the bonding among members of the class, the public festival is a declaration, a presentation of self and one's work, a celebration of authorship. Students give copies of their story as gifts to parents and grandparents, spouses, and children—a contribution to the family archive. Each student also receives a DVD containing all the movies from the class. (Prior to that, however, each student fills out a detailed release form specifying how their story can be used and in what public contexts.) The DVD becomes a form of publishing, a tangible product that can then circulate and be viewed by others. Some of these stories make their way into the following year's syllabus, to be viewed and discussed in the company of the famous writers. Thus, a new generation of voices becomes inscribed into the corpus of Latin@ testimonial literature.

SITUATED KNOWLEDGE—EMBODIED THEORIZING

The theorizing/reflection paper is the most difficult and challenging assignment of the class. Even though we analyze and interpret readings throughout the semester, and we collectively theorize each story after production, students are challenged to stand back and put the personal story they have just produced into wider context. While they are fairly comfortable with theoretical concepts, such as borderlands, intersecting oppressions, hybrid identities, situated identity, nationalism and transnationalism, border feminism, or underground feminism, students are asked to discuss their own narratives of these abstract concepts—to reenact the signature process of theorizing from the flesh.

A sampling of their theorizing essays evidences a greater awareness of how their individual lives and stories are shaped by larger social structures and forces, both within and outside their familial communities. They can articulate connections and disconnections from their cultural histories, and they begin to acquire a new explanatory language and critical standpoint. While they are not yet making new theoretical contributions to the field, they are learning a process for doing so.

To illustrate this embodied theorizing process, I focus on a tiny sample of three *testimonios* from Latin@ students—Liliana Cabrera-Murillo, José Garza, and Juanita Velasco (Students' names are their own; they have granted permission to cite their stories and to upload online.) I will quote and draw from their story scripts and their final theorizing papers to make the case. In a previous article (Benmayor, 2008), I analyzed Cabrera-Murillo's story and reflections in greater depth, citing many of the passages included here but examining the relationship between the theoretical and the artistic dimensions. For this article, I selected these three stories because they are conceptually and aesthetically strong *testimonios* that both "write back" to difficult experiences that are common to Latin@ youth and "write for" their peers and younger generations (for a discussion of "writing back" and "writing for" see Benmayor, 2009). These stories address issues of national, ethnic, and gender identities that widely concern young Latin@s. I also chose these stories because their authors' theorizing papers demonstrated strong intellectual ability to tease out underlying meanings in their narratives and insightfully contextualize their stories within a larger collective experience and body of literature. These stories also exemplify the three constitutive dimensions of signature pedagogy for Latin@ Studies—situated knowledge production, embodied theorizing, and collective referents.

Liliana Cabrera-Murillo's (2004a) story, "Dancing into *mi cultura*" (http://blogs.umass.edu/ equity), addresses issues of identity within and outside one's national community and the role that strong family traditions and ancestral memory can play in constructing a place of belonging. It is also an eloquent example of the impact of Chicana thinkers and writers—specifically Anzaldúa's (1986) *Borderlands*—in the process of coming to consciousness, especially for second, third, and fourth generation Latin@s.

Cabrera-Murillo opens her story with difficult memories of school, often the place where children first experience themselves as part of a social world outside the family in which they feel they do not belong. She talks about feeling unrepresented in the history books, shunned in Catholic school where she was the only Latina, and once again in public school, where her fourth-generation experience set her apart from her immigrant classmates. In her theorizing essay, Cabrera-Murillo synthesizes and names her struggle, acknowledging the importance of higher education in making sense of her past:

> My Digital Story is concerned with the progress of my *Chicanisma* through the relationships of culture, education, society, and family. Family has been a foundation for my personal traditions and a source of support in pursuing my cultural heritage. School provided me an education that kept my academic self separate from my cultural being. ... I had to find a way to claim an identity that embraced a rich Mexican heritage as well as a fourth generation citizen experience ... I was finally given a chance to rewrite a history that had been erased and hidden in Eurocentric textbooks. (Cabrera-Murillo, 2004b; cited in Benmayor, 2008, pp. 191–192)

She goes on to talk about her involvement as a teenager in *baile folclórico* and finds in it a pathway to embrace her *cultura* and define her identity. Through dance, she reconnects to her immigrant farm laboring ancestors, lifting the curve of their spine with the hem of her skirt. She writes:

I now recognize my space. The space that includes oppressions, privilege, and transcendence. My experience entails the suffering of my parents and the educational opportunities that their struggles provided me. My experience is that of the transgression of cultural traditions as I chose to train my legs to dance rather than strengthen them to hold future oppressions (or a husband) on my back. I accept the "westernized" aspects of my education and use my new consciousness to turn it on its side, finding a way to tell the real histories. (Cabrera-Murillo, 2004b; cited in Benmayor, 2008, p. 194)

The concept of new *mestiza* consciousness offered her a new and empowering framework for understanding. She cites Anzaldúa's (1986) famous passage about *mestiza* consciousness:

La mestiza . . . has a plural personality, operates in a pluralistic mode—nothing is thrust out, the good, the bad and the ugly, nothing rejected, nothing abandoned. Not only does she sustain contradictions, she turns the ambivalence into something else. (p. 101)

Through this, Cabrera-Murillo arrives at an extraordinary insight. She says: "It now seems ironic that the name that I've found to identify my experience is a consciousness that requires me to embrace a comfort in ambiguity" (Cabrera-Murillo, 2004b; cited in Benmayor, 2008, p. 193). By writing, producing, and theorizing her story, Cabrera-Murillo bears witness to her past and constructs a new space of belonging. In her interview for Georgetown's national digital storytelling project, conducted two years later, she explains how she comes to this realization:

It was more like she [Anzaldúa] was telling me, "This is you," when I was reading it. Having that duality and not really . . . I knew it, I knew that I had the me that I presented at school, and then I had the me that I presented at home, with people that I was comfortable bringing into my culture. When I was in elementary school, I would have friends come over and spend the night. But when they spent the night, we would have like, chicken and rice and broccoli and make cakes. But when I was with my cousins or somebody else that was in my culture, we'd wake up and we'd have *chorizo* [sausage] and *pan dulce* [sweet rolls, pastries].

I knew that that was there, but she [Anzaldúa] made me comfortable. She made me happy and feel just so prideful in the hybridity of having all of that and not feel that I had lost anything but knowing that it was there. Because it existed, she gave me the tools to go back and find it. (Cabrera, 2006; cited in Benmayor, 2008, p. 194)

These examples make visible the intellectual steps Cabrera-Murillo takes to move from narrative story to "theorizing from the flesh." In applying new *mestiza* consciousness to her own situation, she finds a way out of a long-standing emotional bind. She not only becomes an author of her own story but in the process becomes a sophisticated interpreter of her own experience. As she explains, Anzaldúa's (1986) text triggered a bodily reaction, an immediate recognition and connection. This new awareness enables her to tell the story of exclusion and confusion with a new ending and, in so doing, to *testimoniar*, to "write back" to the forces that oppressed her. The theorizing essay plays a critical role in understanding this signature process, as it is in the explanation of the *testimonio* that we find a second story, a meta-story of situated new knowledge. Interestingly, Cabrera-Murillo's theorizing from the flesh is not just a metaphor for experiential knowledge but directly involves the body through dance and its ability to express ancestral history.

José Garza's (2010a, 2010b) *testimonio* also involves a search for identity and finding community through a real body experience. "Welcome to the Family," (http://blogs.umass.edu/equity/) deals with "my mistaken understanding of assimilation, humanity, body, and existence" (2010b,

p. 1). In his case, the story of a physical attack to his body triggers a new symbolic awareness of identity and belonging. In analyzing the meaning of his story, he says, "This *testimonio* reminds me that realizing my ethnicity, my race, gave me back what assimilation had taken away, compassion" (pp. 1–2). Below is the script of Garza's story (2010c), displayed in the verse format used to facilitate the recording performance:

> I never considered myself a Mexican,
> but maybe that was because my parents raised me that way.
> The only group I ever classified myself under was Garza
> until I met Rodney.
> Rodney was what we in the emergency room called a frequent flyer,
> meaning he came to be seen about 10 to 15 times a week.
> Every time he came in, I would ask what he needed to be seen for:
> "Well sir" he'd reply ". . . headaches, chest pains, shortness of breathe, schizophrenia,
> sore throat, fever, back pain, blurry vision, dizziness, dehydration, earache, vomiting,
> diarrhea, sneezing, and I need clean bandages."
> After I placed Rodney's armband around his wrist he'd ask:
> "Sir, can I get a cup of coffee?"
> I always told him, "No."
> See, even though Rodney was the politest Mexican man I knew, he was a schizophrenic.
> Which meant that if I let him leave to get a cup of coffee
> he was likely to not come back till the next day.
> One early Wednesday morning,
> Rodney made his regularly scheduled appearance.
> We did our friendly routine,
> I checked him in,
> He asked if he could get coffee
> I told him, "No."
> Then a call came in over the ER loudspeaker.
> There was a shooting and GSW victims were being brought in by ambulance.
> While my coworker was registering the gunshot victims, I was calming down the
> families, and performing crowd control.
> One gentleman,
> apparently the brother of one of the victims,
> was furious he could not go back to the trauma room to see his brother.
> At one point he made a rush for the door.
> I responded by stepping in his path.
> And without hesitation he reached into his pocket and pulled out a pen and with all his
> strength stabbed it into my upper thigh.
> I fell to the ground.
> I remember the warm sensation of blood running down my leg as he kicked me in the face over
> and over again.
> Right before I passed out, I saw a cloud come over him.
> When I came to I was still on the floor in the waiting room.
> On my left a group of Hispanic men were beating the man that had attacked me
> And while none of my coworkers or emergency staff came to my aid—there was Rodney.
> He had removed the pen from my thigh and used his clean bandages to wrap my wound.
> The men that had taken down my attacker came back and helped Rodney lift me up and
> place me on a row of chairs.

And for the first time Rodney didn't refer o me as "sir" but rather "brother,"
not just him but all the men who were helping me.
At that moment my outlook changed forever.
For in my time of need none of my Emergency staff was there for me;
it wasn't the white, black, or Asian patients and visitors who stood up in my defense.
No,
It was Rodney, and the rest of my brethren.
In the end, it didn't matter that I didn't speak Spanish and they didn't speak English.
We are Mexican. We are family.

The idea for the story, Garza says, came to him while reading "Missing Body" (Souza, 2001), for our class discussion around the body as a site of memory. He also connects his *testimonio* to Moraga's "La Güera" (1983), and Anzaldúa's (1986) *Borderlands*. In Moraga, he resonates with the parental desire to shield children from racism by emphasizing assimilation into white society. He says, "By placing me into Catholic school and moving into a predominantly white community, my parents . . . wanted a higher education and safer life for us" (Garza, 2010b, p. 2). This, in effect, removed him from his own ethnic community and led him to believe that he could be "equal to everyone else." Not coincidentally, like Cabrera-Murillo, Garza takes aim at his early Catholic school education and the myth of assimilation. With the advantage of analysis, he asserts now that the intersection between assimilation and racism is thorny. "When it comes to assimilation, racism does not allow for it. For if it had, when I needed help, my 'so-called comrades' [other ER staff] would not have abandoned me" (p. 3). His scar becomes a site of memory:

> When I looked at my scar, it allowed me to see that Rodney helping me brought back my body and showed me the compassion I thought was lost. This scar serves now as a site of memory, a site of triumph, and the site of the epiphany that assimilation can take the body away. (2010b, p. 4)

Finally, he forges a link with Anzaldúa (1986), in calling the ER a "borderland where a number of cultures collided and were in a state of constant tension . . . Having been what I now see as a victim of assimilation, I was very much stuck in a borderland, as at the moment I was attached, I had no cultural affiliation" (2010b, p. 4).

Garza wants his *testimonio* to "write back" [speak back] to those who allowed him and other Latin@s to believe in the possibility of assimilation. He adds, "Lastly, my story writes back to me. This *testimonio* reminds me that realizing my ethnicity, my race, gave me back what assimilation had taken away, compassion. Not so much my compassion, though it has, but the compassion and humanity of others" (Garza, 2010b, p. 2). As was the case for Cabrera-Murillo, Garza's *testimonio* narrates an epiphany, a bodily "ah-ha" moment that allows him to embrace his heritage, construct a new sense of belonging, and understand more clearly how he fits into larger structures of exclusion/inclusion. Garza's story offers a somewhat novel turn on the body, a thematic cornerstone of Chicana/Latina feminist theory. Whereas the reclaiming and remembering of the Latina body may have inspired this piece, Garza takes it in an entirely different direction. Instead, he associates the body with a loss of ethnic identity through assimilationist erasure, an experience with which he is intimately familiar. His story is not about sexualized appropriation or rebellion but about violent masculine aggression, male compassion, and the politics of ethnic solidarity. The body becomes a site of community memory, the scar on his leg a tattoo of cultural belonging.

While the theme of reclaiming identity is a common thread in many stories, Juanita Velasco (2010c) offers a different set of themes in her *testimonio* titled, "Home is inside me" (http://blogs.umass.edu/equity/). The text of her story (2010b), transcribed here in prose for the sake of conserving space, voices the traumatic and life-changing move of the immigrant child sent to *El Norte* (to the United States), to improve her life chances. In contrast to Cabrera-Murillo and Garza's intact families, Velasco's is marked by parental death, absence, and family separation. *La frontera*, the border that the child crosses, is actually multiple, as she leaves behind not only a country but also an indigenous past. Perhaps one of the unifying themes that coheres this story is the importance of motherhood and the nurturing of women as a constant amid the uprooted life. Velasco shapes her story from the beginning as a recursive, cyclical structure:

> My journey began with an ending. In the deep-seated, sunlit, *verde gris* [green-gray] mountains of breathtaking, indigenous Oaxaca, a young mother full of dreams gave her life for me. Her spirit along with all those brave mothers who have lost the battle to childbirth has joined the feared *Cihuateteo* [the spirits of women who died in childbirth] on a daily journey with the setting of the sun. Mamá Avelina named me Juanita because it means "God is gracious" and to honor my mother. She took me under her wing, nurturing and disciplining me with the help of *tías* [aunts]. My bare feet were -always running across rocks, and wet dirt cuddled my toes. I ate *mole*, *mangos*, *quesillo* [fresh cheese], *chapulines* [grasshoppers], black beans, about every nourishment that our soil gave us. I was an only child, but I was never lonely. I had *primas* [cousins] to play with, pigs, chickens, and roosters to feed, and the tamarind, lemon, avocado, palm trees, and all the flowers to water. At the end of each day, Mamá Velina gave me her blessing and taught me how to pray. I felt secure in her embrace as I slept hugging her on our *petate* [straw mat], next to her candlelit altar. These were the memories that would soon haunt me and make me ache for home.

> One day, Mamá Velina said she was sending me to *El Norte* because she had hopes and dreams of a better future for me. She told me my father lived there, and I wouldn't be alone. I didn't want to leave. I begged and cried. I tried to make her understand that I didn't need anyone but her. The first few years I was moved around from one family to another. It turned out my father spent his free time in *cantinas* [bars] and the few times I saw him I felt confused. My *tías* [aunts] took me in and raised me until I was 18. I shared a room with six *primas* [cousins] and their moms. It looked like an orphanage with so many kids running around. I never had any privacy; we even went to the restroom together because nobody wanted to wait in line. Though we all complained about the situation and wanted a "normal" family, we have unforgettable memories.

> It was only when I saw my *primas* [cousins] hugging, kissing, and sharing secrets with their mothers that I felt homeless. Many times I felt like a lonely spectator, and my heart would travel back to Mamá Velina's embrace where she would wipe away my tears. Maybe the desire for love made me become a mother at a young age. I have three beautiful *niñas* [girls] and I share with them all the memories of my first home, and I tell them "*no hay como una madre*" [there's nothing like a mother's love]. I've now come to understand that "Home is here—this place inside of me, inside each of us, that we curl into. The place that keeps us whole. That keeps us happy. That keeps us ... on our way."

Velasco directs her story to "all homeless children" in the hopes that her story may inspire them to persevere with their own educational dreams. Velasco became a teen mom and had three daughters before returning to school to become a teacher. Her story is lodged within this process of self-realization and commitment to successive generations of immigrant children. In her theorizing essay she writes:

My hope is that my story produces compassion from the larger society within the United States, while combating xenophobia that still exists today in our country. Children in unfortunate cases are the victims of the circumstances they are born into and it is the responsibility of adults in their lives to make responsible choices for the well being of children. This is for all homeless children. May they overcome hardship and find a voice in my testimony. (Velasco, 2010b, pp. 2–3)

Completing a teacher credential program, Velasco's imagined audiences for the story are immigrant parents and children that she will be dedicating her professional life to serving. She adds that her story speaks to the dilemma of Latina teenage motherhood, of being caught between a cultural norm in the Mexican context and a heavily stigmatized condition in U.S. society. The personal story of teenage pregnancy and motherhood offer a counter-story to the view that young Latinas are promiscuous or lack proper upbringing. Stories like Velasco's become validating and empowering to other mothers in the class and open the minds and hearts of everyone.

From a gendered perspective, Velasco affirms the centrality of communities of women—mythological, indigenous, and immigrant—to help her cope with the losses in her life. "Women have played a big role in my life, and they made decisions that would forever shape [me]" (Velasco, 2010b, p. 7). Deprived of human connection, the symbolic ties to female ancestry become more significant: "To me it's important to keep alive the memory of the brave women we descend from. . . . As I became a mother myself, I understood our genealogical bond that brings us all together" (p. 7).

Velasco's reflections, like those of Cabrera-Murillo and Garza, provide us with a sort of "director's cut" of the movie they have each made. They guide us to the meanings that they find in their own story, amplifying our understanding of the story's content and its significance to the author. All of the students establish some form of interconnection between their personal story and larger social structures of oppression and privilege. Some *testimonios* are more visibly oppositional than others, speaking to mainstream injustices and also to the oppression from within their own cultures. Others reaffirm cultural values from their particular situated standpoints. In all cases, theory does not drive the narrative, but rather the analysis is derived from the experience. After reading dozens of theorizing essays, it seems clear that the students find real value in the process of making meaning from the flesh. While the reality of their lives may be invisible to the mainstream society, the explanations for those realities have also been invisible to most Latin@ students. Therefore, the engagement with theorizing through narrative opens a new window of understanding for these student authors.

From a pedagogical perspective, the pairing of creative production with interpretive commentary is fundamental to reproducing the signature pedagogy of embodied intellectual theorizing. The results are often uneven, as analyzing one's own work and moving from expressive language to the language of interpretation are difficult critical and rhetorical tasks. Maturity and life experience certainly enhance one's critical skills, but what matters is that both novice and more expert theorizers (Benmayor, 2009) have the opportunity to consider their own lives in a larger framework, to understand that theirs is not an isolated story.

The theorizing process also suggests a critical dimension of Latin@ signature pedagogy—the collective referent. Community takes various forms. The stories themselves unfold in the context of multiple communities that are named, for example, the family, the ethnic community, a gendered community, or school. Each story necessarily places the dramatic conflict in relation to the world outside, to which the author is "writing back" or "writing for." *Testimonio* contains both a contestatory, oppositional dimension, and a propositional one (Benmayor, 2009). In addition, in their stories, authors are addressing very concrete collective audiences—cultural communities that have had negative impact on their lives (mainstream forces as well as dimensions of home culture that are oppressive) and supportive ones (e.g., siblings, parents, Latina women and men, schoolchildren). In all three of the *testimonio* examples above, the authors are offering their cultural communities of family, peers, and future generations "stories to live by," revealing the fundamental impulse that community consciousness plays in Latin@ Studies.

SO, WHAT ABOUT THE DIGITAL?

At the beginning of this essay I wrote that the digital medium matters in re-enacting the process of embodying and creating knowledge. Teaching *testimonio* to the YouTube generations is a happy endeavor. The marriage of multimedia and *testimonio* has turned the Latina Life Stories into a space of active learning and creativity, giving voice—figuratively and literally—to young Latin@ and other students of color who rarely encounter a space in the academy to tell their truths and be heard. The digital world offers a democratizing opportunity for young Latin@s to tell their stories in their preferred "language" of multimedia. Moreover, the digital medium offers many more possibilities for authorship than the traditional publication format that Latin@s found, and still do find, so hard to break into. The digital format enables the story to move outside the classroom space, where it circulates in the form of a DVD or can be uploaded to a website or to YouTube and potentially reach multiple audiences. The idea of authorship—of conceptualizing, writing, producing, and publishing a tangible work—becomes much more attainable.

Not confined by the printed page, the medium also encourages a synergy of creative talents, combining spoken word performance with visual esthetics and music. The dramatic dimensions of the personal voice, the play of images, and the musical soundtrack increase the intensity of the experience and produce other forms of meaning. Students analyze the visual texts, not only for form but also content. As we watch stories in class, we discuss the effects of the visuals to our understanding of the stories. (The array of videos associated with this article are located at http://blogs.umass.edu/equity). We might discuss, for instance, how Cabrera-Murillo's story uses the music of the *baile folclórico* [folk dancing] and vivid color to accentuate the moment when the pain of agricultural labor is transformed into the promise of future generations through dance. We note how the semi-surreal treatment of jerky movement and blurry close-in shots in Garza's video re-enactment heighten the drama of the story, and how his choice to film in black and white lends a cinema-verité quality, drawing attention to the narrative voice. We comment on how the softness of Velasco's voice in combination with images of rural Oaxaca transmit the nostalgia she feels. We eventually come to the conclusion that the voice is the centerpiece of the story, what gives it its authenticity.

There is another aspect to the digital that matters particularly to Latin@ pedagogy: analysis and interpretation—the theorizing process. Viewing a digital story sets off a chain reaction. It sparks experiential recognition and pulls out the story within. It stimulates the imagination of how one might express that inner story visually and orally. And it sparks discussion about what the story means and how it resonates collectively. Students of today are more eager and adept at analyzing multimedia texts as opposed to written ones. Although they may lack the expert language or wide knowledge base for deep theorizing, they are comfortable with making sense out of what they see and hear. In other words, the digital *testimonio* invites the signature elements of Latin@ pedagogies: telling from the flesh, giving concrete form to the story, contributing a new perspective about common realities, and sharing that understanding with others. When transposed into the classroom, the digital *testimonio* process becomes even more intentional. The classroom provides a framework for telling, producing, and theorizing.

Testimonio, and particularly digital *testimonio*, also opens a space for closer listening. As students begin to share their stories and disclose personal experiences, the attention level of the class heightens. Everyone is interested in each other's personal lives, but the level of reception is remarkably different from other classes in which difference easily becomes a topic of contention. In this class, *testimonio* establishes the opportunity for real cross-cultural respect and understanding to take place. Perhaps the students who sign up for the course self-select and are initially receptive to a course that specializes in Latinas. But I believe that life story has a special power to set a different tone and atmosphere for listening. In Latina Life Stories, the students quickly build community because they listen with open hearts and minds.

Introducing students to multimedia authoring has had concrete benefits beyond the classroom and the digital lab. They have taken advantage of the democratizing power of the Internet and posted their stories online. More importantly, students have taken the practice of digital *testimonio* into Latino communities, offering workshops to students in elementary schools, public libraries, non-profit organizations, and to other universities. Judith Flores Carmona and Silvia Garcia organized and led for several years a digital *testimonio* group at the University of Utah, producing DVDs and culminating in a collection of *testimonios* (Alemán, Delgado Bernal, Flores Carmona, Galas, & Garza, 2009). Flores Carmona also introduced digital storytelling to second, third, and fourth graders at a local elementary school with a large Latino population, as part of the *Adelante* partnership with that university. Olivia Dávalos currently offers digital storytelling workshops in schools and libraries throughout Monterey County, inspiring countless youth to tell their stories.

Over the years, and based on approximately 300 student stories, I have come to understand digital *testimonio* as a pedagogical watershed. It invites students to become authors, to *testimoniar* from the flesh, to create and represent through the flesh, and to construct and interpret their identities in mind and body. Elías Morales (2008) reflects on the impact of this pedagogical experience on her life, saying:

> I can see myself playing this movie for many years to come. This story has certainly changed the trajectory of my life's journey, and I hope it will also do this for others in my family. … It is a testimony to how loving parents can overcome any, and all things with strength, courage, discipline, and the will to be more than someone who occupies space on this earth, but that desires to be someone who gives to others. God has truly blessed me with this journey and has instilled a desire in my heart to continue writing for the purpose of empowering others. My mother's legacy will be brought to life in my writings, and my parent's love and devotion will live through my every action as I continue to work towards being a teacher. (p. 5)

Many of the students in Latina Life Stories have or will become teachers. They will take digital *testimonio* into their classrooms and reproduce the process that Anzaldúa, Moraga, and all the Latina writers of that generation have unleashed. Younger generations will theorize their own realities and bring new concepts into the picture.

In summary, Shulman's (2005) three dimensions of a signature pedagogy—surface structure (the concrete operational acts of teaching and learning), deep structure (the assumptions about how to impart a body of knowledge and know-how), and implicit structure (the moral dimension that shapes beliefs, attitudes, and values about the profession), are intertwined and embedded in the digital *testimonio* process. I have detailed the stages of the digital *testimonio* learning and production process to argue that these acts are not just good pedagogical strategies but that they intentionally re-enact a signature process in Latin@ Studies of situated knowledge production through embodied theorizing. These pedagogies also re-enact a tradition of Latin American *testimonio*, in emphasizing the urgency to speak out and make visible the acts of oppression and injustice that subjugate, marginalize, and silence communities. Digital *testimonio* enacts one of the fundamental pedagogical approaches in Latin@ Studies—that embodied learning is central to the empowerment of Latin@ students and communities. In the process of telling truths about their experiences, students become aware that they speak not only for themselves but also for others. The shared experience of authoring digital *testimonios* creates a powerful community of understanding. The story and the collaborative practices involved in creating *testimonios* deepen inter-cultural understanding across social categories of identity and difference in ways that I have not experienced in any other course over my more than 30 years of teaching. The invisible becomes visible, creating a space for empathic listening, learning, and understanding. If there is anything that Latin@ Studies seeks to teach, it is this. And finally, the multiple creative languages of digital storytelling encourage historically marginalized subjects, especially younger generations, to inscribe emerging social and cultural identities and challenge unified cultural discourses in new and exciting ways, in an idiom that is ideal for *testimonio*. For all the above reasons, I believe digital *testimonio* is indeed a signature pedagogy for Latin@ Studies in the twenty-first century, and I wish that through it Latin@ students all over the country may tell new truths.

REFERENCES

Alemán, S., Delgado Bernal, D., Flores Carmona, J., Galas, L., & Garza, M. (Eds.). (2009). *Latinas telling testimonios. Unidas we heal: Testimonios of mind/body/soul*. Salt Lake City, UT: University of Utah.

Anzaldúa, G. (1986) *Borderlands: La frontera. The new mestiza* (2nd ed.). San Francisco, CA: Aunt Lute Books.

Benmayor, R. (2008). Digital storytelling as a signature pedagogy in the new humanities. *Arts and Humanities in Higher Education, 7*(2), 188–205.

Benmayor, R. (2009). Theorizing through digital stories: The art of "writing back" and "writing for." *Academic Commons* [Online]. Retrieved from http://www.academiccommons.org/commons/essay/theorizing-through-digital-stories#attachments

Cabrera-Murillo, L. (2004a). Dancing into mi cultura. [Digital story]. Retrieved from http://youtu.be/h6oynUJhXxA

Cabrera-Murillo, L. (2004b). Unpublished paper. HCOM 328, Latina Life Stories, Spring.

Calder, L. (2006). Uncoverage: Toward a signature pedagogy for the history survey. *Journal of American History, 92*(4), 1358–1371.

Digital Storytelling Multimedia Archive. (2006). Liliana Cabrera, clip 4. Retrieved from https://commons.georgetown.edu/projects/digitalstories/clips/199/

Elías Morales, A. (2008). Revelations of my identity. Unpublished paper. HCOM 328, Latina Life Stories, May 6.

Garza, J. (2010a). *Welcome to the family.* [Digital story]. Retrieved from http://youtu.be/j0AQOe15Blg

Garza, J. (2010b). Welcome to the family. Unpublished paper. HCOM 328, *Latina Life Stories.*

Garza, J. (2010c). *Welcome to the family.* Unpublished story script. HCOM 328, Latina Life Stories, Spring.

Latina Feminist Group. (2001). *Telling to live: Latina feminist testimonios.* Durham, NC: Duke University Press.

Latina Life Stories. (no date). Retrieved from http://classes.csumb.edu/HCOM/HCOM328-01/world/index.html

Moraga, C. (1983). *La Güera.* In C. Moraga & G. Anzaldúa (Eds.), *This bridge called my back: Writings by radical women of color* (pp. 27–34). New York, NY: Kitchen Table Women of Color Press.

Shulman, L. (2005). Signature pedagogies in the professions. *Daedalus, 134*(3), 52–59.

Sommer, D. (1988). Not just a personal story: Women's testimonios and the plural self. In B. Brodsky & C. Schenk (Eds.), *Life lines: Theorizing women's autobiography* (pp. 107–130). Ithaca, NY: Cornell University Press.

Souza, C. (2001). Missing body. In Latina Feminist Group (Eds.), *Telling to live: Latina feminist testimonios* (pp. 266–268). Durham, NC: Duke University Press.

Tamayo, J. (2007). Theorizing cuentos del barrio. Unpublished paper. HCOM 328, Latina Life Stories.

Turchin, S. (Producer, Photographer, & Editor). (2010). *U-Stories: Latina life stories.* Retrieved from http://www.youtube.com/watch?v=bLbh2gw8EsA

Velasco, J. (2010a). *Home inside me.* [Digital story]. Retrieved from http://youtu.be/f6aWzBBPeKg

Velasco, J. (2010b). Theorizing my digital story. Unpublished paper. HCOM 328, Latina Life Stories.

Velasco, J. (2010c). *Home inside me.* Unpublished story script. HCOM 328, Latina Life Stories.

Wikipedia. (2011). *Digital storytelling.* http://en.wikipedia.org/wiki/Digital_storytelling

Testimonio: Origins, Terms, and Resources

Kathryn Blackmer Reyes and Julia E. Curry Rodríguez

San José State University

People of color in the United States have utilized the liberationist *testimonio* as both methodology and narrative development. This essay provides a discussion about the roots of *testimonio* in Latin America and how it has been transformed, integrating qualitative research approaches, oral history, spoken word, and memoir writings by Chicanas and Latinas. The major objective of this essay is to provide guidance for the bibliographic search as a reference guide to the research scholar. Beginning with an exploration of terms used for bibliographic searches, the essay provides insight on navigating Library of Congress terms and desired outcomes in situated knowledge. A special feature of this essay is a primer bibliography organized in three sections. Part One identifies a selected list of Latin American *testimonios* identified as Roots/Origins. The second section focuses on Chicana/o Scholars' Uses of Narrative/*Testimonio*, focusing on experiential reflections in diverse institutions, locations, and in personal writing as a methodology to conduct research and to bear witness to their experiences. The third section is called *Testimonio* and Dissertations by Chicana/o and Latina/o scholars, using *testimonio* as a methodology in educational research.

The use of personal narratives in U.S.-based scholarship in the areas of critical race theory, Chicana and Chicano Studies, and other critical studies is informed by the practice of *testimonio* as a legacy of reflexive narratives of liberation used by people throughout the world. Chicanas, in particular, might also be influenced by the deliberate use of personal theoretical insight as prescribed by Collins (1991) in her paramount work, *Black Feminist Thought*. This type of writing entails a first person oral or written account, drawing on experiential, self-conscious, narrative practice to articulate an urgent voicing of something to which one bears witness. Presented at times as memoirs, oral histories, qualitative vignettes, prose, song lyrics, or spoken word, the *testimonio* has the unique characteristic of being a political and *conscienticized* reflection that is often spoken. To be sure, the *testimonio* does not remain in its oral state; but rather, it is often taken (as in interviewed, recorded, and transcribed) or written from the outset perhaps in diaries, letters, or journals. What is certain is that *testimonio* is not meant to be hidden, made intimate, nor kept secret. The objective of the *testimonio* is to bring to light a wrong, a point of view, or an urgent call for action. Thus, in this manner, the *testimonio* is different from the qualitative method of in-depth interviewing, oral history narration, prose, or spoken word. The *testimonio* is intentional and political.

The objective of this article is to discuss how students and scholars might encounter testimonial narratives as well as theoretical works useful in the analysis of said scholarship from the point of view of the bibliographic search. Moreover, our objective is to assist in translating how the term *testimonio* is used in reference materials, sometimes referring to any oral form (as in oral history, interviews, accounts, or vignettes) and also in relation to the categorization of work based on oral accounts in any form. We bring to this discussion extensive work as bilingual and bicultural scholars who have gained insight into the uses of *testimonio* in our scholarship and our professions. We use the term "*testimonio*" as a unique expression of the methodological use of spoken accounts of oppression. We also use the words "testimonial," "narrative," and "testimony" because of the focus on the predetermined terms used in library research as defined by the Library of Congress.

For most scholars, the introduction to *testimonios* has been in English translations of Spanish language narratives produced by various people outside of the United States. Examples of some often cited writers are Partnoy (1986), Poniatowska (1979, 1980), Castellanos (1961), Freire and Horton (1990), Barrios de Chúngara (1978) and Menchú Tum (Burgos-Debray, 2009). These writers and narrators frame a way of writing that originates in the individual but takes from the social events interpreted as unjust or illicit as stamps of oppression. Within Chicana and Chicano Studies, some authors using *testimonio* narratives include Galarza (1971), Villarreal (1959), and Moraga and Anzaldúa (1983). During the 1980s and 1990s, as cultural studies and postmodern methodologies began to frame critical scholarship as subjective and political, Chicanas in particular drew on the reflexive form of *testimonio* using such concepts as agency, subaltern, or native (Anzaldúa, 1999; Lomas, 1994; Pardo, 1998; Pérez, 1999; Sandoval, 2000). Feminist epistemology influenced Chicanas and empowered them to develop the narrative format as redemption—as takers of the stories, as readers of the narratives, and as creators of the analysis.

In the following section, we first suggest that origins matter, briefly exploring the roots of *testimonio*. This section lays the ground for a discussion of terms and an identification of bibliographic sources that can be useful to students and scholars who are engaged in the use of *testimonio* as methodology, to theorize, and as a means of conscientization. We also discuss the fragile commitment of the subject headings imposed by the Library of Congress as obscuring the sources we seek.

ROOTS/ORIGINS

Scholars argue that the Latin American *testimonio* is comparable to the North American memoir. However, the main feature of the testimonial text is the construction of a discourse of solidarity. Although it is difficult to mark a historical moment of its inception, the *testimonio* has been inscribed and sanctioned as a literary mode since the 1970s, in large part as a result of the liberation efforts and the geopolitical resistance movements to imperialism in Third World nations. We come to understand this form of writing as part of the struggle of people of color for educational rights and for the recovery of our knowledge production. Authors of U.S.-based *testimonios* include Hurston (1970), Medrano (2010), Villegas de Magnon (Lomas, 1994), Martin (1992), Douglass (1994), King (Carson, 1998), Chinchilla (1998), Alvarado (1989), García (1994), Galarza (1971), Sanchez (1940/1966), Ortiz (1995), Pérez, (1996), Zavella (1987) and Decierdo (1980). Many of the *testimonios* are speeches, newsletter columns, *corridos*, spoken word, or other shorter forms of writing and would most likely go unidentified if we used conventional search or categorization approaches to find them. Empowered by the womanist framing of knowledge exemplified by Patricia Hill Collins and members of the Memphis Center for Research on Women, Chicana scholars embrace *testimonio* as "emerging power" that makes them "agents of knowledge" allowing them to "speak to the importance that oppression, [and] the importance that knowledge plays in empowering oppressed people" (Collins, 1991, p. 221).

Some scholars define *testimonio* by focusing on the form of the narrative. Specifically, it is an account told in the first person by a narrator who is the real protagonist or witness of events. This definition focuses on *testimonios* as evolving from events experienced by a narrator who seeks empowerment through voicing her or his experience. Thus, the politicized and self-conscious element in this point of view is paramount in this definition. A *testimonio* must include the intention of affirmation and empowerment.

In Chicana and Chicano education research, *testimonio* is situated in the liberationist pedagogy exemplified by Brazilian educator Paulo Freire. Indeed *testimonio*, liberationist pedagogy, and its corollary epistemological project evolved at approximately the same time. This pedagogy advocates writing as a means of liberation—dialogically informing a narrative that is first spoken and then used to make literacy meaningful as a dynamic entry to conscientization and liberation from oppression. *Testimonio* allows the narrator to show an experience that is not only liberating in the process of telling but also political in its production of awareness to listeners and readers alike. Moreover, like Freire's (1970) *Pedagogy of the Oppressed*, *testimonio* empowers the speaker or narrator to transform the oral to its written representation not as an act of oppression and ignorance but rather as an acknowledgment of the revolutionary aspect of literacy.

The collective goal of *testimonio* is to name oppression and to arrest its actions whether as genocide, racism, classism, xenophobia, or any other type of institutionalized marginalization. The aim is to speak for justice against all crimes against humanity. The truth of the survivor story may not be empirically, scientifically, or legally true. Nevertheless, the speakers are aware that the very manner in which they tell the story may hold for them a harrowing reality of reliving the oppressive experience. It is, to paraphrase Anzaldúa (1990), an act of removing a mask previously used as a survival strategy. Voicing the experience provides a kind of active journey from torture, oppression, or marginalization that ultimately leads the speaker or writer to become the empowered survivor. The *testimonio* is not to be kept secret but requires active participatory readers or listeners who act on behalf of the speaker in an effort to arrive at justice and redemption.

Another important characteristic of *testimonio* is the role of memory and reconstructive episte-mology. Some scholars argue that memory may recast the experiences in less than absolute truth. The very nature of human survival enables human beings to recast their memory to accentuate their experiences as merciful vignettes allowing them redemption. Engaging in testimonial acts both empowers and destroys. For the speaker or narrator, the very act of telling is a double-edged sword. Thus, testimonial writing may have psychoanalytical value. Fundamentally, however, the objective of *testimonio* includes the knowledge that reflection and speaking lead, eventually, to liberation. For education scholars this method is a pedagogical aid to help students develop an analytical frame that demystifies structural marginalizations. Perhaps this is the most important characteristic of *testimonio* in educational research or in the classroom, for it holds the Freirian promise of conscientization to hope, faith, and autonomy. From these endeavors come documents, memories, and oral histories that can be used to recast and challenge pervasive theories, policies, and explanations about educational failure as a problem, not of individuals but of systemic institutionalized practices of oppression.

Once introduced to *testimonios,* both the narrator and the listener experience cathartic epiphanies that open their eyes to the power of individual accounts that ensure that social and political events become part of the greater human consciousness. Although a *testimonio* is technically an account made by one person, it represents the voice of many whose lives have been affected by particular social events, such as totalitarian governments, war violence, displacement, or other types of broad social affronts on humanity. *Testimonios* often serve as awakenings for tellers and readers alike. For example, Partnoy's (1986) narrative *testimonio* demonstrates the power of the personal account as a tool, not just in storytelling but also as an aid in the process of healing. In her *testimonio* she describes the torture she experienced at the hands of the Argentinian military and in the very descriptions reclaims her own humanity.

The years of violent turmoil in Central and South America yielded important examples of the use of testimonies. Who could argue the power of *I, Rigoberta Menchú: An Indian Woman in Guatemala/Me llamo Rigoberta Menchú, y así me nació la consciencia* (Burgos-Debray, 2009) or *Si Me Permiten Hablar/Let Me Speak* (Barrios de Chúngara, 1978) as accounts of the implications of military interventions and multinational capitalism? While Menchú's account has been challenged as not being her own authentic story, the point is that *testimonio* holds elements of experiences shared by the collective group to whom one belongs. Thus, the *testimonio* of racism and xenophobia expressed by Chicana scholars and students alike may constitute composite elements that can be triangulated with other evidence (Cuádraz, 1993). However, the cornerstone of *testimonio,* like oral history, is not the speaking of truth, but rather, the telling of an account from an individual point of view whose conscience has led to an analysis of the experience as a shared component of oppression.

In the United States, Chicanas and Chicanos use *testimonio* as a tool to express marginalization resulting from race, gender, and sexuality, such as the book *Telling to Live* (Latina Feminist Group, 2001) and as a means of expressing agency, for example in *This Bridge Called my Back* (Moraga & Anzaldúa, 1983) and *Gay Latino Histories/Dying to be Remembered* (Roque Ramírez, 2010). In other cases, narrative is used to locate social membership as racialized and classed subjects experiencing social mobility, such as *Narratives of Mexican American Women* (A. García, 2004), *Voicing Chicana Feminisms* (Hurtado, 2003), *Migrant Daughter* (Tywoniak & M. García, 2000) and *Memories of Chicano History* (M. García, 1994). Most recently, immigrant youth have deployed *testimonio* successfully to address undocumented student experiences beginning with short narratives in the University of Southern California *Handbook on Undocumented Students,* followed by *Underground Undergrads: UCLA Undocumented Immigrant Students Speak Out* (Madera, Wong, Monroe, Rivera-Salgado, & Mathay, 2008). In all of these cases the act of self-naming, as Chicanas and Chicanos, and as AB540/DREAM students (rather than the racist formulations of racial/ethnic and immigrant political classification, such as "illegal alien" or "Hispanic") provide important evidence of the power of collective self-naming.

THE LOGIC OF SEARCH TERMS: THE POWER OF THE KEYWORD

Although we may take great care to understand what *testimonio* is and is not, clearly from the discussion above, identifying resources in this area must be broadly defined. Researchers are constrained by mainstream terms defined by librarians who may or may not understand the nuanced bilingual and bicultural use of a term, such as *testimonio*. To merely translate the term into its English counterpart, *testimony,* does not capture the theoretical underpinnings of this term. The terminology constraints that all researchers encounter are embedded in the knowledge-base of people who serve as indexers for materials in the research databases and the Library of Congress subject headings. As Chicana and Chicano scholars produce their own epistemological tracks, they recast terms, introduce new forms and transform extant categories. However, to conduct exhaustive research, scholars must think like the mainstream to find resources to provide context and validity to our experiences. To search extant resources for our scholarship and possibly for the placement of our own research, we must resist the idea of self-invention. Therefore, we must use the terms *testimonio,* testimony, testimonial, narrative, and biography interchangeably, while understanding that in doing so we are in direct violation of the very practice of *testimonio*.

To identify references for this non-exhaustive report on testimonial writing, we begin with an examination of terms. The search for materials for the bibliography encompasses a range of resources because there is no consistent subject term or keyword to locate testimonial narratives. As an entry point, a valuable resource for locating similar titles is to begin with a known text. For this project we began with the library catalog record for the book *Telling to Live* (Latina Feminist Group, 2001). The objective was to determine how the mainstream indexers classify this book, which we know is a collection of *testimonios*. Search on this source produced the terms "Hispanic American Women," "Social Conditions," "Feminists," "Sex Discrimination Against Women," and "Ethnic Relations," all of which would be useless in locating additional resources in search of *testimonios*. Two somewhat useful terms derived from this title were: "biography" and "anecdotes"—yet, the latter term reflects a Library of Congress assessment that *testimonio* is not a reliable approach to produce knowledge and expertise. Moreover, the use of the term anecdote also places this book in the area of fiction, which may then dismiss the liminal accounts told by the authors, all of whom are prominent Latina feminist scholars whose intention was to write testimonies of their life experiences. In its common understanding, the term "anecdote" is a term used to refer to accounts of questionable validity.

The book *Telling to Live* (Latina Feminist Group, 2001) includes the word *testimonio* in its subtitle and therefore ties itself to this tradition of writing. But the Library of Congress indexers did not identify the text in the library catalogue. It is important to note that there are significant limitations in the classification of scholarship and that the use of keywords may result in problematic outcomes. Drawing on the practices we use in college bibliographic instruction, our best advice here is to state that a bibliographic search for sources begins by considering all subjects, topics, and terms simultaneously. It is also important to remember the need to use "the master's tools" (Lorde, 1984, p. 110), not because we agree with them but because we want to have a productive bibliographic search.

An illustrative example of this approach is using the term "Hispanic" when we seek to find Chicanas and/or Latinas. The prominent sociologist Joe R. Feagin (2011) argues that terms are politically and culturally defined. Given that indexing terms are determined by the Library of Congress (LC), and that those terms tend to be informed by and for the mainstream, they may be read as a reiteration of the dominant frame (Feagin, 2010). Yet, we wish to point out that this instruction allows for empowerment and redemption as well. We must use the research terms, while knowing that subject headings used by LC indexers draw on "official" designations to classify scholarship regardless of their accuracy. Applying a critical understanding about how terms are developed is both empowering and frustrating. Indeed, Chicana/o scholars use their multicultural expertise to navigate the mainstream research terms, thereby demonstrating their cultural competency of both the mainstream and their own experience.

We subjugated this knowledge to explore the outcome of using "*testimonio*" and "narratives" as primary search terms. Our use of the terms was to demonstrate that the terms yield inaccurate bibliographic searches. That is, we intentionally used terms we knew were not conventional Library of Congress index terms. The initial results of our search were as unsatisfactory and frustrating as we expected. Like the redemptive role of *testimonio,* we reflected on the bibliographic instruction advice. The initial search results were limited, but they yielded small treasures. Aware of the exploratory nature of research, we had to accept good and missed outcomes—always hoping for good. We can definitively assert that there is no perfect term for the topic of *testimonios*. The word "narrative" yields sources in *testimonio* proper, but it also identifies literary sources because "testimony" is a genre of literature.

The initial effort led us to select other terms closely related to *testimonio*. Using the terms, "memories," "story," "oral history," "autobiography," "voices," "memoirs," and "interviews" provided a whole new set of sources. None of these terms perfectly exemplify *testimonio,* but they provide results that could be examined to determine if they meet the type of narrative we seek.

We construct the search by drawing on terms used by contemporary scholars of color in the United States to the broader area of life documents used to record unknown, ignored, marginal, and seemingly inconsequential accounts as defined by traditional scholarship. Consider the valuable resource that the contemporary form of testimonial accounts, expressed in spoken word, will yield as accounts of organic knowledge and expressions of resistance in the future. Youth rightfully see this approach as a highly effective means to narrate/speak their realities of city life, poverty, violence, racism, and other issues they confront in both general society and schools. Yet, unlike traditional *testimonio,* this approach is more like poetry or haiku, depending on its length. Nevertheless, this form of expression, because it is oral, poses a possibility for testimonial analysis.

The point is that while there is no exhaustive approach when conducting a search to compile a bibliography on using the testimonial approach as methodology, drawing on scholarship by critical race scholars offers terms useful to this endeavor. Each research scholar must struggle with alternative forms of expressing what is being searched. There is never a "wrong" or "bad" search when going beyond the limitations of our library research tools. Yet, the researcher can shape the parameters of the search. The idea of research is never about getting the absolute answer, but rather it is about identifying ideas, forming a foundation for the research that the scholar wants to explore and, ultimately, about being faithful to the approach. Here, we offer examples of relevant reference sources, but each researcher must explore and refine a search that is suitable to her or his needs. The critique of extant LC indexing terms is paramount as a means of establishing authority drawing from the parameters of critical race scholarship that have also redressed scholarship over the years.

RESOURCES

Our intention with this essay is to frame a discussion and to propose a reference tool. We recommend and identify resources that may be overlooked, ignored, or discarded but that may have a great deal to contribute to the scholarship of educational *testimonio*. For example, the radio has been an important distributor of narratives to the general population. An important example is Studs Terkel's *Almanac*, which, in the 1950s, provided a space for the *testimonios* of ordinary people to be heard throughout the country, telling their lives during the Jim Crow era, as union workers, and in many other situations. The current *StoryCorps* broadcast by National Public Radio (NPR) records people's stories, airs them, and then houses them at the Library of Congress, and these could most definitely be seen as abbreviated *testimonios*. Focusing on immigration, *The Golden Cradle*, an NPR project about immigration provided narratives of immigrant women whose experiences of diasporic lives also contribute to this situational *testimonio* approach. Maria Hinojosa's Latino USA (latinousa.org) also draws on journalistic approaches to highlight testimonies in contemporary accounts on both Public Broadcast Television and NPR.

Various library archives include important oral histories that are *testimonios*. The University of California, Berkeley's Bancroft Library houses oral histories by Paul Taylor and Manuel Gamio and more recent efforts to document people of color in the Bay Area, for example the World War II accounts by the ship workers of Richmond. UCLA's Chicano Studies Research Center Library houses various interviews and oral histories, including the forced sterilization records of Mexican women. The Harry Ransom Center of the University of Texas at Austin is an important repository of Texas-based narrative materials that document Mexicans in the Communist Party, most notably Emma Tenayuca. The Schomburg Museum and Library houses Black Culture, Afro-Latino and Garifuna narratives. Many local libraries and archives also yield important accounts of people who thought of future generations by documenting their lives on tape or paper. For example, History San José (a local Silicon Valley historical organization) contains a collection of oral histories conducted this decade on the cannery workers of Santa Clara County—many of who are Mexicanas and Chicanas.

Focusing on youth and children as chroniclers of history, the *Foxfire* series by Eliot Wigginton started as an experiential magazine and published interviews and essays describing life in the Appalachian region. More than ten books have been published in this series over the course of the project. How is this *testimonio*? We need only examine the oral history interviews that tell comparable class oppression experienced by rural, poor, white people to understand that privilege is not shared as the product of whiteness, but rather it is informed by economic and political inequality. In their important "talked" book, *We Make the Road by Walking*, Freire and Horton (1990) tell of their work on liberation pedagogy, identifying similarities between the residents of Appalachia and the South American peasants—both groups affected by institutional barriers of discrimination based on class, neglect, educational exclusion, and ethnocentrism. A powerful deployment of *testimonio* has been used by the undocumented student movement. UCLA's underground undergrods, (Madera et al., 2008) and USC's The College and Financial Aide Guide for AB540 Undocumented Students (Oliverez, Chavez, Soriano, & Tierney, 2006) drew on this methodology to address the particular form of repression resulting from unofficial immigration.

Other important sources include slave narratives (for example, Project Gutenberg, Henry Louis Gates, and the Library of Congress); narratives of Japanese Americans in camps (for example, Sherna Gluck and Ronald Takaki); and the World War II project narratives of Chicanas and Chicanos directed by Maggie Rivas-Rodriguez at University of Texas at Austin. The Oral History Association provides important resources for documenting, teaching, preserving, and also serves as a publication outlet for narratives. Most importantly, these sources also provide valuable research terms and categories that are useful in situating narratives and lived experiences.

A last resource for rescued, challenged, and innovative terms can be found in dissertations by Chicanas and Chicanos whose use of the personal narrative has become a chosen methodology to tell the stories of the Chicana/o and Latina/o communities. Likewise, the term "*testimonio*" in current scholarship as a keyword has experienced a growth in usage. A keyword search *in ProQuest's Dissertations & Theses* identifies "*testimonio*" as appearing in 36 dissertations and theses in the periods of 1990–1999; the number explodes to 835 only a decade later in the 2000–2009 period. By 2010, 206 dissertations or theses have been indexed using this term.[1] Chicana scholars transform the scholarship and the codification of their work.

CONCLUDING OBSERVATIONS

We began with an exploration into the conventional understanding of *testimonio*. Using both the traditional *testimonio* and other methodological cousins, such as oral histories and interviews, we conclude that the important aspect of this endeavor is precisely the objective of *testimonio*: It provides an outlet for affirmative epistemological exploration. Thus, this essay means to recast the narrative endeavors of Chicana and Chicano scholarship as having roots in the liberationist urgency of Latin American *testimonio* while addressing the memories of racialization in U.S. lived experiences. We do not lay claim to having produced an exhaustive bibliography, but rather to have addressed the importance of knowing the terms for bibliographic exploration and situating knowledge. Below, we identify selected titles to assist in the work of scholars using *testimonio* as methodology. We include narratives created by Chicanas and Latinas because they provide an important space for narrative works in contemporary scholarship. That *testimonio* is an important multifaceted approach to educational research is perhaps the most important affirmation. If classrooms and educational research reproduce oppressions, then the use of *testimonio* as methodology[2] by Chicana/o researchers in their scholarship makes an attempt to speak about the oppressive cataloguing by mainstream terminology. Unlike the cultural hegemony of empiricist research, the *testimonio* provides both a methodology and a theory for hope and liberation. We provide citations that include non-Chicanas/Latinas because the sources are important in their shared experience as bibliographic contributions. The bibliography is organized in three sections. Part One, identifies a selected list of Latin American testimonies identified as Roots/Origins. The second section (on Chicana/o scholars' uses of narrative/*testimonio*) focuses on experiential reflections in diverse institutions, locations, and in personal writing as a methodology to conduct research inspired by, and to bear witness to, their experiences. Some of the sources in this section specifically relate to education or educational experiences, and they are indicated with an asterisk. The third section is composed of dissertations by Chicana/o and Latina/o scholars using *testimonio* as a methodology in educational research.

NOTES

1. An analysis of these citations confirms that the use of *testimonio* is as diverse as discussed above. The term *testimonio* is deployed without necessarily reflecting a methodology.
2. For a more exhaustive bibliography see the bibliography chapter in *Telling to Live* (Latina Feminist Group, 2001). We use some of the same titles; however, we also include other historical materials not included in *Telling to Live*, and we offer more recent titles.

SELECTED BIBLIOGRAPHIC (RE)SOURCES

Latin American *Testimonios*—Roots/Origins

The sources identified in this section provide a backdrop of "classic" works used in the postcolonial writing developed in or by Latin American people to publicize oppressive regimes. These sources readily appear in the conventional search of *testimonio*.

Alvarado, E. (1989). *Don't be afraid, gringo: A Honduran woman speaks from the heart: The story of Elvia Alvarado* (M. Benjamin, Trans.). New York, NY: Harper & Row.

Barrios de Chúngara, D., with M. Viezzer. (1978). *Let me speak!: Testimony of Domitila, a woman of the Bolivian mines* (V. Ortiz, Trans.). New York, NY: Monthly Review Press.

Beverley, J., & Zimmerman, M. (1990). *Literature and politics in the Central American revolutions.* Austin, TX: University of Texas Press.

Burgos-Debray, E. (Ed.). (2009). *I, Rigoberta Menchú: An Indian woman in Guatemala/*Me llamo Rigoberta Menchú así me nació la consciencia. (A. Wright, Trans.). New York, NY: Verso.

Freire, P. (1996). *Letters to Cristina: Reflections on my life and work* (D. Macedo, with Q. Macedo & A. Oliveira, Trans.). New York, NY: Routledge.

Manz, B. (2004). *Paradise in ashes: A Guatemalan journey of courage, terror, and hope.* Berkeley, CA: University of California Press.

Melville, T., & Melville, M. (1971). *Guatemala: the politics of land ownership.* New York, NY: Free Press.

Ortíz, D., with Davis, P. (2002). *The blindfold's eyes: My journey from torture to truth.* Maryknoll, NY: Orbis.

Partnoy, A. (1986). *The little school: Tales of disappearance & survival.* Pittsburgh, PA: Cleis.

Partnoy, A. (2009). Disclaimer intraducible: My life/is based/on a real story/. *Biography, 32*(1), 16–25.

Poniatowska, E. (1979). *Hasta no verte Jesús mío.* Mexico City, Mexico: Editorial Era.

Poniatowska, E. (1998). *La noche de Tlatelolco: Testimonios de historia oral* (2nd ed.). México, D.F.: Ediciones Era.

Randall, M. (2003). *When I look into the mirror and see you: Women, terror, and resistance.* New Brunswick, NJ: Rutgers University Press.

Tula, M. T., with Stephen, L. (1994). *Hear my testimony: Maria Teresa Tula human rights activist of El Salvador.* Cambridge, MA: South End Press.

Tupac, D. M. (Ed.). (2000). *The autobiography of Maria Elena Moyano: The life and death of a Peruvian activist* (P. S. T. Edmisten, Trans.). Gainesville, FL: University Press of Florida.

Chicana/o and Latina/o Narrative/*Testimonios* in Education

Chicana/o and Latina/o scholars have used narrative approaches to telling their own stories and the stories of others (drawing on qualitative research methods, including oral history and in-depth interviews) to produce *testimonios* primarily focused on educational and social mobility. Citations specifically geared toward education or that draw on educational experiences are marked with an asterisk.

Anzaldúa, G. (2000). *Interviews = Entrevistas.* New York, NY: Routledge.

Anzaldúa, G. (2010) Movimientos de rebeldía y las culturas que traicionan. *Race/Ethnicity, 4*(1), 1–7.

Barron-Mckeagney, T. (2002). *Telling our stories: The lives of midwestern Latinas.* New York, NY: Routledge.

Behar, R. (1993). *Translated woman: Crossing the border with Esperanza's story.* Boston, MA: Beacon.

*Bejarano, C. L. (2005). *¿Qué onda?: Urban youth cultural and border identity.* Tucson, AZ: University of Arizona Press.

*Benmayor, R. (2002). Narrating cultural citizenship: Oral histories of first generation college students of Mexican origin. *Social Justice, 29*(4), 96–121.

Broyles-González, Y., & Rodriguez, D. (1990). The living legacy of Chicana performers: Preserving history through oral testimony. *Frontiers: A Journal of Women Studies, 11*(1), 46–52.

Cantú, N. E. (1995). *Canicula: Snapshots of a girlhood in la frontera*. Albuquerque, NM: University of New Mexico Press.

Cintrón-Vélez, A. N. (1999). Generational paths into and out of work: Personal narratives of Puerto Rican women in New York. In I. Browne (Ed.), *Latinas and African American women at work: Race, gender, and economic inequality* (pp. 244–269). New York, NY: Russell Sage Foundation.

Cortéz, J. (1999). *Virgins, guerrillas & locas: Gay Latinos writing on love*. San Francisco, CA: Cleis.

Cruz, A. (2007). *Queer Latino testimonio, Keith Haring, and Juanito Xtravaganza: Hard tails*. New York, NY: Palgrave Macmillan.

Cuádraz, G. H. (1993). *Meritocracy (un)challenged: The making of a Chicano and Chicana professoriate and professional class*. Unpublished dissertation. University of California, Berkeley.

*Cuádraz, G. H. (2006). Myths and politics of exceptionality: Interpreting Chicana/o narratives of achievement. *The Oral History Review, 33*(1), 83–105.

*Delgado Bernal, D., Elenes, C. A., Godinez, F. E., & Villeñas, S. (Eds.). (2006). *Chicana/Latina education in everyday life: Feminista perspectives on pedagogy and epistemology*. Albany, NY: State University of New York Press.

Fiandt, J. (2006). Autobiographical activism in the Americas: Narratives of personal and cultural healing by Aurora Levins Morales and Linda Hogan. *Women's Studies, 35*(6), 567–584.

*Flores, J., & García, S. (2009). Latina testimonios: A reflexive, critical analysis of a "Latina space" at a predominantly white campus. *Race, Ethnicity & Education, 12*(2), 155–172.

*Flores Niemann, Y. (1999). The making of a token: A case study of stereotype, threat, stigma, racism, and tokenism in academe. *Frontiers: A Journal of Women Studies, 20*(1), 111–134.

Flores-Ortíz, Y. (2003). Re/membering the body: Latina testimonies of social and family violence. In A. J. Aldama (Ed.), *Violence and the body: Race, gender, and the state* (pp. 347–359). Bloomington, ID: Indiana University Press.

*Gándara, P. C. (1995). *Over the ivy walls: The educational mobility of low-income Chicanos*. Albany, NY: State University Press.

*García, A. M. (2004). *Narratives of Mexican American women: Emergent identities of the second generation*. Walnut Creek, CA: Altamira.

*González, M. S., Plata, O., García, E., Torres, M., & Urrieta, L. (2003). Testimonios de inmigrantes: Students educating future teachers. *Journal of Latinos and Education, 2*(4), 233–243.

*Hart, E. T. (1999). *Barefoot heart: Stories of a migrant child*. Tempe, AZ: Bilingual Press/Editorial Bilingüe.

Heidenreich, L. (2007). *"This land was Mexican once": Histories of resistance from northern California*. Austin, TX: University of Texas Press.

*Hurtado, A. (2003). *Voicing Chicana feminisms: Young women speak out on sexuality*. New York, NY: New York University.

Ikas, K. R. (2001). *Chicana ways: Conversations with ten Chicana writers*. Reno, NV: University of Nevada Press.

Jarrell, R., & Reti, I. (Eds.). (2002). *Grace Palacia Arceneaux: Mexican-American farmworker and community organizer, 1920–1977*. Santa Cruz, CA: University of California Santa Cruz, University Library.

*Latina Feminist Group. (2001). *Telling to live: Latina feminist testimonios*. Durham, NC: Duke University Press.

Lomas, C. (Ed.). (1994). *The rebel: Leonor Villegas de Magnón*. Houston, TX: Arte Publico Press.

*Madera, G., Wong, K., Monroe, J., Rivera-Salgado, G., & Mathay, A. A. (2008). *Underground undergrads: UCLA undocumented immigrant students speak out*. Los Angeles: UCLA Center for Labor Research and Education.

Méndez-Negrete, J. (2006). *Las hijas de Juan: Daughters betrayed* (Rev. ed.). Durham, NC: Duke University Press.

Mendoza, L. (1993). *Lydia Mendoza: A family autobiography*. Houston, TX: Arte Público Press.

Moraga, C. (1997). *Waiting in the wings: Portrait of a queer motherhood*. Ithaca, NY: Firebrand.

Padilla, G. M. (1993). *My history, not yours: The formation of Mexican American autobiography*. Madison, WI: University of Wisconsin Press.

*Pendleton Jiménez, K. (2007). On late nights: Living in my queer teacher body. In I. Killoran & K. Pendleton Jiménez (Eds.), *"Unleashing the unpopular": Talking about sexual orientation and gender diversity in education* (pp. 63–71). Maryland, MD: Association for Childhood Education International.

Pendleton Jiménez, K. (2008). Latina landscape: Queer Toronto. *Canadian Journal of Environmental Education, 13*(2), 114–129.

*Pérez Huber, L. (2009). Disrupting apartheid of knowledge: *Testimonio* as methodology in Latina/o critical race research in education. *International Journal of Qualitative Studies in Education, 22*(6), 639–654.

*Pérez Huber, L. (2010). Sueños indocumentados: *Using LatCrit to explore the testimonios of undocumented and U.S.-born Chicana college students on discourses of racist nativism in education.* Unpublished dissertation. University of California, Los Angeles.

*Pérez Huber, L. (2010). Using Latina/o critical race theory (LatCrit) and racist nativism to explore intersectionality in the educational experiences of undocumented Chicana college students. *Educational Foundations, 24*(1–2), 77–96.

Pizarro, M. (2005). *Chicanas and Chicanos in school: Racial profiling, identity battles, and empowerment.* Austin, TX: University of Texas Press.

*Quiróz, P. A. (2001). The silencing of Latino student "voice": Puerto Rican and Mexican narratives in eighth grade and high school. *Anthropology & Education Quarterly, 32*(3), 326–349.

Rebolledo, T. D., & Márquez, M. T. (Eds.). (2000). *Women's tales from the New Mexico WPA: La diabla a pie.* Houston, TX: Arte Público Press.

Relaño Pastor, A. M. (2003). Living in a second language: Self-representation in reported dialogues of Latinas' narratives of personal language experiences. *Issues in Applied Linguistics, 14*(2), 91–114.

*Reyes, X. A., & Ríos, D. I. (2005). Dialoguing the Latina experience in higher education. *Journal of Hispanic Higher Education, 4*(4), 377–391.

Romero, M., & Stewart, A. J. (Eds.). (1999). *Women's untold stories: Breaking silence, talking back, voicing complexity.* New York, NY: Routledge.

Roque Ramírez, H. N. (2003). *Un idioma de (in)visibilidad: Las imágenes LGBTs Latinas en las noticias de televisión y prensa impresa en Español.* New York, NY: GLAAD Center for the Study of Media & Society.

Roque Ramírez, H. N. (2003). "That's my place!" Negotiating racial, sexual, and gender politics in San Francisco's Gay Latino Alliance, 1975–1983. *Journal of the History of Sexuality, 12*(2), 224–258.

Roque Ramírez, H. N. (2010). Gay Latino histories/dying to be remembered: AIDS obituaries, public memory, and the queer Latino archive. In G. M. Pérez, F. A. Guridy, & A. J. Burgos (Eds.), *Beyond el Barrio: Everyday life in Latina/o America* (pp. 103–128). New York, NY: New York University Press.

Roque Ramírez, H. N. (Ed.). (2010). Homoerotic, lesbian, and gay ethnic and immigrant histories [Special Issue]. *Journal of American Ethnic History, 29*(4).

Russel y Rodríguez, M. (2007). Messy spaces: Chicana testimonio and the undisciplining of ethnography. *Chicana/Latina Studies: The Journal of Mujeres Activas en Letras y Cambio Social, 7*(1), 86–121.

*Sandoval, A. (1999). Building up our resistance: Chicanas in academia. *Frontiers: Journal of Women Studies, 20*(1), 86–92.

*Santiago, D. A. (2007). *Voces (voices): A profile of today's Latino college students.* Washington, DC: Excelencia in Education. Retrieved from http://www.eric.ed.gov/PDFS/ED506010.pdf

*Tywoniak, F. E., & García, M. T. (2000). *Migrant daughter: Coming of age as a Mexican American woman.* Berkeley, CA: University of California Press.

*Valenzuela, A. (1999). *Subtractive schooling: U.S.-Mexican youth and the politics of caring.* Albany, NY: State University of New York Press.

Vicioso, S. C. (2010). Discovering myself: Un testimonio. In M. Jiménez Román, & J. Flores (Eds.), *The Afro-Latin@ reader: History and culture in the United States* (pp. 262–265). Durham, NC: Duke University Press.

Yosso, T. J. (2006). *Critical race counterstories along the Chicana/Chicano educational pipeline.* New York, NY: Routledge.

Dissertations

This section features selected dissertations within a broader scope in education using *testimonio* as a research methodology. These dissertations are available through *ProQuest Dissertations and Theses* as full text.

Araujo, D. (2009). *Chicanas/Latinas in higher education.* (Ed.D., University of California, Irvine and University of California, Los Angeles).

Burciaga, M. R. (2007). *Chicana Ph.D. students living nepantla: Educación and aspirations beyond the doctorate.* (Ph.D., University of California, Los Angeles).

Creel, K. J. (2010).*"This is our home!" Chicana oral histories: (Story)telling life, love and identity in the Midwest.* (Ph.D., University of Minnesota).

Cruz, C. (2006). *Testimonial narratives of queer street youth: Toward an epistemology of a brown body.* (Ph.D., University of California, Los Angeles).

Flores, E. (1999).*Chicana testimonio and autobiography: Memory, representation, and identity in Lucas, Ruiz, Moraga, and Anzaldúa.* (Ph.D., Arizona State University).

Flores Carmona, J. (2010).*Transgenerational educación: Latina mothers' everyday pedagogies of cultural citizenship in Salt Lake City, Utah.* (Ph.D., University of Utah).

Guerra, R. J. (2008). *Literature as witness: Testimonial aspects of Chicano self-identity narratives.* (Ph.D., University of Nebraska—Lincoln).

Guzmán-Martínez, C. (2011). *Chicana and Chicano "pedagogies of the home": Learning from students' lived experiences.* (Ph.D., University of Texas at San Antonio).

Mah y Busch, J. D. (2003). *Valuing concientización: The cultivation of a materialist moral epistemology in Chicana/o narrative.* (Ph.D., Cornell University).

Napoli-Abella, C. (2009). *Motherhood, mourning, testimonio, and the representation of silenced histories.* (Ph.D., University of California, Irvine).

Oliva Alvarado, K. E. (2007). *Transnational lives and texts: Writing and theorizing United States/Central American subjectivities.* (Ph.D., University of California, Berkeley).

Pearlman, J. (2010). *Chronicles of resistance: A borderlands testimonio.* (Ph.D., University of Pittsburgh).

Pérez Huber, L. (2010). *Sueños indocumentados: Using LatCrit to explore the testimonios of undocumented and U.S.-born Chicana college students on discourses of racist nativism in education.* (Ph.D., University of California, Los Angeles).

Prieto, L. (2009). *Conciencia con compromiso: Maestra perspectives on teaching in bilingual education classrooms.* (Ph.D., University of Texas at Austin).

Ramírez, L. G. (2004). *Women of 18 Street: Narratives of education and struggle.* (Ph.D., University of Illinois at Chicago).

Roybal, K. R. (2011). *Land, gender, and the politics of identity formation: Uncovering Hispana/Mexicana voices in the southwest.* (Ph.D., University of New Mexico).

Scholz, T. (1996). *The rhetorical power of testimonio and ocupación: Creating a conceptual framework for analyzing subaltern rhetorical agency.* (Ph.D. University of Colorado).

Turner, M. R. (2010). *Embracing resistance at the margins: First-generation Latino students testimonios on dual/concurrent enrollment high school programs.* (Ph.D., University of Denver).

REFERENCES

Alvarado, E. (1989). *Don't be afraid gringo: A Honduran woman speaks from the heart: The story of Elvia Alvarado.* New York, NY: Harper & Row.

Anzaldúa, G. (ed). (1990). *Making face, making soul Haciendo caras: Creative and critical perspectives by women of color.* San Francisco, CA: Aunt Lute Foundation Books.

Barrios de Chungara, D., with Viezzer, M. (1978). *Let me speak!: Testimony of Domitila, a woman of the Bolivian mines* (6th ed., V. Ortiz, Trans.). New York, NY: Monthly Review Press.

Burgos-Debray, E. (Ed). (2009). *I, Rigoberta Menchú: An Indian woman in Guatemala*/Me llamo Rigoberta Menchú, y así me nació la consciencia. (A. Wright, Trans., 2nd English-language ed.). New York, NY: Verso.

Carson, C. (Ed.) (1998). *The autobiography of Martin Luther King, Jr.* New York, NY: Intellectual Properties Management.

Castellanos, R. (1961). *BalúnCanán.* México: Fondo de Cultura Económica.

Chinchilla, N. (1998). *Nuestras utopias: Mujeres guatemaltecas del siglo XX.* Guatemala, C.A.: Agrupacion de Mujeres Tierra Viva.

Collins, P. H. (1991). *Black feminist thought: Knowledge, consciousness, and the politics of empowerment.* New York, NY: Routledge.

Cuádraz, G. H. (1993). *Meritocracy (un)challenged: The making of a Chicano and Chicana professoriate and professional class.* Unpublished dissertation. University of California, Berkeley.

Decierdo, M. A. (1980). *The struggle within: Mediating conflict in California fields, 1975–1977.* Berkeley, CA: Chicano Studies Library Publications, University of California.

Douglass, F. (1994). *Autobiographies: Narrative of the life of Frederick Douglass, an American slave.* New York, NY: Library of America.

Feagin, J. R. (2010). *The white racial frame: Centuries of racial framing and counter-framing.* New York, NY: Routledge.

Feagin, J. R., & Feagin, C. B. (2011). *Racial and ethnic relations* (9th ed.). Boston, MA: Pearson.

Freire, P. (1970). *Pedagogy of the oppressed* (M. B. Ramos, Trans.). New York, NY: Continuum.

Freire, P., & Horton, M. (1990). *We make the road by walking: Conversations on education and social change.* Philadelphia, PA: Temple University Press.

Galarza, E. (1971). *Barrio boy.* Notre Dame, IN: University of Notre Dame Press.

García, A. M. (2004). *Narratives of Mexican American women: Emergent identities of the second generation.* Walnut Creek, CA: Altamira.

García, M. T. (1994). *Memories of Chicano history: The life and narrative of Bert Corona.* Berkeley, CA: University of California Press.

Hurston, Z. N. (1970). *Dust tracks on a road: An autobiography.* Urbana, IL: University of Illinois Press.

Hurtado, A. (2003). *Voicing Chicana feminisms: Young women speak out on sexuality and identity.* New York, NY: New York University Press.

The Latina Feminist Group. (2001). *Telling to live: Latina feminist testimonios.* Durham, NC: Duke University Press.

Lomas, C. (Ed.). (1994). *The rebel: Leonor Villegas de Magnón.* Houston, TX: Arte Público Press.

Lorde, A. (1984). *Sister outsider: Essays and speeches.* Trumansburg, NY: Crossing Press.

Madera, G., Wong, K., Monroe, J., Rivera-Salgado, G., & Mathay, A. A. (Eds.). (2008). *Underground undergrads: UCLA undocumented immigrant students speak out.* Los Angeles, CA: UCLA Center for Labor Research and Education.

Martin, P. P. (1992). *Songs my mother sang to me: An oral history of Mexican American women.* Tucson, AZ: University of Arizona Press.

Moraga C., & Anzaldúa, G. (Eds.). (1983). *This bridge called my back: Writings by radical women of color* (2nd ed.). New York, NY: Kitchen Table, Women of Color Press.

Medrano, M. F. (2010). *Américo Paredes: In his own words, an authorized biography.* Denton, TX: University of North Texas Press.

Ortíz, F. I. (1995). *Mexican American women: Schooling, work, and family.* Charleston, WV: Clearinghouse on Rural Education and Small Schools, Appalachia Educational Laboratory.

Pardo, M. S. (1998). *Mexican American women activists: Identity and resistance in two Los Angeles communities.* Philadelphia, PA: Temple University Press.

Partnoy, A. (1986). *The little school: Tales of disappearance & survival.* Pittsburgh, PA: Cleis.

Pérez, F. (1996). *Dolores Huerta.* Austin, TX: Raintree Steck-Vaughn.

Pérez, E. (1999). *The decolonial imaginary: Writing Chicanas into history.* Bloomington, IN: Indiana University Press.

Poniatowski, E. (1979). *Hasta no verte, Jesús mío.* Mexico: Era.

Poniatowska, E. (1980). *Fuerte es el silencio.* Mexico City, Mexico: Ediciones Era.

Roque Ramírez, H. N. (2010). Gay Latino histories/dying to be remembered. In G. M. Perez, F. A. Guridy, & A. J. Burgos (Eds.), *Beyond el barrio: Everyday life in Latina/o America.* (pp. 103–128). New York: New York University Press.

Sánchez, G. I. (1940/1996). *Forgotten people: A study of new Mexicans.* Albuquerque, NM: Horn.

Sandoval, C. (2000). *Methodology of the oppressed.* Minneapolis, MN: University of Minnesota Press.

Tywoniak, F. E., & García, M. T. (2000). *Migrant daughter: Coming of age as a Mexican American woman.* Berkeley, CA: University of California Press.

Oliverez, P.M., Chavez, M.L., Soriano, M., & Tierney, W.G. (Eds). (2006). *The college & financial aid guide for AB540 undocumented students.* Retrieved from http://www.usc.edu/dept/chepa/pdf/AB%20540%20final.pdf

Villarreal, J. A. (1959). *Pocho.* Garden City, NY: Doubleday.

Wigginton, E. (Ed.). (1992). *Refuse to stand silently by: An oral history of grass roots social activism in America, 1921–1964.* New York, NY: Doubleday.

Zavella, P. (1987). *Women's work and Chicano families: Cannery workers of the Santa Clara Valley.* Ithaca, NY: Cornell University Press.

Radio Broadcasts

Latino USA. http://www.latinousa.org/
    National Public Radio. (1984). The Golden Cradle Immigration stories.
    StoryCorps. http://storycorps.org/about/
    Terkel, S. (1952). Studs Terkel's Almanac WFMT Radio Station.
    Youth Radio. http://www.youthradio.org/

Libraries and Archives

History San José. http://www.historysanjose.org/
    Schomburg Center for Research in Black Culture: Museum and Library. http://www.nypl.org/
locations/schomburg
    University of California Berkeley, Bancroft Library. http://bancroft.berkeley.edu/
    University of California, Los Angeles: Chicano Studies Research Center. http://www.chicano.
ucla.edu/
    University of Texas at Austin, Harry Ransom Center. http://www.hrc.utexas.edu/

Index

INDEX

Pillow, W. 133
Poindexter, P.M. 126, 132
Poniatowska, E. 125, 163
predominantly white institutions (PWIs): teacher
    educators and co-creation of *testimonios* 49–65
Prieto, L. 50, 52, 54, 55, 56–8, 59–60, 61, 62
Public Broadcast Television 168

race, class and gender: negotiation of stigma 118–20
racist nativism 56–8, 63; microaggressions: student
    testimonios 3–4, 30–44
radio 168
Randall, M. 102
Ranero, J.J. 84, 86, 88
rape 17–18
reciprocity 6, 16, 57, 126, 130, 134, 136–7, 140
reflexión and status of Latinas in academia 5,
    81–94; creating threads of connection 84–6;
    healing fractured minds, bodies and spirits
    86–92; replicating process of *reflexión* 92–3;
    scholarly contributions of *testimonio* 83–4
reflexivity 79, 93, 97, 105, 162, 163; self- 130
Rendón, L.I. 5, 6, 50, 64, 84, 85, 86, 87, 94, 121
Reyes, X.A. 50, 52
Richardson, M. 71
Rivas-Rodriguez, M. 126, 168
Roberts, D. 32
Rodriguez, D. 50
Rodríguez-Johnson, E. 116, 118
role models 22
roots/origins of *testimonio* 163–5
Roque Ramírez, H.N. 165
Rorty, R. 105
Rosaldo, R. 58, 99
Ruiz, E. 116, 118
Russel y Rodríguez, M. 4

Saavedra, C.M. 70
SACNAS (Society for the Advancement of
    Chicanos and Native Americans in Science) 113,
    114, 119–20
Saito, N.T. 32
Sánchez, G.I. 163
Sánchez, G.J. 32
Sandoval, C. 33, 163
Santiago, D. 110
Scarry, E. 103
Schmidt Camacho, A. 15
schools 5, 8, 135, 145, 152, 153, 155, 159;
    California: student *testimonios* on effects and
    responses to microaggressions 3–4, 30–44;
    Ciudad Juárez: two high-school girls 3–4,
    11–26; curriculum 6, 97–106; science,

technology, engineering and math (STEM) fields
    109–22, 116, 117–19, 121–2; teacher educators:
    testimonial co-creation 49–65
science, technology, engineering and math (STEM)
    fields 6–7, 102–11; discussion 120–2; finding,
    forging and walking *Paths to Discovery* 111–14;
    findings and analysis of *testimonios* from *Paths to
    Discovery* 115–18; negotiation of stigma: class,
    race and gender 118–20; parents, family and
    community 116; teachers and mentors 116–19,
    121; *testimonios* theory as analytic lens 114–15
Shulman, L. 146, 159–60
signature pedagogy for Latin@ Studies, digital
    testimonio as 144–60
slave narratives 168
Smith, L.T. 12, 14, 24
Smith-Maddox, R. 31
social advocacy 42–3, 44
social justice practice, *testimonio* as 104–5
socialization, academic 5, 81–94
Society for the Advancement of Chicanos and
    Native Americans in Science (SACNAS) 113,
    114, 119–20
Solórzano, D.G. 4, 31, 32, 33, 39, 42
Sommer, D. 58, 98, 146
Souza, C. 155
spiritualism 76
Spivak, G. 4
Stacey, J. 14
Staudt, K.A. 15
Stephanson, A. 98
stigma 157; science, technology, engineering and
    math (STEM) fields 118–20
Stoll, D. 98–9, 106
StoryCorps 168
student *testimonios* on effects and responses to
    microaggressions 3–4, 30–44; Chicana
    feminisms 33–4; *conocimiento* 34, 35, 38–9,
    42–3, 44; findings on effects 36–9; focus groups
    35–6; Latina/o critical theory 31–3, 34; racist
    nativism 32, 34; responses 39–42; *testimonio* as
    methodology 34–6

Takaki, R. 168
Tamayo, J. 150
Taylor, Paul 168
teacher education: co-creation of *testimonios* 49–65;
    digital storytelling 145; multiculturalism 77
teacher educators: co-creation of *testimonios*
    49–65; *cariño* (authentic care) 61–2, 64;
    conciencia con compromiso (consciousness with
    responsibility/commitment) 58–61, 62, 63–4;
    cultural dissonance: *me retumba la cabeza* (my